THE HEALTHY HOUSE PLANT

A Guide to the Prevention, Detection, and Cure of Pests and Diseases

JEAN F. BLASHFIELD

DRAWINGS BY SUZANNE CLEE
PHOTOGRAPHS BY MARIN VARBANOV

Little, Brown and Company — Boston – Toronto

FIRST EDITION

LIBRARY OF CONGRESS CATALOGING IN PUBLICATION DATA
Blashfield, Jean F
    The healthy house plant.

    Includes index.
    1. House plants—Diseases and pests. 2. House plants. I. Title.
SB608.H84B52   635.9′65   79-23782
ISBN 0-316-09955-4

MV
Designed by Susan Windheim

*Published simultaneously in Canada
by Little, Brown & Company (Canada) Limited*

PRINTED IN THE UNITED STATES OF AMERICA

To my husband,
Wallace B. Black,
without whom this book
would have been completed
much sooner . . .
but with less joy

~~∂~~ CONTENTS

THE HEALTHY HOUSE PLANT

ᏄᏋ 1. YOU'RE THE DOCTOR

Nirvana has arrived for the grower of house plants. Among the many gadgets and gimmicks now available to make life easier are:

· pots with built-in reservoirs to keep soil continuously moist;

· probes that measure moisture in a plant's soil and tell you when to water again;

· a more complex probe that "purrs" when there is balanced food supply in the soil;

· tiny indoor hoses, fifty and seventy-five feet long, so you can water from your kitchen sink without frantic trips back and forth to refill the watering can;

· books, books, and more books;

· the services of plant hotels and plant-sitters (for when you must be away from your green family);

· small plastic tents in which your plants can play at camping when you travel away from them;

· plant stands that sing to your plants when you're not around to fill the air with chatter — and one that thanks *you* for taking care of the plants on it, as if the plants were speaking (if I wanted my plants to talk, I'd teach them myself!);

The healthy — and happy — house plant is one that lives with others and shares the benevolent, wise attention you bestow. The happy person is one who lives with and enjoys such plants.

· plant health and accident insurance, sometimes available from reputable plant stores (but only covering those leafy gems costing fifty dollars or more).

Perhaps the *pièce de résistance* is a special lamp featuring a growth light mounted above a pot for low plants: the lamp is turned on and off by touching a leaf — *any* leaf — on the plant. Now that's downright spooky.

But regardless of what help you've had from gadgets, *you* get the credit when your plants are bloomingly beautiful — and so *you* are responsible for their health. You must be the doctor when they're beginning to show signs that something is wrong. It may take patience and a bit of work at times, but you'll be rewarded if you take time and enjoy the whole process.

Perhaps the most exciting development to arise from the recent plant boom is the new career field "horticultural therapy": therapists, both amateurs and professionals, are working with drug addicts, prisoners, the aged, the emotionally ill, and the handicapped, teaching them how to care for plants. These rehabilitators recognize that growing plants — and being concerned about them — is a relaxing, mind-expanding, effective therapy, as well as a joy. And with the proper outlook, all household plant doctors can derive similar benefits for themselves.

Relax — You Can Bury Your Mistakes

I can hear the gasps of horror in response to that section heading: "What? But plants are living things and shouldn't be treated so lightly!" Well, one of the more unfortunate aspects of the recent plant boom has been the spread of a "flower-child approach" — the expectation that every leaf pinched off a house plant can be propagated as a new plant. Nonsense. Nature doesn't work that way. If you've ever planted seeds (quite a fun challenge when growing house plants), you've discovered that *even if you are lucky* only about half of the seeds will germinate, perhaps half of those will develop into strong seedlings, and maybe half of those will finally grow into healthy plants. So there's a lot of waste — but no cause for alarm: it's all part of the process of natural selection.

In a forest, to cite another example, only those small trees that have the strength to reach for the sun and actually shunt other ones out of their growing space will grow into the giant trees that create our forests. Those left out will die, or at least be stunted — but the species as a whole becomes stronger as a result.

And speaking of forests, it might be wise at this point to bring up one of the most fatal plant diseases of all: "unable-to-resist-itis." These days you walk into almost any kind of store — a five-and-ten, a supermarket, a florist's, a hobby shop, a hardware store, maybe even a plant store — and invariably come out with a new little green something. Perhaps it's a variety of house plant you already have . . . but, "Oh, it's just so cute." That reaction is almost inevitable when you're first getting started growing plants; or you may, in fact, intentionally want to expand your greenery by picking up some of the new hybrids that are stronger than old ones (or perhaps even some weaker hybrids, because they'll soon disappear from the market). But eventually, too much "Oh, but it's so cute" — too much "unable-to-resist-itis" — will create problems: when the plants take over and drive you out of your home; or when the watering takes so long that you're late for work each day; or when sheer probability puts at least ten plants in the sick bay at all times; or when you find yourself having to forego weekends at the seashore because you promised your plants that you'd scrub the white stuff off the outside of their pots.

Just who's running whom? For my money — and my pleasure — *I'm* running the plants, not vice versa. And that makes me solely responsible when they begin to ail and I must play the doctor.

Plants can be downright cantankerous. One symptom may mean that any of a number of different things are wrong. At first, you will probably choose the wrong cause to pursue, and there's a good chance you'll lose a plant, or two, or three. But you'll learn. Don't dwell on your mistakes; bury them and get on with gaining more experience.

Keep in mind that you don't have to rely on books alone when trying to evaluate a plant's health:

· Check with a neighbor who has a similar plant and see what he or she is doing right or wrong.

· Call your nearest botanical garden or horticultural society. Most now have experts who will try to answer your questions if you are prepared to describe the exact species of plant and its growing conditions — light, feeding (fertilizing), watering. Don't lie if you suspect you've been doing something wrong; you might as well find out the truth.

· Go to a greenhouse you trust for advice. (I wouldn't bother with an in-town plant store unless it's one that has been in business for years and has a good reputation; the clerks in new stores probably know less than you.)

If every plant you have seems to develop a problem (and in that case you can't bear to bury your mistakes), you might consider starting fresh with a list of easy-to-grow plants. Their sheer amiability will turn you into an expert. And if you succeed with them, your own confidence may reach such a level that you can begin again to experiment with the more persnickety plants.

The table on the next page *(The Twenty Hardiest House Plants)* is derived from a list compiled by an expert at the Chicago Botanical Garden, who in turn developed it using material from the University of Minnesota. The plant qualities required for inclusion on the list were as follows:

1. Relatively resistant to insect and disease attack
2. Normally immune to spider mite
3. Tolerant of low humidity (the scourge of most homes in winter)
4. Resistant to shedding leaves in reaction to an occasional missed watering
5. Able to grow well without added artificial light
6. Able to remain attractive in spite of the above conditions

The recommended plants — each of them almost, but not quite neglectable — are listed in alphabetical order by their botanical name.

THE TWENTY HARDIEST HOUSE PLANTS

BOTANICAL NAME	COMMON NAMES
Aglaonema commutatum	Chinese evergreen
Aloe vera	burn plant, unguentine plant, medicine plant, aloe
Araucaria excelsa	Norfolk Island pine, araucaria
Beaucarnea recurvata	ponytail palm, bottle palm, elephant's foot
Chlorophytum comosom	spider plant
Cissus rhombifolia	grape ivy
Clivia miniata	clivia, Kaffir lily
Coffea arabica	coffee tree, coffee plant
Dracaena deremensis warneckii	Warnecki dracaena
Dracaena fragrans massangeana	corn plant
Howea forsteriana	Kentia palm
Monstera deliciosa	split-leaf philodendron, Swiss-cheese plant, ceriman, Mexican breadfruit
Peperomia obtusifolia	common peperomia
Philodendron oxycardium	heart-leaf philodendron, common philodendron, heartleaf, sweetheart vine
Plectranthus australis	Swedish ivy
Rhoeo spathacea	Moses-in-a-boat, boat lily
Sansevieria trifasciata	snake plant, mother-in-law's tongue
Scindapsus aureus	pothos, devil's ivy, variegated philodendron, marble queen
Stapelia gigantea	carrion flower, Aztec lily, stapelia
Syngonium podophyllum	nephthytis, arrowhead, African evergreen

If you get far into house plants at all, you'll go beyond this basic list. And you'll need to know what makes plants tick.

A Brief (Very Brief) Botany Primer

A little basic botany never hurt anybody — and it might someday help you to understand, at least superficially, what is going on with your plants.

There really aren't all that many major parts to a plant: leaves, flowers (on some), stems, roots, and root hairs. Most of the plants that you regard as foliage plants are technically flowering plants, although you

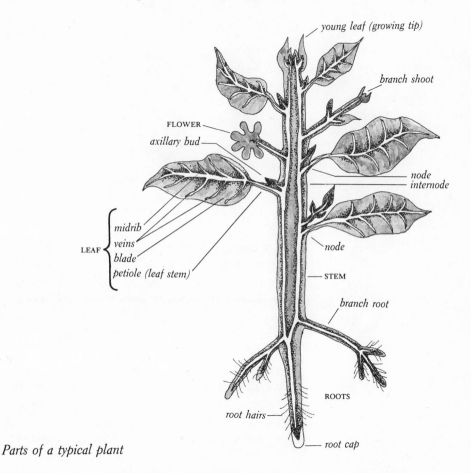

young leaf (growing tip)

branch shoot

FLOWER

axillary bud

node
internode

node

LEAF
midrib
veins
blade
petiole (leaf stem)

— STEM

branch root

ROOTS

root hairs

— *root cap*

Parts of a typical plant

may never see their flowers. The major exception is the ferns, which are more primitive than flowering plants. Ferns don't flower, and their "leaves" are actually leaflets on the larger "leaf," or *frond*.

The function of a plant's leaves is basically to carry

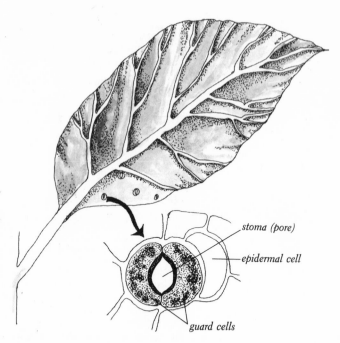

Enlarged surface view of a leaf underside, showing a stoma and surrounding cells. Stomata open and close to control the movement of oxygen, carbon dioxide, and water through the plant.

out *photosynthesis,* thus making food for the plant to use for energy and growth. Leaves generally try to grow at right angles to the sun's rays so that the largest surface area possible is being struck by the available light. Leaves give plants their remarkable talent for taking carbon dioxide, the stuff we and other animals exhale, from the air. The gas enters the leaves through tiny pores located mostly on their undersides (a major reason for always washing the back of a leaf when you give a plant a bath). These pores, called *stomata,* or *stomates, (stoma* or *stomate,* when discussing only one — but there are many thousands on even one small leaf), open and close according to the plant's needs. At the same time, water rises up into the leaf from the roots, where it has been taken from the soil by the root hairs. In the plant cells is a green material called *chlorophyll;* it's what makes most plants green. But even more important, chlorophyll, in the presence of light, can take carbon from carbon dioxide (CO_2) and hydrogen from water (H_2O) and combine them to make the complex sugar *glucose* $(C_6H_{12}O_6)$. The sugar in turn breaks down into starch (a substance that feeds the world) and the tough material called *cellulose* that forms plant cell walls. Oxygen, given off as a by-product of the process, is released from the leaf through the same stomata through which carbon dioxide entered.

The substance that makes the whole engine run is water, which must always be present in the soil for most plants to thrive. Along with any nutrients it carries, water is absorbed by the root hairs and transported up the roots to the stems, then up the stems to the leaves. (And sugars are transported in the reverse direction.) Any water that isn't used by the leaves in photosynthesis or in keeping the plant cells stiff (turgid) is given off to the atmosphere through the stomata in a process called *transpiration.* The hotter and drier the air around leaves, the more water the plant transpires in its attempt to keep the water content both inside and outside the leaf in balance. The equivalent of half a plant's weight might be transpired in one day. On very hot days, or in low humidity, thin-leaved plants can't keep up with the water demand and they wilt; and drafts, hot or cold, increase the rate of transpiration. Also, on hot days the stomata in the leaf surfaces close to protect the leaf's moisture content, and when they do, no carbon dioxide can enter. If this goes on long, the plant cannot feed itself and it won't grow. Thus, a proper plant environment and an adequate water supply are important factors you must always consider.

Plants don't just take in carbon dioxide and give off oxygen, however. They also, like us, *take in* oxygen and *give off* carbon dioxide in the process *respiration* — which is more than just simple "breathing," as we often think of it. Respiration actually involves taking in oxygen as well as burning starches; in plants (and in humans, too) starch can't be burned without oxygen. The energy resulting from burning is used by the plant for maintenance or growth, and carbon dioxide is given off as a waste product. Obviously, stomata play a vital role in plants' lives; the cleanliness and crispness of leaves are of prime importance to a plant.

Lots of things, then, can go wrong with a plant — not even counting attack by the most aggravating enemy, insect pests. The way you treat your plants can often do more harm than the worst disease. (We'll worry about insects and diseases in chapters 6 and 7, respectively.) Things will sometimes go wrong with your plants, but you need not fret if you're prepared to deal with the problems that occur.

The Plant Infirmary

When a plant is feeling less than well, it cannot handle the full regimen of its normal life: lots of bright light; regular, complete watering; frequent, albeit mild, feeding. An ailing plant is not equipped to deal with those routine aspects of horticulture. You must make it well first.

A sick plant should be allowed an infirmary — a place of its own, in brightness but not direct light, preferably in a spot that's draft-free, very humid, and fairly cool (though certainly not cold). Almost any ill a plant can fall heir to may be at least partially alleviated by its residing for a period in very humid air. If you must encase it in plastic to give it that benefit, do so. Just be sure that some fresh air is allowed to circulate freely around the plant periodically in order to prevent the additional scourge of mold. A plant's "place of its own" need not necessarily be apart from its friends — it may just be a plastic enclosure. Insect or disease attack, however, *must* be treated in full isolation from other plants.

In addition, both for use in your plant's regular "preventive health-care program" or for specially ministering to an unwell one, consider keeping on hand in the plant infirmary the following items:

· A magnifying glass with a power of at least ×10. Some insects are too small to be seen by the naked eye.

· A sharp knife, always kept clean, for performing minor or major plant surgery when needed. Don't use a dirty one: it can only transmit problems from one plant to another.

· Clean, always-ready pots, for quickly repotting plants whose roots have been exposed for examination or treatment. Don't leave a wounded plant with its roots dangling while you hunt for a fresh pot.

· A large mister, for regular humidification of your plants; and possibly a small sprayer (such as an old, sterilized perfume atomizer), for specially treating wounded plants that perhaps can't take the full blast of your standard mister.

· Stakes and string to prop up wounded or weak-stemmed plants that are getting too tall for their own strength. Preferably, both stakes and string (or wire-lined "twist-ems") should be green, so that they're inconspicuous.

· A hygrometer, preferably combined with a thermometer. It's safer for a sick plant if you really know — not just guess — how humid and how warm it is in the plant's sickroom (as well as everywhere else that you grow plants).

· Plastic — sheets that you can tape around large plants and bags that you can use to cover smaller ones. Plastic-covered frame tents that you can easily prop over plants are now available in many plant stores, or you can readily create your own out of coat hangers and plastic.

· An acid/base testing kit for checking your soil pH.

· Fungicide for dusting wounds after you remove rotting material from diseased plants.

· Insecticide — but only as a last resort. (Please read chapter 8, on chemicals, and chapter 6, on insect pests, before you decide to keep a can of poison around.)

· Nondetergent soap for use both in cleaning plants regularly and in initially treating for pests (see chapter 6).

· Patience — enough to wait for several weeks before returning a seemingly cured plant to its friends, especially after an insect attack (pests may be lying in wait for another chance to strike). And patience to see if one treatment works before starting another.

· Clean hands, for whenever you deal with a sick plant. (Clean them again before you proceed to touch your other green friends.)

· And a little bit of green-thumb luck certainly wouldn't hurt.

◈ 2. THE REGULAR CHECKUP FOR SYMPTOMS

IF YOU'VE TRIED TO DISCOVER WHAT'S BEST FOR YOUR plants, you learned very early that they can't be watered according to a single, simple routine, such as watering every second day in summer, every third day in winter. You learned that plants in clay pots use up their water more quickly than plants in plastic pots, that small pots dry up more quickly than large ones, that dormant plants need less water than actively growing ones, and that some plants need to be allowed to dry more completely between waterings than others.

Therefore, you know — and you put into practice what you know, don't you? — that each time you walk around with the watering can (or hose nozzle, if you're caught on those cute little indoor hoses), you must carefully inspect the soil in each pot, or at least give each plant individual consideration. While you're at it, it takes but a little more time to inspect the whole plant, not just its soil-bound feet. Watering offers a great chance to give your plants a regular checkup for symptoms of bad health or neglect. Look at each plant — really look — and ask yourself these questions:

· Are new leaves the proper size and color?

· Are the angles between stems and leaves, as well as the backs of leaves, clean?

· Do leaves angle out from stems crisply, as if at attention, or do they hang limply?

· Is the pot in aesthetic balance with the size of the plant (a good indication that the plant is in the right-sized pot)?

· Are all leaf tips green instead of charred brown and dry?

· Are leaves clean and shiny without oils being applied? or clean and dust-free, if it is a matt-finish, hairy-leaved plant?

· Is the outside of the pot clean, scrubbed free of the salty white residue left by watering?

· Is the distance between leaves about the same all over the plant?

· Is growth equal on all sides of the plant?

· Is each plant displayed so it has room to breathe and be admired?

If you manage to say yes to each of these inspection questions, congratulations — you've won the Green Thumb Healthy Plant Award! But you needn't expect to win the award for all your plants, all the time. If you didn't expect health problems once in a while, you wouldn't be reading this book (unless you're just super-cautious) — and if you *always* had healthy specimens, you would probably be growing plastic plants. So if you have to say no to one or more of the inspection questions, don't worry, you're in good company. Even the best of us pick up charred leaf tips (from low humidity) in winter. Spider mite can come charging out of the woodwork at the drop of a relative humidity percentage point. A new purchase can have scale insects on it, missed by too cursory an examination in the greenhouse when you picked it out. (I'm smarting from that problem on a mother fern as I write: I was so busy admiring the fronds, which were laden with spores and marvelous baby leaflets, that I failed to notice the small, brown lumps marching, albeit slowly, up a couple of frond stems. Fortunately, a few scales can be picked off simply. Other pests aren't so agreeable.)

Anyway, when you do discover signs of poor plant health, begin to analyze, one by one, the symptoms you perceive.

If Your Begonia Has Pneumonia

It takes human medical diagnosticians at least eleven years to become fully qualified to practice, and even then they must continue to supplement their education for the rest of their days. You, however, probably have no training at all in treating plant ills, yet are obligated to diagnose and try to help a plant that obviously has something wrong. Well . . . no, I guess it's not absolutely necessary — you can discard the plant. But the economic facts behind a thirty-nine-dollar display plant may discourage that option. Although I'll accept the reasoning that you'll try to help a sick plant because you don't want to spend a second small fortune to replace it, I'd prefer to think you want to help because you like the plant and think it deserves to live.

Whatever your motivation, start by accepting the probability that you won't discover the answer to your plants' woes on the first attempt. But you can at least try, and sometimes you may succeed. For instance, there are, in the table on the following pages, at least nine observable plant symptoms that can each be caused by too low a relative-humidity level in your home; if you notice most of these symptoms, chances are good that low humidity is your problem. The symptoms are listed separately so that you, as an apprentice plant doctor, may observe only one of them yet come scurrying to this book for guidance to a correct diagnosis and cure.

On the other side of the coin is the sad fact that a single symptom, such as yellowing leaves, may have such an incredible number of possible causes that it's hard to pinpoint the specific one. In such a case, look for more symptoms and try to link them with a common cause; yellowing, for instance, rarely occurs in isolation (except perhaps for the phenomenon of the lone yellow leaf, which is usually normal aging of that leaf alone). If you find three or four specific symptoms in a plant and each has as its possible cause "overwatering," you are using probability rather than just possibility when you focus upon too much water as the culprit. Treat the plant as specified for overwatering, be patient as you wait for it to react to the treatment, cheer if the remedy works — and begin searching again if it doesn't.

How does one describe a plant symptom? We all differ in our use of language, which is a disturbingly imprecise tool these days. And symptom description is even more difficult than it might otherwise be, because each plant suffers in its own way: what appears yellow in one plant might verge toward tan in another. You can overcome the language problem if you try to get to know the list of possible symptoms and learn what they look like individually in each of your plants.

Even more important, acquaint yourself with the healthy plant you bought or were given as though it were an intimate friend. Learn all you can about it quickly, so that later, when (if) things go wrong, you'll know what's still right and will more easily perceive what's wrong. Then you'll be able to begin quickly the search for the primary causes of its sickness.

Problems of a
Sick Plant
The following tables must, of necessity, serve only as a starting point for you to begin to question the way you have been treating your plants and what you should do to set things right. More detailed general information should be sought in the chapters indicated (a table is no place to try to squeeze in everything). In addition, chapter 11 specifically covers almost two hundred kinds of house plants and considers some of the important and common things that can go wrong with them. In that listing, I have not repeated "yellowing leaves caused by overwatering" in each instance, though it is the most common cause of difficulties; instead, I have concentrated on the problems peculiar to specific plants. By referring to the following tables and the chapter 11 list, then, you should be able to analyze and cure the particular problem of most any ailing house plant.

Good luck! May the next Green Thumb Healthy Plant Award be yours.

LEAF PROBLEMS

SYMPTOM	POSSIBLE CAUSE	WHAT TO DO ABOUT IT

Color Change

SYMPTOM	POSSIBLE CAUSE	WHAT TO DO ABOUT IT
Older (lower) leaves turn yellow, usually one at a time	Normal aging	Remove yellowed leaves at base of leaf stem
Older (lower) leaves turn yellow, dry, and drop off; remaining leaves may wilt	Overwatering	Let soil dry until it will hold together as a ball. Remove plant from pot. Inspect root ends for the mushiness that indicates root rot. If none exists, repot plant in fresh pot, preferably clay, with an extra layer of pebbles in the bottom to handle drainage. Water only when soil has dried to the extent required for the specific plant. If some root has rotted, trim off the damaged portion. Repot plant in a fresh clay pot at least one size smaller than the one used before. Revamp your watering practices. *See also chapter 4*
	Underwatering	Carry out root check described immediately above to be sure cause is not too much water. If no mushiness exists and soil is completely dry, return plant to pot; increase frequency of watering just slightly, but be sure that each watering is thorough: drench the soil, let excess run out drainage hole. *See also chapter 4*
	Humidity too low (especially if yellowed leaves cling to plant)	Increase the relative humidity in all ways possible: mist plant often; put plant on a pebble tray faithfully kept filled with water; lower room temperature. Be sure air circulates well to avoid fungus problems. *See also chapter 4*

SYMPTOM	POSSIBLE CAUSE	WHAT TO DO ABOUT IT

Color Change

SYMPTOM	POSSIBLE CAUSE	WHAT TO DO ABOUT IT
Older (lower) leaves turn yellow, dry, and drop off; remaining leaves may wilt (cont.)	Drafts; abrupt temperature change	Keep plant protected from blasts of hot or cold air from doors, windows, heating or air-conditioning units. If a plant can replace its leaves, it will soon do so; one that doesn't will probably need air layering eventually (see chapter 10). *See also chapter 3*
	Too little light (especially if plant is in north light)	Spend five or six days gradually moving plant into brighter location, until it receives enough light to carry on adequate photosynthesis. *See also chapter 3*
	Overfeeding (fertilizer accumulation)	Buildup of fertilizer salts in the soil has had a toxic effect on some roots and the leaves they support. Leach the soil: sink pot to rim in tub of lukewarm water. Leave it for an hour or until water is visible on top of the soil. Remove and let drain. If salt crust on rim can't be easily scraped off, repot plant in fresh soil and fresh pot. Prevent repeat of salt accumulation by fertilizing soil less often or with weaker food solutions; leach the soil periodically during the growing season. *See also chapter 5*
	Underfeeding	Increase the strength or frequency (not both) of feeding with a well-balanced fertilizer. *See also chapter 5*

SYMPTOM	POSSIBLE CAUSE	WHAT TO DO ABOUT IT

Color Change

SYMPTOM	POSSIBLE CAUSE	WHAT TO DO ABOUT IT
Older (lower) leaves turn yellow, dry, and drop off; remaining leaves may wilt (cont.)	Compacted soil (especially if water remains on soil surface after watering)	Repot plant in a more porous soil; be sure to remove most of the old, denser soil from the roots. *See also chapter 5*
	Air pollution	Keep air conditioning on, adding a carbon filter to the unit, if possible. Keep all windows closed on smoggy days, and just hope that the pollution clears. Wash leaves often. *See also chapter 3*
	Insect attack	Inspect plant thoroughly with a magnifying glass; treat in appropriate manner only for specific pest identified. *See also chapter 6*
Older (lower) leaves turn yellow or light green, dry, and drop off; some leaves become orange or red; others fade	Nitrogen deficiency	Feed plant with a well-balanced fertilizer. Do not regard the condition as an emergency requiring massive doses of food: roots can be burned and damaged. *See also chapter 5*
Older (lower) leaves turn yellow except at the veins, which remain green	Zinc or manganese deficiency	Feed lightly but often with a full-formula fertilizer. *See also chapter 5*
Older (lower) leaves turn yellow except at the veins, which remain green; leaves fall without withering	Magnesium deficiency	Feed lightly but often with a full-formula fertilizer. *See also chapter 5*

Color Change

SYMPTOM	POSSIBLE CAUSE	WHAT TO DO ABOUT IT
Newer (upper) leaves turn yellow except at the veins, which remain green	Iron deficiency	Feed with a chelated iron product according to instructions on label. Adjust soil pH so that iron given in the future can be absorbed. *See also chapter 5*
Newer (upper) leaves turn yellow; older leaves curl upward	Sulfur deficiency	Feed lightly but often with a full-formula fertilizer. *See also chapter 5*
Leaves turn yellow and curled	Aphids	Inspect plant thoroughly with a magnifying glass; treat in appropriate manner for aphids, if identified. *See also chapter 6*
	Powdery mildew	Increase air circulation and move plants apart; dust with fungicide. *See also chapter 7*
Leaves turn grayish and dull, twisted or wrinkled, perhaps curled and brittle	Cyclamen mites (especially on African violets)	Inspect plant thoroughly with a magnifying glass; if cyclamen mites are identified, discard affected plant. *See also chapter 6*
Leaves turn pale or bleached and new growth is weak and spindly	Too little light (especially in summer)	Spend five or six days gradually moving plant into brighter location, until it receives enough light to carry on adequate photosynthesis; or give plant a boost with artificial light. *See also chapter 3*
	Too much light	Some plants cannot take the full brightness and accompanying heat of summer sun. Move plant back from window or, if necessary, shield plant from about 10:00 A.M. to 2:00 P.M. Review growing requirements of each plant. *See also chapter 3*

SYMPTOM	POSSIBLE CAUSE	WHAT TO DO ABOUT IT

Color Change

Leaves turn pale or bleached and new growth is weak and spindly (cont.)	Overwatering (especially in winter)	Even a plant that doesn't really go dormant requires less water in winter than in summer; let soil dry until plant almost wilts, water thoroughly, and then start watering less often than you did before. If condition persists, check for possibility of root rot. *See also chapter 4*
	Underfeeding (especially in summer)	Feed lightly but often with a full-formula fertilizer during growing season. However, if plant is an acid-lover, feed with acid fertilizer to be sure that the nutrient given can actually be used. *See also chapter 5*
	Temperature too high (especially in winter)	All plants can suffer from the high temperature home heating systems create in winter. Lower the thermostat, especially at night; increase humidity as much as possible. *See also chapter 3*
	Consistent exposure to ripe apples	Ethylene gas given off by ripening apples can damage plants. Move the fruit bowl, or keep apples in the refrigerator. *See also chapter 3*
Leaves bleach and become mottled with yellow	Whitefly (if pests fly away when plant is shaken); aphids (if shaking has no effect)	Inspect plant thoroughly with a magnifying glass; treat in appropriate manner for specific pest identified. *See also chapter 6*

SYMPTOM	POSSIBLE CAUSE	WHAT TO DO ABOUT IT

Color Change

Leaves bleach and become mottled with grayish yellow tinge; close inspection reveals cobwebs	Spider mites	Inspect plant thoroughly with a magnifying glass; treat in appropriate manner for spider mites, if identified; increase humidity in all ways possible. *See also chapter 6*
Leaves turn brown, possibly with curled edges and mushy spots, and may drop off	Frostbite (especially if leaves touched a windowpane on a cold night)	Cut off damaged leaves, even if they are numerous (they won't revive). Place newspaper between plant and window glass at night during cold spells. (Don't move the plant every night to protect it — that can be more harmful in the long run than cold temperatures). *See also chapter 3*
Leaves turn bluish green, then purple, perhaps bronze or mottled, beginning with older (lower) ones	Phosphorus deficiency	Feed lightly but often with a full-formula fertilizer. *See also chapter 5*
Variegated leaves turn all green	Too little light	Spend five or six days gradually moving plant into a brighter location, until it receives enough light to carry on adequate photosynthesis in just those parts of the leaves that should be green. *See also chapter 3*

Leaf Problems (cont.)

SYMPTOM	POSSIBLE CAUSE	WHAT TO DO ABOUT IT

Falling Leaves

Leaves suddenly drop off plant in large numbers	Abrupt change in light	Condition usually will occur when a plant is moved suddenly from brightness to dimness. Have patience and wait for new leaves to appear under the new conditions. Next time, move plant gradually to avoid this horrible experience (which is fairly common in new plants brought from greenhouse to home). *See also chapter 3*
	Abrupt change in temperature	Keep plant protected from hot or cold air from doors, windows, heating or air-conditioning units. If a plant can replace its leaves, it will soon do so; one that doesn't will need air layering eventually (see chapter 10). *See also chapter 3*
	Cold-water watering	Have patience while awaiting natural replacement growth. When watering, always use water that's lukewarm or at least at room temperature. *See also chapter 4*
	Cold drafts	Check air movement in the room. Move plant to a more protected location or install screens to block drafts. *See also chapter 3*
	Humidity too low (especially if plant has just been acquired)	Increase relative humidity in all ways possible: mist plant often; put plant on a pebble tray faithfully kept filled with water; lower room temperature. Be sure air circulates well to avoid fungus problems. *See also chapter 4*

SYMPTOM	POSSIBLE CAUSE	WHAT TO DO ABOUT IT

Falling Leaves

SYMPTOM	POSSIBLE CAUSE	WHAT TO DO ABOUT IT
Leaves suddenly drop off plant in large numbers (cont.)	Underwatering	Plant had probably adjusted to continuous moisture and then didn't get it. Return to normal and safer watering practices. *See also chapter 4*
	Overwatering	Let soil dry until it will hold together as a ball. Remove plant from pot. Inspect root ends for the mushiness that indicates root rot. If none exists, repot plant in fresh pot, preferably clay, with an extra layer of pebbles in the bottom to handle drainage. Water only when soil has dried to the extent required for the specific plant. If some root has rotted, trim off the damaged portion. Repot plant in a fresh clay pot at least one size smaller than the one used before. Revamp your watering practices. *See also chapter 4*
	Transplanting shock	Some plants just don't like being handled. Have patience. Reassure plant and keep general conditions healthful. *See also chapter 4*
	Environmental shock	Some plants, such as polyscias, just firmly object to having their environments changed, as when moved from store to home. Treat plant well and it will return to beauty. *See also chapter 3*
	Exposure to natural-gas fumes	Move plant to a healthier location and check for gas leaks. *See also chapter 3*

Leaf Problems (cont.)

SYMPTOM	POSSIBLE CAUSE	WHAT TO DO ABOUT IT
	Falling Leaves	
Leaves suddenly drop off plant in large numbers (cont.)	Underfeeding (especially sulfur deficiency)	Feed lightly but often with a full-formula fertilizer. *See also chapter 5*
	Spider mites, mealybugs, or thrips	Inspect plant thoroughly with a magnifying glass; treat in appropriate manner only for specific pest identified. *See also chapter 6*
	Drying and Wilting	
Leaves dry up and crumble	Temperature too high (especially if combined with underwatering)	Lower the thermostat (in winter) or move plant from hot window location (in summer). Water more often, making sure that soil drains easily. *See also chapter 3*
	Spider mites	Inspect plant thoroughly with a magnifying glass; treat in appropriate manner for spider mites, if identified; increase humidity in all ways possible. Leaves should regrow if humidity is kept high and pests eliminated. *See also chapter 6*
Leaves wilt, usually followed by withering and dropping	Drafts	The difference in temperature between drafts and normal air causes leaves to lose more moisture than plant can absorb through its roots. Locate and block draft or move plant. Put plastic bag over plant temporarily until it revives. *See also chapter 3*

Drying and Wilting

SYMPTOM	POSSIBLE CAUSE	WHAT TO DO ABOUT IT
Leaves wilt, usually followed by withering and dropping (cont.)	Humidity too low (especially if soil isn't dried out—see "Compacted soil" below	Increase relative humidity in all ways possible: mist plant often; put plant on a pebble tray faithfully kept filled with water; lower room temperature. Be sure air circulates well to avoid fungus problems. *See also chapter 4*
	Nematodes	Discard plant (burn if possible) after taking cuttings. If plant is particularly valuable, treat with nematocide according to package directions. *See also chapter 7*
	Compacted soil (especially if water remains on soil surface after watering)	Repot plant in a more porous soil; be sure to remove most of the old, denser soil from roots. Be certain when watering that you are thorough, so root ball has no chance to dry out and compact. *See also chapter 5*
	Damage from physical contact; careless or frequent handling	Cut off damaged leaves; keep your cotton-pickin' hands off! *See also chapter 3*
Leaves wilt but revive later in day	Temperature too high	Afternoon sun can bring on temporary wilting; the leaves revive naturally in the cooler evening. However, this cannot go on indefinitely without harming the plant. Move plant to a cooler location; increase humidity in all ways possible. *See also chapter 3*

Leaf Problems (cont.)

SYMPTOM	POSSIBLE CAUSE	WHAT TO DO ABOUT IT
Drying and Wilting		
Leaves wilt and some older (lower) ones turn yellow	Overwatering; root or stem rot	Let soil dry until it will hold together as a ball. Remove plant from pot. Inspect root ends for the mushiness that indicates root rot. If none exists, repot plant in fresh pot, preferably clay, with an extra layer of pebbles in the bottom to handle drainage. Water only when soil has dried to the extent required for the specific plant. If some root has rotted, trim off the damaged portion. Repot plant in a fresh clay pot at least one size smaller than the one used before. Revamp your watering practices. *See also chapters 4, 7*
Leaves wilt and edges turn brown; new leaves may be small	Persistent underwatering	Water more often, but don't start overwatering to compensate. Between waterings, let soil dry as required for the specific plant. *See also chapter 4*
	Pot-bound	A pot-bound plant tends to be underwatered because there is not enough soil to hold water. Repot plant in a larger pot. *See also chapter 5*
Newer (upper) leaves wilt, others become vivid dark green	Copper deficiency	Feed lightly but often with a full-formula fertilizer. *See also chapter 5*

Tip Changes

SYMPTOM	POSSIBLE CAUSE	WHAT TO DO ABOUT IT
Leaf tips and edges turn brown and dry	Humidity too low	Almost inevitably, some plants will have browned leaf tips from the low humidity of most homes — especially in winter. Put all plants except cacti on pebble trays faithfully kept filled with water. Mist often (except for those hairy-leaved plants that don't like it). Set thermostat low to increase relative humidity, buy a room humidifier, and so forth. Trim off tip damage with sharp scissors. *See also chapter 4*
	Overwatering	Let soil dry until it will hold together as a ball. Remove plant from pot. Inspect root ends for the mushiness that indicates root rot. If none exists (and it probably won't unless some leaves have turned yellow), repot plant in fresh pot, preferably clay, with an extra layer of pebbles in the bottom to handle drainage. Water only when soil has dried to the extent required for the specific plant. If some root has rotted, trim off the damaged portion. Repot the plant in a fresh clay pot at least one size smaller than the one used before. Revamp your watering practices. *See also chapter 4*
	Bruising from physical contact	Remove damaged leaves. Move plant out of the traffic pattern. *See also chapter 3*

Leaf Problems (cont.)

SYMPTOM	POSSIBLE CAUSE	WHAT TO DO ABOUT IT

Tip Changes

Leaf tips and edges turn brown and dry (cont.)	Temperature too high; hot drafts from room heat	Eliminate drafts; reduce temperature of room. If difficult to do, be sure to increase humidity in all ways possible to compensate. *See also chapter 3*
	Overfeeding (fertilizer accumulation)	Buildup of fertilizer salts in the soil has had a toxic effect on some roots and the leaves they support. Leach the soil: sink pot to rim in tub of lukewarm water. Leave it for an hour or until water is visible on top of the soil. Remove and let drain. If salt crust on rim can't be easily scraped off, repot plant in fresh soil and fresh pot. Prevent repeat of salt accumulation by fertilizing less often or with weaker food solutions; leach the soil periodically during the growing season. *See also chapter 5*
	Root damage	Avoid breaking roots when repotting plants; if you've been careless, wait patiently for new roots to grow. Cut damage off leaves. *See also chapter 4*
	Air pollution (if you live in a smog-bound city)	Keep air conditioning on, adding a carbon filter to the unit, if possible. Keep all windows closed on smoggy days, and just hope the pollution clears. Wash leaves often. *See also chapter 3*

SYMPTOM	POSSIBLE CAUSE	WHAT TO DO ABOUT IT

Tip Changes

SYMPTOM	POSSIBLE CAUSE	WHAT TO DO ABOUT IT
Leaf tips and edges turn brown and dry (cont.)	Aerosol-spray damage	Remove damaged edges or leaves. Avoid using aerosol sprays for treating insect pests (try regular "pump" sprayers); if you must use an aerosol device, hold it at least eighteen inches from plant. *See also chapter 4*
	Fluoride damage (if all else is well), especially in plants of the Arum family	Use rainwater when watering, or add lime to the soil to increase its alkalinity and effectively stop the fluoride effect
Leaf tips and edges turn tan or bronze (or even red), beginning with older (lower) leaves	Potassium deficiency	Feed lightly but often with a well-balanced fertilizer. *See also chapter 5*
Leaf tips and edges turn yellow, then brown or spotted, and curly	Calcium deficiency	Feed lightly but often with a full-formula fertilizer. *See also chapter 5*
Leaf edges curl; some leaves may drop off	Drafts	Keep plant protected from blasts of hot or cold air from doors, windows, heating or air-conditioning units. If a plant can replace its leaves, it will soon do so. One that doesn't will probably need air layering eventually (see chapter 10). *See also chapter 3*

Leaf Problems (cont.)

SYMPTOM	POSSIBLE CAUSE	WHAT TO DO ABOUT IT

Tip Changes

SYMPTOM	POSSIBLE CAUSE	WHAT TO DO ABOUT IT
Leaf edges curl; some leaves may drop off (cont.)	Humidity too low	Increase relative humidity in all ways possible: mist plant often; put plant on a pebble tray faithfully kept filled with water; lower room temperature. Be sure air circulates well to avoid fungus problems. *See also chapter 4*
	Sucking insects (especially aphids)	Inspect plant thoroughly with a magnifying glass; treat in appropriate manner only for specific pest identified. *See also chapter 6*
	Underfeeding	Feed lightly but often with a full-formula fertilizer. *See also chapter 5*
Leaf tips, edges, and veins turn reddish or bronze, beginning with older (lower) leaves; new growth is stunted	Phosphorus deficiency	Feed lightly but often with a full-formula fertilizer. *See also chapter 5*

Spotting and Coating

SYMPTOM	POSSIBLE CAUSE	WHAT TO DO ABOUT IT
Leaves develop yellowish or tan patches	Sun scorch	Move plant to a shadier location or, if that's not possible, for several hours at midday put a shield between plant and any bright window nearby. Cut off damaged leaves if necessary. *See also chapter 3*

Spotting and Coating

SYMPTOM	POSSIBLE CAUSE	WHAT TO DO ABOUT IT
Leaves develop brown, dry spots	Overwatering	Let soil dry until it will hold together as a ball. Remove plant from pot. Inspect root ends for the mushiness that indicates root rot. If none exists, repot plant in fresh pot, preferably clay, with an extra layer of pebbles in the bottom to handle drainage. Water only when soil has dried to the extent required for the specific plant. If some root has rotted, trim off the damaged portion. Repot plant in a fresh clay pot at least one size smaller than the one used before. Revamp your watering practices. *See also chapter 4*
	Too much light (especially if plant is not clean)	Move plant gradually to a shadier location; give it a cooling bath with soap and water. *See also chapters 3, 4*
Leaves develop dry, brown or black, sunken spots, possibly rimmed with dark rings	Anthracnose	Avoid this fungus problem by making sure plant is not chilled or kept too humid. Remove spotted leaves; spray remaining ones with a fungicide. Increase temperature and air circulation and withhold humidifying mist until new spots stop forming. *See also chapter 7*

Leaf Problems (cont.)

SYMPTOM	POSSIBLE CAUSE	WHAT TO DO ABOUT IT

Spotting and Coating

Leaves develop light-colored, usually circular spots; or spots, different from rest of leaf in color and texture, that are rimmed with light-colored rings	Fungal leaf spots	Don't allow moisture drops to remain on leaves in darkness or if it's cold. Avoid cramped plant rooms with no air circulation. Move plants apart; increase ventilation without creating drafts. Spray with fungicide, especially during gray, humid weather. Remove damaged leaves. *See also chapter 7*
	Cold-water watering (especially of gesneriads)	When watering, always use water that's lukewarm or at least at room temperature (this is critical for African violets and their relatives). *See also chapter 4*
	Bacterial disease (if spots increase in size)	Remove affected leaves if attack is mild; discard plant if serious. *See also chapter 7*
Leaves develop rusty spots, usually with brown edges	Overfeeding (fertilizer accumulation; leaf rot from rubbing incrusted pot rim)	Buildup of fertilizer salts in the soil has had a toxic effect on some roots and the leaves they support. Leach the soil: sink pot to rim in tub of lukewarm water. Leave it for an hour or until water is visible on top of the soil. Remove and let drain. If salt crust on rim can't be easily scraped off, repot plant in fresh soil and fresh pot. Prevent repeat of salt accumulation by fertilizing less often or with weaker food solutions; leach the soil periodically during the growing season. *See also chapter 5*

Spotting and Coating

SYMPTOM	POSSIBLE CAUSE	WHAT TO DO ABOUT IT
Leaves develop swellings (edema) — irregular spots of watery growth, possibly with corklike edges	Overwatering (especially of ivy geraniums)	Cut down on watering; remove damaged leaves. (Geraniums should be kept in porous, quickly draining soil.) *See also chapter 4*
Leaves develop raised, blisterlike, irregular patches	Leaf miners	If damage is minimal, just remove affected leaves. If attack is major, treat in appropriate manner for leaf miners. *See also chapter 6*
Leaf surfaces become sticky and glossy (honeydew patches), perhaps with spreading patches of blackish or dark gray, powdery coating (sooty mold)	Sucking insects	Inspect plant thoroughly with a magnifying glass; treat in appropriate manner only for specific pest identified. Wash all leaves with soap and water. *See also chapter 6*
Leaves develop a whitish, dustlike coating	Powdery mildew	Increase air circulation and move plants apart; dust with fungicide. *See also chapter 7*
Leaves develop a gray-tan coating; light or dark brownish spots form on leaves, turning grayish black, perhaps watery	Botrytis blight	Increase air circulation and move plants apart; dust with fungicide. *See also chapter 7*

SYMPTOM	POSSIBLE CAUSE	WHAT TO DO ABOUT IT
	Spotting and Coating	
Leaves develop silvery streaks or transparent spots on top surface; rusty or whitish spots form on backs	Thrips	Treat in appropriate manner for thrips. *See also chapter 6*
Fresh chew marks appear on leaves	Someone is eating them	Search for the presence of chewing pests (you may need to do this at night, because many hide during the day), such as snails or slugs. (You'll also see slime trails from these pests.) Treat in appropriate manner for specific pest identified. *See also chapter 6*
Small brown or gray lumps, usually hard, appear on leaves and stems	Scale insects	Inspect plant thoroughly with a magnifying glass for scale insects; treat in appropriate manner for scale, if identified. *See also chapter 6*

STEM PROBLEMS

SYMPTOM	POSSIBLE CAUSE	WHAT TO DO ABOUT IT
Stems wilt	Same as for leaves; see LEAF PROBLEMS, *Drying and Wilting*	—
Stems and leaves are broken	Pets, children, careless or frequent handling	Trim off broken parts. A Band-Aid won't help.
Brown or black discoloration, possibly watery, creeps up stem from soil level and stem collapses	Stem rot from overwatering	Let soil dry until it will hold together as a ball. Remove plant from pot. Cut away damaged stems with sharp knife. If that destroys plant completely, take cuttings of remaining healthy tissue and discard remainder of plant. If some plant remains, dust wounded part with fungicide. Carry out root check to see if damage has been done to roots. Repot as described elsewhere under "Overwatering" items. Revamp your watering practices. *See also chapters 4, 7*
	Stem rot from rubbing pot rim (especially over-fed African violets)	Smooth pot rim with candle wax or paraffin. Clip off damaged stems. Avoid fertilizer accumulation. *See also chapters 5, 7*
Stems lean	Too little light	Insufficient light causes stems to lean as much as possible toward the light source. Gradually move plant into brighter location; or give it a boost with artificial light. Turn plant frequently to avoid permanent lean. *See also chapter 3*

Stem Problems *(cont.)*

SYMPTOM	POSSIBLE CAUSE	WHAT TO DO ABOUT IT
Small brown or gray lumps, usually hard, appear on stems and leaves	Scale insects	Inspect plant thoroughly with a magnifying glass for scale insects; treat in an appropriate manner for scale, if identified. *See also chapter 6*
Stems turn hard and inflexible	Sulfur deficiency	Feed lightly but often with a full-formula fertilizer. *See also chapter 5*
Stems die from the tip down	Temperature too low	This unusual situation is most apt to occur in winter when a plant is too close to a window. Move it farther into the room; cut off any damaged portion.

ROOT PROBLEMS

SYMPTOM	POSSIBLE CAUSE	WHAT TO DO ABOUT IT
Roots grow out of drainage holes	Pot-bound	Repot plant in a larger pot. If that is undesirable, trim off some roots and return plant to same-size pot. *See also chapter 4*
Roots appear on soil surface	Underwatering (soil ball is too dry at the bottom)	Plant probably has not been watered sufficiently to soak the root ball; therefore the roots turn upward to seek water near the soil surface. Leach the soil: sink pot to rim in tub of lukewarm water. Leave it for an hour or until water is visible on top of the soil. Remove and let drain. When watering, use enough water so that excess runs out the drainage hole. *See also chapter 4*
	Pot-bound	Repot plant in a larger pot. If that is undesirable, trim off some roots and return plant to same-size pot. *See also chapter 4*
Roots lack holding power, plant easily uproots; roots appear dark and mushy when checked	Root rot from overwatering	Let soil dry until it will hold together as a ball. Remove plant from pot. Inspect root ends for the mushiness that indicates root rot. Trim off damaged portion. Repot plant in a fresh clay pot at least one size smaller than the one used before. Revamp your watering practices so that plant is watered only when soil has dried to the extent required for the specific plant. *See also chapters 4, 7*
Roots become stunted, gnarled, distorted, covered with galls, and diminish in number	Nematodes	Discard plant (burn if possible) after taking cuttings. If plant is particularly valuable, treat with nematocide according to directions on package. *See also chapter 7*

FLOWER AND BUD PROBLEMS

SYMPTOM	POSSIBLE CAUSE	WHAT TO DO ABOUT IT
Few or no buds or flowers form on a flowering plant	Too little light	Spend five or six days gradually moving plant into a brighter location, until it receives enough light both to carry on photosynthesis and to bud. *See also chapters 3, 9*
	Temperature too high without a nighttime drop	Turn down thermostat each night to guarantee that plant is exposed to at least a ten-degree-Fahrenheit drop in temperature. *See also chapters 3, 9*
	Pot too roomy	Many flowering plants require a certain degree of pot-boundness in order to bloom; otherwise, they're just too busy growing to bloom. *See also chapter 9*
	Overwatering	Plants need more water to flower than they do at other times, but they will not flower if they are busy trying to save roots from rotting in soggy soil. Let the soil dry almost to the danger point, then water less often but throughly. Be sure the pot drains well. *See also chapters 4, 5, 9*
	Humidity too low	Increase relative humidity in all ways possible: mist plant often; put plant on a pebble tray faithfully kept filled with water; lower room temperature. Be sure air circulates well to avoid fungus problems. *See also chapters 4, 9*
	Nitrogen overdose (if leaf growth is excessive)	Feed plant less often and change to a fertilizer with a high phosphorus content. Check, too, that it's the right time of year for the plant to bloom. *See also chapter 5*

SYMPTOM	POSSIBLE CAUSE	WHAT TO DO ABOUT IT
Few or no buds or flowers form on a flowering plant (cont.)	Wrong day-night duration	Some flowering plants will bloom only when days and nights are of a certain length, either longer or shorter than normal, and they cannot be forced to bloom indoors unless you give them the required day length. Check each plant's requirements. *See also chapter 9*
Buds blast (wither) or drop off before opening; those that do open shrivel or drop off quickly	Humidity too low	Increase relative humidity in all ways possible: mist plant often; put plant on a pebble tray faithfully kept filled with water; lower room temperature. Be sure air circulates well to avoid fungus problems. *See also chapters 4, 9*
	Drafts; abrupt temperature change or temperature too high	Keep budding plants out of all but the safest air currents; make sure that ventilation is in the form of gentle air movement, not gusts, and avoid extremely high temperatures. *See also chapters 3, 9*
	Overwatering	Plants need more water when budding than they do at other times, but the soil still must drain very well. If soil is soggy, let it dry almost to the danger point; then water less often but thoroughly. If buds still continue to blast, assume that root rot set in before you discovered the situation and repot as necessary. *See also chapters 4, 5, 9*

Flower and Bud Problems (cont.)

SYMPTOM	POSSIBLE CAUSE	WHAT TO DO ABOUT IT
Buds blast (wither) or drop off before opening; those that do open shrivel or drop off quickly (cont.)	Too little light	Spend five or six days gradually moving plant into brighter location; or give the plant a boost with artificial light. In increased sunlight, do not turn plant often (the buds can actually twist off). *See also chapters 3, 9*
	Underwatering	Water more frequently to give buds enough moisture to maintain their shape and growth, but make sure that drainage can handle the excess water. *See also chapters 4, 9*
	Environmental shock	Try to ease the strain of sudden changes such as when moving the plant from greenhouse to home. Keep plant in a plastic-bag greenhouse for several days; open bag a little longer each day, giving plant time to adjust to the change. *See also chapters 3, 4, 9*
	Natural-gas damage	Move plant to a healthier location and check for gas leaks. *See also chapter 3*
Buds turn black	Cyclamen mites (especially on African violets)	Inspect plant thoroughly with a magnifying glass; if cyclamen mites are identified, discard the affected plant. *See also chapter 6*
Buds are distorted	Nematodes	Discard plant (burn if possible) after taking cuttings. If plant is particularly valuable, treat with nematocide according to directions on the package. *See also chapter 7*

SYMPTOM	POSSIBLE CAUSE	WHAT TO DO ABOUT IT
Flower petal tips turn brown	Underwatering	Increase frequency of watering just slightly, but be sure that each watering is thorough: drench the soil, let excess run out drainage hole. *See also chapters 4, 9*
	Overfeeding (fertilizer accumulation)	Buildup of fertilizer salts in the soil has had a toxic effect on some roots and the flowers they support. Leach the soil: sink pot to rim in tub of lukewarm water. Leave it for an hour or until water is visible on top of the soil. Remove and let drain. If salt crust on rim can't be easily scraped off, repot plant in fresh soil and fresh pot. Prevent repeat of salt accumulation by fertilizing less often or with weaker food solutions; leach the soil periodically during the growing season. *See also chapter 5*
	Humidity too low	Increase the relative humidity in all ways possible: mist leaves (but not flowers) often; put plant on a pebble tray faithfully kept filled with water; lower room temperature. Be sure air circulates well to avoid fungus problems. *See also chapters 4, 9*
Flower petals develop brown spots	Overwatering	Plants need more water when flowering than they do at other times, but the soil still must drain very well. If soil is soggy, let it dry almost to danger point; then water less often but thoroughly. If flowers continue to char, assume that root rot set in before you discovered the situation and repot as necessary. *See also chapters 4, 5, 9*

Flower and Bud Problems (cont.)

SYMPTOM	POSSIBLE CAUSE	WHAT TO DO ABOUT IT
Flower petals develop brown spots; flowers smaller than usual	Too much light	Check requirements for the specific plant; not all flowering plants can tolerate hot, south-facing light. *See also chapters 3, 9*
Flower petals curl up	Drafts; abrupt temperature change	Keep flowering plants out of all but the gentlest air currents and check your thermostat. Keep flowering plants in even temperature, if possible, preferably fairly low (except for gesneriads). *See also chapter 3*
Flowers develop a gray-tan coating or brownish spots; buds become distorted	Botrytis blight	Increase air circulation and move plants apart; dust with fungicide. *See also chapter 7*
Flowers develop a whitish, dustlike coating	Powdery mildew	Increase air circulation and move plants apart; dust with fungicide. *See also chapter 7*
Flowers become distorted and streaked	Thrips	Treat in appropriate manner for thrips. *See also chapter 6*

GROWTH PROBLEMS

SYMPTOM	POSSIBLE CAUSE	WHAT TO DO ABOUT IT
Growth slows or stops	Normal dormancy (especially in fall)	Cut down on watering; stop feeding. Plant will indicate when to resume normal treatment by starting to grow again. *See also chapter 4*
	Pot-bound	Repot plant in a larger pot. If that is undesirable, trim off some roots and return plant to same-size pot. *See also chapter 4*
	Overwatering	Let soil dry until it will hold together as a ball. Remove plant from pot. Inspect root ends for the mushiness that indicates root rot. If none exists, repot plant in fresh pot, preferably clay, with an extra layer of pebbles in the bottom to handle drainage. Water only when soil has dried to the extent required for the specific plant. If some root has rotted, trim off the damaged portion. Repot plant in a fresh clay pot at least one size smaller than the one used before. Revamp your watering practices. *See also chapter 4*
	Underfeeding	Feed lightly but often with a full-formula fertilizer. Do not try to remedy the situation with a single strong feeding. *See also chapter 5*

SYMPTOM	POSSIBLE CAUSE	WHAT TO DO ABOUT IT
Growth slows or stops (cont.)	Compacted soil (especially if water remains on soil surface after watering)	Repot plant in a more porous soil; be sure to remove most of the old, denser soil from roots. When watering, be thorough, so the root ball never has a chance to dry out and compact. *See also chapter 5*
	Nematodes	Discard plant (burn if possible) after taking cuttings. If plant is particularly valuable, treat with nematocide according to directions on the package. *See also chapter 7*
	Wrong soil pH	Using a soil test kit, determine the exact soil pH in the pot and compare with the requirements for the specific plant; or just repot plant in fresh soil with the proper acidity for the plant. *See also chapter 5*
	Insects	Inspect plant thoroughly with a magnifying glass; treat in appropriate manner for specific pest identified. *See also chapter 6*
New growth is stunted, pale, possibly curled or otherwise distorted	Underfeeding	Feed lightly but often with a full-formula fertilizer. Do not try to remedy the situation with a single strong feeding. *See also chapter 5*
	Wrong environment (too cold, too dry, too dark)	Check the cultural requirements of the specific plant and try to determine which environmental aspect is wrong. (Note that African violets show stunted growth when the light is too bright.) *See also chapter 3*

SYMPTOM	POSSIBLE CAUSE	WHAT TO DO ABOUT IT
New growth is stunted, pale, possibly curled or otherwise distorted (cont.)	Mealybugs or other sucking pests	Inspect plant thoroughly with a magnifying glass; treat in appropriate manner only for specific pest identified. *See also chapter 6*
	Nitrogen or boron deficiency	Feed lightly but frequently with a full-formula fertilizer. *See also chapter 5*
	Overfeeding (fertilizer accumulation)	Buildup of fertilizer salts in the soil has had a toxic effect on some roots. Leach the soil: sink pot to rim in tub of lukewarm water. Leave it for an hour or until water is visible on top of the soil. Remove and let drain. If salt crust on rim can't be easily scraped off, repot plant in fresh soil and fresh pot. Prevent repeat of salt accumulation by fertilizing less often or with weaker food solutions; leach the soil periodically during the growing season. *See also chapter 5*
New growth is stunted and thicker than normal	Compacted soil (especially if water remains on soil surface after watering)	Repot plant in a more porous soil; be sure to remove most of the old, denser soil from the roots. *See also chapter 5*
New growth is weak and spindly, with long gaps between pale leaves	See LEAF PROBLEMS, *Color Change* (Leaves turn pale . . .)	—

Growth Problems (cont.)

SYMPTOM	POSSIBLE CAUSE	WHAT TO DO ABOUT IT
New growth is stunted, with distances between leaves shorter than normal	Potassium deficiency	Feed lightly but often with a full-formula fertilizer. *See also chapter 5*
All growth stops; plant appears dead	Neglect	Plant may still be alive. Snip a bit of stem with a sharp knife or scissors and see if any internal greenness remains. If so, it might be possible to revive the plant with wise treatment and tender loving care.

PROPAGATION PROBLEMS

SYMPTOM	POSSIBLE CAUSE	WHAT TO DO ABOUT IT
Cuttings wilt	Normal propagation (initially)	A new cutting naturally wilts until its stem bottom adjusts to taking in water directly. Keep humidity high to assist the cutting during its adjustment period. *See also chapter 4*
Cuttings wilt and die	Humidity too low	Keep cutting in its rooting medium with a plastic bag placed over it (but let air in occasionally to prevent mold). Keep the plastic-protected cutting out of direct sunlight. *See also chapter 4*
Cuttings fail to root	Wrong medium	Not all cuttings can be rooted in water. If nothing happens after a while, make a fresh cut on the stem end and insert into a solid medium such as soil, sand, or vermiculite.
	Cutting too moist	After taking the cutting, let it dry in the air for up to twenty-four hours before inserting it in a rooting medium. (Some cuttings, especially from succulents, will not root unless the necessary callus is encouraged to form over the cut.)
Seedlings suddenly turn watery and wilt, collapse at the soil line, or die overnight	Too little light	Seedlings need all the light possible to get started right; move them to a brighter location or provide a boost with artificial light. (If leggy seedlings are allowed to develop, the plants will probably be leggy all their lives.) *See also chapter 3*
	Damping-off disease (from unsterilized soil)	There is no cure: start again using only peat moss or sterilized potting soil for starting seedlings. *See also chapter 7*

~~3. ANALYZING YOUR HOME ENVIRONMENT

ALTHOUGH USUALLY YOU'RE THE DOCTOR WHEN IT comes to your plants' health — at least you were until recently, when botanical gardens started answering questions from amateurs — you may have the choice of sending your unwell plants to a health farm. I know of several plant hospital/hotels where you can take well plants to be boarded while you're away or where you can take sickly ones to be made well . . . if possible. One of the major attributes of a plant hotel is that it provides a horticultural environment that's quite possibly better than the one at home. If you send your plants away for a cure, they are likely to return home considerably healthier than when they left you merely because they've been away from their harmful routine surroundings.

It's a shock to think that the home we love may be death to a plant we also love. But such may be the case if insufficient thought is given to choosing plants that suit the individual home environment. During the recent boom in house-plant popularity, the number of long-legged but weak-kneed plants rose alarmingly. It was *the* thing to do to have plants, so have plants people did — even if they could not provide appropriate light or if they kept their homes warm and dry like a desert.

House plants in general are very adjustable creatures, but they are at their best when environmental conditions are encouraging. Like Goldilocks, they may find aspects of your home too warm, too cold, too bright, too dark, but with a little thought you can give them conditions that are *juuust* right.

Plants are products of nature, and nature — at least the green and wild sort — is found outdoors, where the sun beats down for a changing but certainly predictable number of hours each day, where winds stir the air, where masses of greenery giving off moisture enhance other plants. Greenhouses do a fairly good job of duplicating natural conditions for many sorts of plants. But when we move those plants into our homes things begin to go wrong: leaf tips turn brown, stems get scrawny, and, even more horrifying, great masses of leaves fall, denuding the expensive acquisitions. It's heartbreaking to watch the slow demise of a beautiful and grandiose plant — especially one acquired as a showpiece — because it can't adjust to your home after long years in a greenhouse. But you can insure that you'll have healthy display plants in a couple of ways:

· First, don't buy big ones. Instead, get nice little ones that can more easily adjust or be helped to adjust to your home (and if they don't, the loss isn't so costly). Be good to them and eventually you'll have the huge decorator plants that draw oohs and ahs, and you'll be able proudly to say, "I grew them from pups."

· Second, if you don't have the kind of patience required for the first way, find out where the plants you like spent their "childhoods" — not ancestral (which you should do with all house plants) but actual. If raised nearby or north of where you are, the plant should adjust fairly easily to the light direction and intensity available at your home. If they're southern plants, on the other hand, and you're a northerner, forget about them — or at least prepare to have some difficulty getting them to adjust.

For example, I recently ran into the most fantastic plant sale: about one hundred four- or five-foot-tall false aralias, with gorgeous bronzy leaves fully skirting the stems down to the pot rim; the delicate, lacy look just about lured me into buying at the excellent savings offered (about one-third of the normal greenhouse price). But the plants had been shipped up from Florida, so I reluctantly passed them up. Probably everyone in Chicago who bought them was going to go through the sad experience of watching lower leaves fall . . . and middle leaves fall . . . until the tall, slender stems became almost naked to the world. (This awful process can often be alleviated, by the way, by covering a new plant with a large plastic bag for a few hours each day. Not all day, though — except in the case of the very persnickety polyscias; just enough to encourage the plant to believe that you care and to convince it that it should adjust to you and your home — that you're doing the best you can for it, so it should reciprocate.)

In any event, before you bring a plant home you really should first understand what your home offers — or doesn't offer — and you should know how to perceive when your environment is threatening to a plant's existence.

A Place in the Sun A plant's need for sunlight (or artificial light, which is a perfectly acceptable substitute since the plant can't tell the difference) relates directly to its place of origin. Most house plants are tropical — which conjures up visions of sun-drenched beaches. Actually, for plants, *tropical* means "lush growth": the plants were just part of a great variety of life residing under a canopy of tall trees — in a rain forest, in fact. The tropical plants didn't actually get much direct sun, but what they got was strong and didn't have to pass through a glass window first, as it does in most homes. Tropical or not, house plants need light.

SYMPTOMS/ TOO LITTLE LIGHT	New growth is weak, pale, and straggly Older (lower) leaves turn yellow Stems lean toward light source, making growth uneven Few or no buds form on a flowering plant Buds blast (wither) or drop off before opening; those that do open shrivel or drop off quickly

A plant receiving too little light grows long stems with big gaps between the leaves, because leaves are, quite literally, just a burden to a plant when they can't perform their basic function of photosynthesis — producing food from a concoction of carbon dioxide, water, and minerals, all stirred with a wand of light. And the plant, when finally moved into enough light, can't make itself beautiful again; the long gaps between stuffy leaves won't disappear. Pinch back the plant and let it reacquire its growth — this time properly.

What is "enough" light? Obviously, that depends upon the kind of plant. The common house plants that need the least light — those suitable for locations where your hand casts a barely visible shadow on a sheet of white paper — are generally plain green and hardy: aspidistra, Chinese evergreen *(Aglaonema),* pothos, nephthytis, India rubber plant *(Ficus elastica),* unvariegated peperomia, aluminum plant (the "aluminum" markings are not real variegation but are very thin air spaces in the leaves), corn plant *(Dracaena fragrans massangeana),* bird's-nest fern, *Chamaedorea* palms, snake plant *(Sansevieria trifasciata),* and philodendron. This list provides quite a variety of colors, shapes, and growing habits for a dim spot. (If you're using a light meter to measure the light your plants are getting, such a dim spot will register between 50 and 200 footcandles [now more commonly called "lumens per square foot" by scientists].) All these plants can survive neglect.

They don't really thrive in such little light, but they tolerate existence: they maintain themselves and that's all. They don't need much water and they eat almost no food; feed them perhaps once a year.

Other plants have light-colored variegations, and thus less chlorophyll in their leaves for making food. They must have more light in order to make enough food for life and growth. Still other house plants are grown primarily for their flowers and require a great deal of energy in order to bloom — energy which must be derived from food made by sun-involved photosynthesis. Such plants require a great deal of sunlight. Oleander *(Nerium)*, Christmas kalanchoe, crown of thorns, clerodendron, and geraniums are among these sun-loving plants.

SYMPTOMS/ TOO MUCH LIGHT	Leaves turn pale, yellow, or bleached New growth is weak and spindly Leaves develop spots, usually brown and dry, or yellowish or tan patches Flower petals and leaves develop brown spots; flowers, if they form at all, may be smaller than usual or may drop off quickly Stems and leaves go limp each day (though they usually revive at nightfall)

The plants that are easiest to care for in a very bright location are those that are free to enjoy dry soil between complete waterings: cacti, succulents — obviously, the thick-leaved plants that hold their own water supply. Although their soil dries out quickly in the full sun of a south window, they do well. Unfortunately, many thin-leaved plants that can't retain water, especially flowering plants, also require very bright light — and they are a lot trickier to keep happy in a bright and consequently hot south window. Their leaves rapidly transpire (give off) moisture in the bright heat, their roots can't keep up with their leaves' demand for water from below, and the plant goes limp. If buds are just

Crassula falcata
with sun scorch

forming at that time, the plant throws them off in order to concentrate its energies on protecting its leaves, which are more important.

CONTROLLING NATURAL LIGHT

Because of the heat buildup in summer daylight, it is a good idea to shield most plants from direct, hot sun from perhaps 10:00 A.M. to 2:00 P.M. — those hours during which the sunlight is most intense and during which heat builds up viciously near the window. You can spread a venetian blind (kept partially open) or a sheer curtain — anything, in fact, that will break up the concentration of light, thus alleviating the heat. You needn't necessarily shield the actual window: you can protect the plant itself from the sun, perhaps by covering it with cheesecloth. However, with the latter method you'll still get heat buildup by the window; shielding the plant itself only breaks up the light, not the heat. If you own your home, consider installing blinds *outside* the windows, with controls on the inside: even the heat buildup will be prevented during those midday hours.

The intensity of light a plant gets is not necessarily the only aspect of light that needs to concern you.

good light in summer

 good light in winter

 light usable only for dimness-tolerating plants

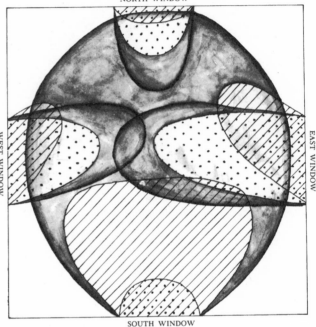

NORTH WINDOW

WEST WINDOW

EAST WINDOW

SOUTH WINDOW

The usable light for growing plants varies according to the season of the year and the direction in which a room's windows face. Shown here, for a room in the northern hemisphere, are the relative areas of useful light provided by unobstructed windows at four different exposures.

Some flowering plants and even a few foliage plants are affected by the *length* of their day; the flowering ones won't bloom unless the day is of a certain length. The spider plant, for instance, won't put out its spiders (shoots) unless it has a short day, only eight hours long. For more information on day length, see chapter 9.

You needn't accept the light availability in your home as an unchangeable condition. You can revamp things considerably and change the light that reaches your plants. As noted above, you can shield them; or you can just move plants back from the window when the light is too strong (though the daily handling required can itself be harmful).

Improving the light requires additional thought. Basically, you want to take advantage of any reflections that might increase the amount of light that reaches your plants. For example, since white surfaces reflect light and dark ones absorb it, if you keep your plants on a white-painted surface, any sunlight that reaches the surface will be reflected back up toward the plants, intensifying its effect on them. A roof overhang above a windowsill containing plants can also be painted white so that reflected sun is directed down toward the plants. Here are some other suggestions for controlling natural light:

· If you have a big plant that can't easily be rotated to keep its growth even, put aluminum foil or a similar bright surface in back of it, so that sunlight reflects from the surface to the back of the plant, keeping growth nice and uniform.

· If necessary, get drastic and cut down bushes that block windows, or trim trees that prevent your house plants from receiving their full share of light.

· Keep your windows clean.

Crassula argentea *(jade plant) overgrown in one direction because it hasn't been rotated*

You can increase the intensity of sunlight reaching a plant by placing a mirror to reflect the available light (left). You can decrease light intensity by shielding the plant with cheesecloth, which breaks up the sun's rays.

· Hang a sheer curtain. Curiously enough, a sheer curtain doesn't just filter the direct light and reduce consequent heat; it also breaks up (diffuses) sunlight into billions of tiny shafts that increase the intensity of light *away* from the immediate vicinity of the window, throughout the room.

· Set up mirrors around windows; for example, to pick up the rays of the setting sun and reflect them indoors; added to illumination from the rising sun, that will give lots more light for plants.

· Paint the fence in your garden white so that it reflects additional light into your house.

You can also, of course, change a plant's lighting diet by moving it, if you live in a house or in an apartment with a variety of window exposures. Whenever you move a plant from very bright to dim light, or vice versa, do so *gradually*, to give the plant time to adjust; otherwise, a plant can easily sunburn — just as you can after a long winter — or lose its leaves from shock. First move the plant to a halfway location for several days, and then make the final step into new light.

Artificial Light The ideas in the preceding section are all expedients to improve on what already exists. The major thing you can do to change light conditions within your home is to play sun-god yourself by giving your plants a boost with artificial light.

A winter day in the North may be only eight or nine hours long; those hours are useless to a plant if the day is gray and drizzly. A pair of fluorescent light tubes (perhaps one Deluxe Cool White, which gives more infrared than the regular Cool White, and one Warm White type to give the plants both the red and blue light needed) will in effect create a day as long as you want. Actually, even a sixteen-hour artificial-light day doesn't really give any more light, in toto, than a few hours of real sunlight. But it does allow you to grow plants in places that get no real sunlight; it lets you force plants to bloom at odd times of the year; it lets you produce flowers on plants that might not otherwise cooperate.

There isn't room here to give you the entire story on artificial light for your plants. But here are some points you should keep in mind to have healthy plants:

· Fluorescent light tubes wear out gradually instead of all at once, as incandescent bulbs do; therefore, change the tubes every eight or nine months, when light efficiency has begun to dwindle. If you wait until the tubes are obviously dimmer, the comparative brightness of new tubes can shock the plants.

· Plants of different sizes should be raised so that their tops are all at the same level in relation to the light tube; otherwise, the lower ones will develop stringy stems from trying to reach the light.

· Most plants can be prevented from having a dormant period when they live under artificial light. Do not cut down on their water and food during the winter months; there's no need to, since the plants no longer "know" the time of year.

· You must be even more faithful about keeping the humidity high (see the next chapter) when growing plants under artificial light, because the drying effect of the lights can readily let in bugs that like dryness.

· Using water around electricity can be dangerous. Follow all the safety rules in working with this combination.

· Distance from the light tubes really matters. A plant ten inches from the light source receives much less light than one only four inches away. You must, therefore, decide whether your plants are under lights to encourage growth (in which case they must be near the tubes and can't easily be shown off) or to merely maintain their present size (which allows for their convenient display, since they can be farther from the tubes).

· Light emitted from the ends of a fluorescent light tube is considerably duller than that put out at the center. In planning your useful plant space, try to use only the central light except for very-low-light-level plants.

· A small incandescent light, perhaps in a lamp on an end table, can also be used as an individual light source for a small plant, such as an African violet or a miniature rose. Just be certain that air circulates well around the plant, because incandescent light is hot light. Don't let the plant grow too close to the bulb; it can burn.

· Group plants with similar requirements together, under different lights; it's easier for you and better for the plants.

· If the leaves of your plants start to curl under, they are probably too close to the lights. Raise the lights or lower the plants.

Controlling Most house plants thrive best in cool, moist atmo-
Temperature spheres. "Moistness" will be covered in detail in the
next chapter; there is often more you can do about
humidity than you can about temperature — especially if you live in an apartment where an unfeeling
robot in the basement determines the temperature of
your home: too warm if he's got a generous soul, too
cold if the owners have been after him to save money.

In regard to temperature, generally if you're comfortable, your plants will be, too — at least in the daytime. Plants prefer a drop in the temperature at night
of approximately ten degrees Fahrenheit (and even
that doesn't compare with the more extensive drop
they would receive in the wild).

SYMPTOMS/ Leaves turn pale, yellow, or bleached
TEMPERATURE New growth is weak and spindly
TOO HIGH Leaves dry up and crumble (especially if combined with
underwatering) or may wilt
Leaf tips and edges turn brown and dry
Few or no flowers form on a flowering plant
Buds blast (wither) or drop off before opening; those that
do open shrivel or drop off quickly

You may be a warmth-loving creature who luxuriates
in high-temperature rooms. If so, you may not be
aware of it when your thermostat, presuming you have
one, is not recording properly; your first task should be
to find out if it is. Obtain an accurate thermometer and
compare it to the readings on your thermostat. You
may find that, as on a finicky oven, the actual readings
are not precisely what you set. You'll have to learn to
compensate for those differences as you do on your
oven. Then you can improve your plants' health by
turning the thermostat down on winter nights.

If you have no thermostatic control over your heating, what can you do? Well, on cold nights when the
heat's up high you can open a window — *in an adja-
cent room* — so that the coolness just seeps into your

plant room instead of blasting its way in. You can turn on a fan to keep the air circulating: moving air is cooler than still air. You can limit yourself to warmth-loving plants such as begonias, cacti, dracaenas, African violets, spathiphylum, peperomias, and even some orchids. Be sure to also increase the humidity of your home as much as possible to compensate for the increased heat.

Regardless of your best efforts, some plants will begin to develop pale or bleached leaves after several months of winter's artificial heating. All you can do until the relief of spring sets in is raise the humidity as much as possible and increase the light supply.

SYMPTOMS/ TEMPERATURE TOO LOW	New growth is stunted Stems may die from the top down Leaves turn brown, possibly with curled edges and mushy spots (frostbite) and may drop off

Temperatures that are too cold for house plants are more likely to occur from drafts, such as from air conditioners, or in spurts, such as when the heat in an office is turned off for the weekend, than from consistently cold room temperatures. We don't often live in conditions that are consistently too cold for comfort (although the British once did, but they were not very lucky with their African violets until they began to use central heating). Most plant enthusiasts are more likely to have problems that arise from drafts — about which more later.

If you must grow plants in a consistently cold room, however, you may still be lucky; if you have sufficient sunlight, you can grow lots of flowering plants that don't do well in the normal heat of most homes: azaleas, fuchsias, cineraria — the gift plants, in fact. Others that will thrive in a cool room (day temperature below 70 degrees Fahrenheit, night down to 40 degrees) are: gold-dust plant *(Aucuba),* silky oak tree *(Grevillea),* the heathers, Norfolk Island pine, and some ferns.

On cold nights, plants in windows can be endangered if they touch the chilly glass. That's when leaves suddenly turn brown and mushy: they're frostbitten. All you can do is remove the damaged leaves from the plant. If you know the temperature at night is going to go down below the reasonable point ("reasonable" by your own definition), you might plan to move those plants that are touching window glass, or at least put newspaper between the plants and the windowpane. (But don't move plants too often — that's often harmful also.) *Never, never* pull down a window shade over plants, blocking them from the warmth of the room. The cold buildup between the shade and the glass at night can be horrendous, killing all plants quickly.

Problems with chilled plants can begin on the way home from the plant store. Never buy a plant when the outside temperature is below zero (Fahrenheit). And if you ever buy a plant when the weather is even just a bit cool, insist that the plant be carefully wrapped; then be sure to take it straight home — don't wander on errands first.

SYMPTOMS/ ABRUPT TEMPERATURE CHANGE	Older (lower) leaves turn yellow, dry, and drop off Leaves suddenly fall off plant in large numbers Anthracnose disease (leaves develop dry, brown or black, sunken spots, possibly with dark rings around them)

Plants prefer temperature consistency, even if that consistency doesn't provide the best of all possible worlds. In other words, 'tis better to err (slightly) about heat factors but keep them constant than it is to keep changing your mind about them and create sudden fluctuations. For example, a plant in the same room as a window air conditioner is much better off if you keep the air conditioner running all the time than if you switch the machine off during the day while you're at work and then turn it on in the evening, then off again at night when you retire. Of course, running the appliance constantly would be wasteful; so remember your plants' needs when you're thinking about making abrupt changes in your life-style such as purchasing air conditioners or choosing a new place to live.

Air — Good and Bad   The quality of the air in your home is something you can't do much about, but its movement — and thus your plants' access to fresh air — is something that you can control. Ventilation is a significant aspect of the growing conditions in your home that you should take into consideration before placing plants in any specific spot.

There is an important difference between an air current and a draft: the former is good, the latter is not. Seeing a misplaced plant die is not the right way to find drafts — seeing the flickering of a candle *before* you position the plant is. Make a complete circuit of your home, particularly all the places where you might want to place plants, while carrying a lighted candle. Move it all around — near windows, doors, and so on. Note where the candle flame flickers: that's where there's a draft, usually from a badly fitting window, a door too far off the floor, a fireplace with currents coming down the chimney, or even a blower on a heating unit. The trouble with drafts, even though they do bring needed fresh air to a plant, is that they quickly slurp up the moisture that a plant transpires through its leaf pores, leaving the plant unable to cope with the increased demand for water elsewhere. If a plant is suffering from high temperatures, the draft enhances the bad effects; if the plant is already cold, the draft chills it, perhaps beyond repair.

SYMPTOMS/ DRAFTS	Older (lower) leaves turn yellow, dry, and drop off; remaining leaves may wilt
	Leaves wilt, usually followed by withering and dropping
	Leaves suddenly drop off plant in large numbers (cold draft)
	Leaf edges curl; some leaves may drop off
	Buds blast (wither) or fall off before opening; those that do open shrivel or fall off quickly
	Flower petals curl up

You'll note from the draft symptom list that many varied symptoms can be caused by drafts. Always check for drafts (even such mild ones as those caused by a door that frequently opens and closes near a plant) when considering other possible causes. Even if other things are wrong, they can be compounded by drafts. Cure the draft and you may well be on the way to solving the problem.

Circulating air — air that moves in gentle air currents throughout your house or apartment, and that moves fresh supplies of carbon dioxide and oxygen to a plant — is a must for healthy plants. In fact, one of the best ways to prevent other problems is to keep air circulating. Never crowd your plants so close together that fresh air cannot get between them to reach all leaves. Air that is trapped by crowded plants becomes stagnant and may encourage fungi to grow (see chapter 7). If air doesn't circulate, dust is free to settle on leaves, where it blocks the stomata, through which leaves breathe both in and out — so the suffering is twofold. Don't let plants, particularly hanging plants consisting of numerous separate plants in one basket, become too thickly grown: air can't get among the leaves to do its good work.

An important ingredient of fresh, circulating air is the carbon dioxide it carries; plants always need fresh supplies in order to carry on photosynthesis. The carbon dioxide is used in making the carbohydrates and starches that the plants use for energy. That's one of the reasons that people who talk to their plants often have good luck with them: the carbon dioxide they exhale is like a breath of fresh air to the plants. In fact, plants that continually live in a closed, nonventilated room (or greenhouse) may actually become puny. And plants raised in greenhouses that provide lots of carbon dioxide (perhaps from evaporating dry ice or carbon-dioxide generators) often grow bigger and better than other plants because part of the stuff of photosynthesis is available in such abundance.

AIR POLLUTION

Air pollution is, of course, much more a problem outdoors than indoors, but in areas that are prone to bad periods of smog, even the inside air may not be fresh and healthy for days on end. The effects of the air pollution on house plants may begin to show in the form of brown-tipped leaves or masses of yellowing and dropping leaves. Ferns are especially vulnerable to continued smog and may succumb quickly. The greasy, dangerous dust in the air may settle on a plant's leaves, blocking its respiration. Certain plants in city homes may react to specific pollutants. For instance, African violets, begonias, and orchids may react to the nitrates from automobile pollution. In the winters of the late 1970s, when the intense cold forced some areas to reinstate the use of high-sulfur-content coal, many house plants may have suffered — especially begonias, which seem to be sensitive to almost everything.

SYMPTOMS/ AIR POLLUTION Leaf tips and edges turn brown and dry
Older (lower) leaves turn yellow, dry, and drop off; remaining leaves may wilt
Leaf surfaces get dirty

If polluted air is a problem where you live, the only things that you can do are to be sure that the carbon filter on your air-conditioning unit is fresh when periods of high pollution occur, mist and wash your plants often so that pollutants can't settle for long on tender surfaces (though some experts say that keeping leaves dry makes the stomata remain closed, thus preventing bad air from entering the plant), keep the air circulating, and work to prevent pollution in your community.

There are some pollutants in your own home that can be harmful without your realizing it. Curiously enough, if you're an apple freak and always have a supply of them around, you can harm your plants. Most ripening apples (I've heard that the exception is Delicious apples, but I don't know why) give off a gas called ethylene that can actually cause the leaves of house plants to turn yellow, pale, or bleached. Perversely, ethylene gas can also be valuable to some house plants. A bromeliad that seems reluctant to bloom may be conned into doing so by placing it in a plastic bag for a few days with a ripening apple; the gas instigates blossoming. (Before you do that, though, remember that a bromeliad, once it blooms, will be nearing the end of its life.) Here are some more pollution tips:

· A kerosene lamp, while pretty, may be harmful if burned for long in the same room as your plants.

· Although the use of coal gas for heating is basically a thing of the past, the current oil shortage may well bring it back in some areas. Plants will suffer from coal gas, although they don't from natural gas.

· Move plants out of a room where you're painting; the fumes may harm them.

· If you smoke, wash your plants more often than you otherwise might. The components of tobacco smoke settle on leaves, blocking breathing pores.

Plants, Pets, and Children — Together

You must take into consideration the other inhabitants in your home when you bring plants into it. If you have young children or nibbling pets, for example, never bring home a dumb cane *(Dieffenbachia),* however enticing — its leaves can paralyze the tongue. All parts of the oleander are poisonous if eaten; unless you live alone or with responsible adults only, keep it out of your home. The leaves of your friendly avocado are poisonous to animals, as are the leaves and unripe fruit (which is especially attractive to children) of the Christmas cherry. Many bulbs are poisonous, and they should always be stored where inquisitive children anxious for a munch cannot get at them. The colorful caladiums, which also often attract children, can induce painful vomiting, as can the sap of the euphorbias (poinsettias and crown of thorns).

Any plant that has been sprayed with an insecticide should be a no-no to all chewers. Keep sprayed plants isolated until they have been cured. Then wash them very, very carefully before returning them to the traffic patterns of your home.

There's plenty of room in a home for plants, pets and children, but some accommodation will need to be made. I've never heard of dogs and house plants having many problems coexisting, except that dogs like to charge around and can knock over plants. Cats, however, are often a problem — one which has brought several ingenious solutions to prevent their munching freely on the greenery:

· Sprinkle red pepper on the plants.

· Spray a mischievous cat with cold water each time it's caught munching, until it learns to stay away from plants (I suspect that any self-respecting cat would learn not to get caught after the first time).

· Feed your cats greens every couple of days — beans, lettuce, or whatever they'll eat — and perhaps they'll lose their desire for the house plants.

· Grow a few plants for the cats' own use and keep them where the felines will munch on them instead of the greenhouse charmers.

Cats particularly adore umbrella plants *(Cyperus)* and spider plants *(Chlorophytum),* although they later vomit up the munched leaves (usually with no serious harm done except to the plant). Cats also tend to go a little batty occasionally and dash blindly about as if

Satan were after them. Plants tumble in their wake. Clay pots will be helpful because they are more difficult for cats to knock over than the lighter plastic ones; but clay pots usually break if they do fall, so be prepared to repot quickly.

I won't bother to discuss boa constrictors and house plants . . .

Children at play cannot be calculated against quite so readily as cats. The most important thing one can do to eliminate damage to house plants by children — or vice versa — is to keep plants out of toddlers' reach. Then, as kids grow older and begin to be curious, interest them in plants of their own. Let them learn the fun and fascination there can be in growing and loving a green friend.

ᴂ 4. ANALYZING THE CARE YOU GIVE YOUR HOUSE PLANTS

TAKE A LIVING THING OUT OF ITS NATURAL ENVIRON-
ment and it must be cared for; it can no longer manip-
ulate its own life if the ingredients making up its former life are not present. House plants have long ago
been uprooted from their natural environment, but in
the process of being bred, grown in mass, and sold to
the world, they have never learned to care for themselves. You must be their caretaker — and the care you
provide determines whether the plants live or die,
shine or droop.

That's quite some responsibility. But fortunately,
plant care is mostly just common sense, based on accepting the fact that each plant has its individual needs
and that not all plants can be treated equally (notwith-
standing the Bill of Rights).

Water,
Water . . .

First, disabuse yourself of the notion that you can
water all your plants every Tuesday and Friday and
that that will be sufficient. A plant's water needs —
the amount and timing — relate to a variety of factors:
the succulence of the plant, its size, the state of its

health, its location in the sunshine, the dryness of the room, whether it's a flowering plant or just foliage, whether it's hanging or "seated among friends," whether its roots require oxygen, the speed with which the soil drains, the size of the pot . . . and I could probably go on all day.

Obviously, each plant must be considered as an individual. If you don't give them that benefit, some plants will be perpetually underwatered and others forever overwatered; each situation can be serious.

OVERWATERING

It should be clear from the list of possible symptoms that overwatering can affect just about any part of the plant — always in a detrimental way, up to and including death. Although people aren't always generous to each other, we tend to be overgenerous with our

SYMPTOMS/ OVERWATERING

Older (lower) leaves turn yellow, dry, and drop off in large numbers

Leaves turn pale, yellow, or bleached and new growth is weak and spindly (especially in winter)

Leaves suddenly drop off plant in large numbers

Leaves wilt (even when soil is damp)

Leaf tips and edges turn brown and dry

Leaves develop spots, usually brown and dry

Leaves develop swellings (edema) — irregular spots of watery growth, possibly with corklike edges, usually on leaf backs

Few or no buds form on a flowering plant

Buds blast (wither) or drop off before opening; those that do open shrivel or drop off quickly

Flower petals develop brown spots

Growth slows or stops

Brown or black discoloration, possibly watery, creeps up stem from soil level and stem collapses (stem rot)

Roots lack holding power, plant easily uproots; roots appear dark and mushy when checked and give off a pungent odor (root rot)

plants, convinced that all ills can be cured by a good, therapeutic soaking of the soil. 'Tain't so.

A plant that has its soil perpetually soaked gets no air at its roots. The root hairs thus feel no need to venture outward seeking water — and growing. The constant water, especially if the plant has any degree of succulence (water-holding tendency), will sooner or later make the roots rot and — also sooner or later — the whole plant will die because it has no functioning roots to sustain it. The lower (older and therefore least tenacious) leaves die first, turning yellow because their supply of nutrients and water is cut off in the plant's effort to sustain only the youngest (and thus healthiest) leaves. If that symptom doesn't signal you in time, other things then begin to happen, often all at once.

Chrysalido-
carpus lutescens
*(areca palm) with older
leaflets dying as a result
of overwatering*

Therefore, recognizing that we can all be overgenerous at times (especially when we wield the watering can while angry or in deep thought), always suspect overwatering as the prime problem whenever any symptom typical of it appears. You'll nearly always be right.

If you suspect that overwatering is the problem, you can just let the soil dry and then promise to behave in the future. But if damage to your plant's superstructure is extensive, it is safest to check the underpinnings in addition.

Carefully knock the pot against a counter edge or in some similar way jar the soil loose. On newspaper, spread out the root ball and gently tap away excess soil. After most soil has been removed, hold the roots under lukewarm tap water to clean them. Inspect the roots: look at them closely; pinch them lightly between your fingers; smell them (yes!). The visual examination may reveal that root endings are discolored — brown or black instead of white or yellowish. The pinching may indicate that the roots' texture is soft and mushy instead of crisp. Your nose may discover the odor of rotting vegetation (in fact, it's sometimes possible to smell rotting roots without unpotting the plant). If you discover these traits, your plant has developed root rot. Perpetual moisture, too much of it, has weakened the roots and a fungus has been allowed to invade them — and permanent destruction is well under way.

Using a clean, sharp knife, cut off the damaged ends of roots, well down into crisp, healthy tissue (if that means there's no root left, try to retrieve some stem or leaf cuttings of undamaged parts; throw the rest of the plant away). You may want to dust the roots with a fungicide. Repot the plant in new soil, in a fresh pot that is smaller than the previous one. Make sure that the drainage is very good and that the pot is not too large; there must be no chance of overwatering again, especially until the plant has completely regained its strength. Place the plant in indirect light, keep humidity high, and don't feed the patient. Soon some leaves will undoubtedly yellow and fall in response to root loss, but soon, too, new growth will appear.

How, then, do you avoid overwatering? Well, first of all, you *don't* overcompensate by sprinkling just lightly whenever you water. That, too, can mean death for the plant. Instead, *whenever you water, water thoroughly,* filling the space between the soil and the pot rim with water, so that there is enough to completely soak down and through the roots, moistening every speck of soil. What must also happen is that any excess — any water that does not adhere to soil or vermiculite particles — must drain away, out the hole in the bottom of the pot.

You don't have a drainage hole in the bottom of your pot? Then that's probably why you are overwatering; whatever excess is in your watering allotment can only settle in the bottom of the pot, endangering the roots, then the leaves, and so forth. If you feel absolutely forced to have a holeless pot — and I strongly recommend that you avoid them — be sure that there

Cutaway view of a potted plant with good drainage

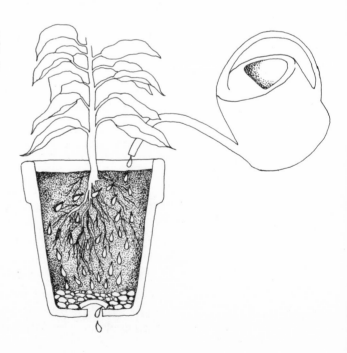

is at least an inch of pebbles in the bottom to serve as a catch basin for the extra water; the bigger the pot, the deeper the layer. And be sure to include some charcoal among the pebbles to prevent the water that does collect there from turning sour. Whenever you read herein that a plant must have excellent drainage, it means that there should be pebbles in the pot's bottom as well as loose particles such as sand or perlite mixed in with the potting soil.

It seems contradictory to say that a medium should have the facility both to hold moisture but also to drain well, but that's what is required. Actually, such a soil is like a sponge: it fills with water until it's wet; excess drains out from between soil particles. Water is held in the soil by the organic matter and vermiculite, but it runs out quickly from around sand and perlite, leaving air spaces.

Although I've never been one for gadgets (I figure that the money is better spent on new plants), I've succumbed to one type of gadget that has become ubiquitous during the recent house-plant boom: the water meter that is inserted in the soil. A meter indicates how wet the soil is (on a scale from 1 to 8 on some, from 1 to 12 on others — both are arbitrary sets of numbers); then you consult a little booklet or read the package to learn when each kind of plant should be watered. For example, a Norfolk Island pine might not need watering until the meter reading gets down to 5. For the perpetual overwaterer, such a meter can be a magic guide to long-awaited success — *if* he or she inserts the device's prong far enough into the soil and then believes the reading and obeys the instructions. Just carry the meter around along with the watering can as you check your plants. If the meter reads too high for a particular plant, don't water it. Some days the meter might dictate a watering after only two days, because the sun has been hot; other times it might take three or four days for the plant to need water, because it's been cloudy and dreary. Eventually, you'll learn to identify thirsty soil by feeling it, without taking a reading; then you can give your meter to a friend who tends to overwater.

UNDERWATERING

Underwatering often creates more clearly visible symptoms than overwatering. For example, a *Spathiphyllum* may completely collapse around the pot rim when it has not been watered for a long time. Succulents may shrivel a bit, as if their skins were too big for them. Thin-leaved plants wilt so badly that you can almost see the tiny pores in their leaves panting for water.

SYMPTOMS/ UNDERWATERING

Older (lower) leaves turn yellow, dry, and drop off
Compacted soil problems develop
Leaves suddenly drop off plant in large numbers (often after turning dark and crisp)
Leaves wilt, followed by withering and dropping
Roots appear on soil surface
Buds blast (wither) or fall off; those that do open shrivel or fall off quickly
Flower petal tips turn brown
New growth is stunted and thicker than normal
Growth slows or stops
Soil separates from the pot sides
Succulent growth shrivels

Pteris cretica (brake fern) with older fronds brown and dried from underwatering

A plant can easily be underwatered even when you think you've been watering properly if you've managed to let the soil ball compact around the roots and form an impenetrable mass. Compacted soil, apparent when the soil separates from the pot sides, often happens when you've already been watering too lightly (perhaps just a sprinkle every day) for a while: the water on the top does not go in deeply enough to moisten the heart of the root ball; then, when you do water correctly and fully, the compacted ball is too tough to let water penetrate, and the plant remains underwatered. Sink the pot in lukewarm water up to the pot rim for thirty minutes, or until water is visible on the surface of the soil, and make an effort to water thoroughly in the future.

OTHER WATERING HINTS

Some Dos and Don'ts to consider when you're analyzing how to handle your plants and their watering supply:

· *Do* water plants that are in north light considerably less than plants that are in south light.

· *Do* water plants from the top occasionally, even if they normally get watered from the bottom. (Watering from the bottom — the method chosen by some growers of African violets and other plants with compacted leaf masses — entails setting the pot in a dish of water so that moisture can soak up into the soil through the drainage hole.) Periodic watering from the top serves to make sure that all the soil is moistened, and it leaches out (rinses away) any fertilizer buildup in the soil. And if you do water from the bottom, be sure to discard any water that does not soak into the soil within half an hour.

· *Don't* ever water house plants with cold water; in their tropical homes the water their roots received was always warm. Cool water in soil (especially in cool soil in winter) can send a plant into shock.

· *Don't* use chemically softened water for watering

plants; the softening works by an ion-exchange process that removes calcium and leaves dangerous sodium (salt) in its place. On the other hand, a de-ionizer in your watering system is great for plants.

· *Don't* pour water that has drained from one pot into another plant's pot. You may just be transmitting problems from one to the other.

· *Don't* water as much during the plant's dormancy period as you do during the rest of the year (dormancy is further discussed later in this chapter).

If you have leaf-tip burning or spotting on plants such as ti plant, aloe, aspidistra, asparagus fern, spider plant, dracaena, snake plant (mainly members of the arum family), and if humidity is high enough and other cultural problems seem to have been avoided, consider that the cause might be fluorides in the water. Not much is yet known about fluoride effect on plants, but, in any event, it can be avoided by using rainwater or distilled water; or you can minimize the effect by keeping the soil slightly alkaline.

I recommend that wick watering be used only when you must be away from your plants for a period of time, or possibly when you are growing constant-moisture-loving plants under lights. Many pots now come with built-in watering wicks, guaranteeing a perpetual, "troublefree" supply of water drawn by capillary action along a wick that goes from a reservoir (at the bottom or to one side of the pot) into the soil. The problem with ordinary use of such devices is that the soil never gets a chance to have any air in it: there is always water between the particles of the soil medium. No plants, except perhaps umbrella plant *(Cyperus)* and baby's tears, like such perpetually watered "feet." And for a plant in less than bright sunlight, perpetual water in its soil may foster mold on its surface.

HUMIDITY

Taking care of the actual watering needs of a plant does not end your responsibility for regulating its water. In spite of the fact that the humidity of the air is one of the basic background environmental factors in your home, you can do a fair amount of finagling to change the humidity around your plants. And change it you must — especially in winter — unless you live in a rain forest, because our tropical-origin plants are constantly in need of as much moisture in the air around their leaves as they can get. The average tropical rain forest gets about eighty inches of rain a year (the United States as a whole averages only about thirty inches). That rainfall keeps the air very humid. Such humidity in your house would rot the furniture, curl your hair, and mildew the mirrors. So we aim for a compromise, one we and the plants can live with comfortably.

SYMPTOMS/
HUMIDITY TOO LOW

Older (lower) leaves turn yellow, dry, and cling to plant
Leaves suddenly drop off plant in large numbers
  (especially if plant has just been acquired)
Leaves wilt, usually followed by withering and dropping
  (especially if soil isn't dried out)
Leaf tips and edges turn brown and dry
Leaf edges curl; some leaves may drop off
Few or no buds form on a flowering plant
Buds blast (wither) or drop off before opening; those that
  do open shrivel or drop off quickly
Flower petal tips turn brown
Cuttings wilt and die
Spider mites attack — leaves bleach and become mottled
  with gray; close inspection reveals cobwebs

First, a clue about recognizing the symptoms of lack of humidity: dryness of plant tissues generally means that the relative humidity is too low, as contrasted with a softness or mushiness of tissues, which generally means overwatering. And unfortunately, the two are not mutually exclusive.

You must be prepared — unless you are content to live only with succulents and cacti or perhaps a few of

Cyperus alternifolius (umbrella plant) with brown leaflet tips from insufficient humidity

the persistent, hardy creatures who accept almost anything you throw at them — to raise the humidity level around the plants in all ways possible. Two methods are basic to life with plants:

(1) Place all plants that like high humidity (and most of them do) on trays containing a layer of pebbles an inch or more deep. When you water the plants, the excess water of a thorough drenching will run out into the pebbles. Then, when the draining has stopped, add enough water directly to the tray of pebbles to raise the water level to within half an inch of the bottom of the pot (no higher, though, because the water can seep back up into the pot creating the horrors of overwatering without your even being guilty). The bigger the area around the plant from which water can evaporate into the air, the better for the plant. For example, a big tray with three or four plants on it is great; a saucer with one plant sitting on pebbles isn't terribly helpful because the surface area from which water can evaporate is small. Some people place a pot of water among their plants, but that doesn't really help a great deal either because, again, the surface area available for evaporation is slight. Another boon of the plant boom has been the development of windowsill trays for holding pebbles; they aren't very deep, but they're better

than nothing at all — which has been the alternative for unhandy people up until now. (Also now available are humidifying trays that incorporate watering wicks extending from tray base to plants set on a raised platform.)

(2) Again, a *must,* not a suggestion: mist your plants at least once every day if they are humidity lovers. A sprayer and a mister are really two distinct devices: A sprayer breaks up water into globules that scatter around the surface you're spraying; the droplets can actually be quite harmful if the sun is shining on them because they magnify the sunlight into a burning pinpoint of light. A mister, on the other hand, breaks water into a fine mist that lingers in the air around the plant; admittedly, the extra humidity doesn't linger long, but while it does the leaf gets a rest from transpiring water from its leaf surfaces. So be sure when you pick a humidifying apparatus that you are actually getting a mister rather than a sprayer, and then use it often: three or four times a week for all plants, to dust them; daily for humidity lovers; even more often for a

Increasing the moisture content of the air around a plant by misting it and placing the pot on a pebble tray

few very-thin-leaved plants if they're in considerable sunshine.

Another possible method for controlling humidity: lower the temperature in your home by turning down the thermostat. The lower the temperature, the higher the *relative* humidity (the term refers to the amount of moisture in the air relative to the amount the air can hold *at a given temperature*). *Voilà:*

> Make the air cooler = Make the relative
> humidity higher

And the power companies will thank you.

You might also consider purchasing a room humidifier. Admittedly, the big, luxurious ones are expensive, but they're worth it for both you and your plants. Besides, again thanks to the plant boom, you can instead get an inexpensive humidifier made particularly to sit among your plants and nourish their moisture needs. Called Humidiplant, it holds enough water to keep going for a number of hours and shuts itself off when empty. Of course, if you live in a house with a built-in humidifier attached to the furnace, be certain that it's in proper working condition.

I won't bother delineating the symptoms of *too much* humidity, because such an event is very, very rare in heated homes. The only high-humidity sign you might need to keep an eye out for is mold or mildew — during muggy spells, if plants are kept too close together, so that no air circulates among them; or if you let a plant reside inside a plastic cover without fresh air for too long a period.

One gadget worth investing in is an inexpensive hygrometer, a device that indicates relative humidity. Watch the dials and learn when relative humidity in your home drops too low, requiring that you assist the plants; and note what conditions increase the moisture in the air, allowing you to take a brief vacation from your efforts to keep the relative humidity above 40 percent at all times.

Plant Transplants and Surgery

Pots seem to be such simple things: you pick one, stuff it with pebbles and dirt, and it just sits there forever keeping the soil from being strewn around the room. Well . . . not quite — not, that is, if you want healthy plants. A healthy plant grows — that's the object of all your watering and feeding — and as it grows it must be moved from pot to pot to pot until it reaches the size you want or until the plant has really just outlived its beauty.

You must make a choice between clay and plastic pots. Clay is good for people with a tendency to over-water, because much water evaporates through the pores in the sides. Also, air gets into the soil through the porous sides and oxygen can easily reach the roots. Plastic pots, on the other hand, retain moisture longer; consequently, plants demanding constant moisture are safer in plastic than they are in clay because they don't need watering as often. On the purely aesthetic side, clay is more natural, rustic, and earthy-looking. Plastic is lighter in weight and is readily washed clean. Clay breaks easily but reveals considerably more about the state of your plants than plastic does — for instance:

A white, powdery deposit will accumulate on the outside of clay pots, a precipitate from the minerals in the water. Just scrub it off whenever it annoys you. But if the deposit starts to build around the *inside* of the pot rim, or if white crystallike scum spreads across the soil, you know you've been fertilizing too much (see chapter 5). This danger does not reveal itself so readily in plastic pots, although the signal is there, too.

Another example: A clay pot that is dry and light-colored and seems to be at room temperature when touched contains dry soil — it's time, perhaps past time, to water the plant. You can't tell that sort of thing from a plastic pot. (When you water again, water thoroughly; in fact, you might even sink the pot in water to its rim so that the pot itself gets thoroughly soaked through — a damp pot sheds water a little less quickly than a dry pot.)

Never use clear-glass or clear-plastic pots. Yes, they

are attractive, but the sunlight hitting roots can either burn them or encourage them to grow more rapidly than the foliage can keep pace with: the plant will be virtually all root, with disproportionately tiny leaves.

Both plastic and clay pots, as long as they have drainage holes in them — and, please, as mentioned before, don't plant in pots without them unless absolutely forced to — will reveal when a plant needs "a new suit of clothes" because it has outgrown the previous one. Roots will begin to push themselves up on the surface of the soil or, much more commonly, will grow out of the drainage hole. When that occurs, the plant needs repotting (unless it is a flowering plant that prefers to be cramped or pot-bound in order to flower, or unless you want to slow the growth of the plant to within manageable bounds).

SYMPTOMS/
POT-BOUND

Roots grow out of drainage holes
Roots appear on soil surface
Soil dries quickly despite frequent watering
Older (lower) leaves turn yellow
Leaves wilt and edges turn brown; new leaves may be small
Growth slows or stops
Plant appears topheavy

Use the symptom-list cues to know when to repot. Then proceed as follows:

Preferably in spring — but anytime for a constantly growing plant such as ivy — transplant into a larger pot, preferably one inch but at least never more than two inches larger than the one used before. Before starting, soak clay pots in water; and make sure either clay or plastic pots are sparkling clean. Insert a drainage-hole cover — a piece of clay pot curved over the hole of a clay pot, pebbles in a plastic pot, or bits of nylon stocking or rustproof window screen over the holes in either — to prevent soil from running out the bottom of the pot. Add pebbles to create a layer into which

Transplanting a pot-bound polka-dot plant (Hypoestes sanguino-lenta) *into a larger pot*

excess liquid from watering can run. Even though it's not really necessary when there is a drainage hole (it's absolutely vital in pots without drainage holes), such a layer provides a safety margin for when a pot is allowed to sit in water for a while: there's somewhere for the water to go other than into the soil, where it can be harmful.

Next add fresh soil atop the pebble layer, letting it curve up on the sides. Tamp the soil down to about the texture of the old soil so that there will be no discrepancy between new and old soil. Carefully tap the plant out of the old pot and remove old pebbles from the clutches of the roots. Insert the old soil ball into the new pot, and brace it so that the final height of the top will be just right with no new soil added to the surface. (While you have the plant out of its pot, you might as well take the opportunity to run a quick check on the condition of the roots — see chapter 10). Then sift in new soil around the old soil ball and tamp it against both the old soil and the pot side, again making sure that there is no distinction in texture. (A root will shy away from a new growing medium if it is of a different texture than its old home.) Water the pot well so that the soils have a chance to settle together. Take care to avoid changing the level of the soil on the stem; for some reason, plants (except for African violets) don't like the elevation of their "turtlenecks" changed.

Eventually, many of your plants will reach a size beyond which you'd rather they didn't venture — such as when you can no longer see out your windows, or when your little tree is beginning to lean sideways to avoid bumping its head on the ceiling. You can make a plant maintain its size by keeping it in the same-sized pot until its leaf sizes begin to change. Just give it a fresh coating of topsoil each spring; an inch is almost as good as a mile in encouraging a plant to maintain its health. Sooner or later, however, the plant will have had too much of life in the same pot and you'll have to do something drastic about it. That calls for surgery:

Remove the pot from the plant — or the plant from

its pot. You can literally just cut off a half-inch, or even an inch, from all around the root ball. Just stand the plant, in its moist soil, on a cutting board and, with a very sharp knife, trim away the desired amount of soil along with the roots it contains. If the plant has long been pot-bound and has grown stupendous roots encircling itself, you may need to first unravel and trim those in order to do the job.

The whole thing seems a horrific way to treat a plant, but you must take a realistic approach; ask yourself: whose home was it first — yours or the plant's? (If it was the plant's, you might want to reconsider.) Anyway, most plants can really take quite a lot of seeming ill-treatment without coming to fatal harm.

After trimming, repot the plant in fresh soil in a smaller pot — one almost painfully small, because the plant will want the tightness as a security blanket to recover from the shock of being chopped up. Keep the plant out of direct sun and water it cautiously, but keep the humidity as high as possible. In a few days, many leaves will start to yellow and fall. Don't panic: the plant is naturally ridding itself of leaves that no longer have roots to support them. Soon it will settle down to life at its new size . . . and you'll have retrieved a plant for another long period of domestic beauty.

A note on surgery in general: All you can really do when surgery is necessary (when leaves have frostbite; when too long a period of low humidity has left almost no leaves on some branches; when stems have broken; when sunburn requires treatment; when operating is a last, desperate hope for a very unhappy plant; whatever) is to be brave, use very clean equipment in order not to compound the problem, and cut cleanly where it seems necessary. Sometimes, a cut in time will save a plant when all else has failed. For example, my frozen *Dieffenbachia* plant lost leaf after leaf as each turned brown and mushy and curled into nothingness; the main stem seemed destined to follow. So I cut all the leaves off in one dramatic gesture, hacked across the stem considerably below where the mushiness was, and threw away the scraps. The sad-looking stems are now bearing several small but happily growing green projections that are about to become more leaves. Plant retrieved.

Surgery might also be required when a plant such as an asparagus fern has long been in bad conditions; stem after stem has turned brown and died. Rather than weep over each, just cut off all stems down to the soil level, change the plant's environment as you determine is necessary (which probably means changing your watering habits more than anything else), and wait for the stems to regrow. They will. Quite prettily. A few final surgical Dos and Don'ts follow:

· *Don't* ever use a knife for surgery that was used before on another sick plant without having cleaned it thoroughly first.

· *Do* keep all patients in dim light and on a restricted water diet for the first several days after surgery to help them recover from shock.

· *Don't* ever feed a patient while it is recovering; a plant must have all its wits about it before it can handle food properly.

A Healthy Plant Is a Clean Plant

Yup. I don't mean to create aphorisms, but that section title is painfully true. Dirty plants can't breathe; they can't utilize the sunlight that reaches them; they're prone to pests; and they just plain look miserable. And all they need is an occasional bath and some other brief attention from you.

Smallish plants with lots of stems and leaves should be taken to the sink, where they can be sprayed with a harsh stream of cooling water, or turned upside down (put a plastic bath cap over the soil) in a pail or tub of soapy water and swished around. Be sure never to get soap into the soil, and be just as sure to rinse all soap off the leaves; otherwise, it will dry and clog the pores that you're trying so hard to clean.

Larger plants, especially big ones with easily countable numbers of leaves, should be washed with a sponge

Left: Cleaning a small plant by inverting it in a pail of soapy water. The soil is protected with plastic wrap.

Right: Monstera deliciosa *(split-leaf philodendron) being* washed with a soft sponge

and soapy water, and then rinsed just as carefully. Big plants can also be taken into the shower with you if you take care to keep soap out of the soil. You can almost hear a plant sigh with relief when it's been bathed.

The force of a humidifying mister should clean off most dust in between full-fledged baths. Be sure to get all around the plant, both back sides and tops of leaves. And while you're misting plants, look for dead leaves or flowers. Pick them off carefully to prevent their dropping onto the soil, where they can rot and start fungal problems. A few plants keep a very tenacious hold even on dead leaves, and you'll need to have scissors to get the dead matter off; prayer plants, for example, are quite distressed at giving up leaves — they try to cling for dear life to the dead ones.

Cleanliness is not just a matter of aesthetics. The stomata, the opening and closing pores on leaves, cannot function properly when they are clogged by dirt or the greasy air of an industrial city. You can do everything else right for your plants, but if you let them remain dirty, your efforts may be doomed to failure.

Vacations — The Plants', Yours, and Everyone Else's

In that great outdoor world where plants lived naturally before being brought indoors, there was often a period of coolness or dryness during which it behooved plants wanting to survive such times to take things easy for a bit — to rest while conditions weren't quite up to par. They would stop or at least slow their growth, requiring less water because there was less available; most survived by just generally cooling it for a couple of months. That response is called dormancy, and many of our house plants still go through it automatically, not realizing that they're guaranteed a better, evener existence indoors. You must take heed of a plant's vacation or chance harming it by overindulgence.

It's safe to assume that all your foliage plants will go somewhat dormant during the winter, perhaps from about November through the middle of February. The lowered light level alone will practically guarantee that they won't be as active as they were in the summer. During that period, cut out all fertilizer of any kind, reduce the amount of water the plants get (if they were being kept continually moist, let the soil dry somewhat on top; if they were succulents being watered only once a week, don't water until you see signs that the outer skin of the leaves is starting to shrivel). Don't repot plants during dormancy unless it's necessary to replace a broken pot; they won't have the energy to adjust to their new surroundings.

There are, of course, exceptions to the dormancy rule. Ivies, for example, and philodendrons, baby's tears, fittonia, and jade plants don't go fully dormant, although their growth may slow just a bit, depending on how much of their light is cut off. They can continue to be fed, though on a gentler scale than during the rest of the year.

Other plants, the spectacular flowerers particularly, need a period of enforced dormancy just after they finish flowering. They'd be willing to go on performing for you, but their bloom won't be as good unless they have a few weeks during which little. is expected of them.

Regardless of the reason for dormancy, the plants will let you know when it is time to resume normal care by starting to put out new leaves again. You may think the dormant plant is not growing at all, but suddenly tiny new green leaves will appear. Start fertilizing again and resume normal watering.

In the case of dormancy, you're adjusting to the plant's needs for a vacation. But what about your own? There is a limit to how much a plant can be asked to sacrifice to your need for a holiday. But you can arrange for brief ones without bringing in plant-sitters if you just make sure that your plants have a covering of plastic for the period you are gone.

Put all your small plants in the bathtub on raised, upside-down pots. Fill the tub with water almost to plant-pot level, cover the whole thing with a sheet of plastic, and go away safely for up to two weeks. Bigger plants can be covered with plastic where they live, or you can invest in some of the plastic tents that are now available (they're useful, too, as hospital tents for sick plants). In any case, water the plants the day before you seal them up. And when you leave, turn the temperature down so that water use is slowed.

You can also go away for longer periods of time by setting up a temporary wick-watering system for all your plants. Fill deep containers (not wide ones — they encourage evaporation) with water and place them among your plants. Lead heavy cotton string or candle wick (unwaxed) from the containers to the soil surface of each pot. Capillary action will send water along the string to the soil.

Everybody gets a vacation if you're lucky enough to be able to take your plants (all except fragile ones and gesneriads) outdoors during the summer. After all chances of frost are long gone, after the nights have begun to stay above 55 degrees Fahrenheit in fact, begin gradually to move the hardy plants outdoors, first to an enclosed porch for a few days, then onto a sheltered step, and then into the garden. Remember that direct sun outdoors is considerably brighter than direct sun indoors. Even the sunshine lovers can't really take it, so keep all plants in shade or semishade — perhaps under shrubs, where they get direct light only part of the day as the sun moves or as the shrub moves about in a light breeze. You can, if you want, sink the pots (clay pots only) of your plants into the soil where they're safe from being blown over, but I see no real reason for going to all that work; it just increases the chances of picking up soil pests. Instead, just water and feed the plants often, as usual during the summer. Let them have rain when it falls, sun when it shines, wind when it blows (though not too much of that, because fragile indoor plants have never developed a toughness born of wind experience).

Try to group indoor plants together, on a patio edge, under one tree, along a porch foundation — wherever it's easiest for you to take care of all the plants at once. If you spread them around, it's entirely too easy to forget that Joe the Jade Plant is under the syringa.

It is definitely a plant-care vacation for you while the plants are outside, but that doesn't mean you can totally neglect them from June to September. There are more kinds of insect pests around to attack your plants outside. A breeze can quickly dry the soil in a pot just after you've watered it. And don't place pots on a white-painted surface: the sun can be reflected upward too strongly, burning the plants. Inspect your plants as frequently as you would indoors.

When it comes time to move them back inside, do it gradually and try to do it when there will be at least two to three weeks for the plants to readjust to indoor life before they're subjected to artificial heat. I know it's difficult to predict the first cold nights of autumn, but, if in doubt, bring the plants inside in August, guaranteeing lots of time. Check each one closely for signs of bugs; isolate and treat it if necessary. Repot each in fresh soil as you bring it in and get it readjusted to indoor conditions.

Seem like a lot of work? Perhaps it will require more effort early in the growing season than would leaving the plants in place, but the benefit is vigorous, healthy plants that are better prepared to survive another winter of that nasty furnace's heat. And perhaps you won't get a vacation for those few days at the end of summer when you have to make sure that plants are in shape for putting back among your collection. But you'll probably be stunned at the glowing vigor they will show after a summer spent in the open air.

~ 5. YOUR HOUSE PLANTS' DIET

Your plants' diet, starting with their soil, must be a frequent consideration, for you must always guarantee that the right nutrients are available.

If your plants were still in their native habitat — perhaps tucked along a stream amid tropical jungle undergrowth — they would need no assistance in planning their menus: nature would provide. The nutrients in the soil would regularly be replenished as fallen leaves and small animals decayed into their constituent elements or as eroding rocks supplied minerals dissolved in rainwater. Soil in pots, on the other hand, is subject to the human desire for tidiness and can't be replenished naturally: you can't let fallen leaves remain on the soil; you'd prefer that the cat use the litter box instead of the plant's dirt. Therefore, you must give your plants the chemical elements they need for health and growth.

Actually, you can't feed a plant; it makes its own food. You merely provide the proper chemical elements, from which the plant, using sunlight and water, concocts its own meals.

The Needed Nutrients If any chemical elements were more important for plant health than others (and they aren't *really*, because all must be in balance), they would have to be the old familiars: oxygen, carbon, and hydrogen. Without them, we would have no life as we know it on earth. Those elements are, however, not really a part of good nutrition as it concerns us here, since they are ever present as part of the air and water you provide.

The most important supplemental elements that you must introduce into the soil are: nitrogen (symbol N); phosphorus (symbol P), which is usually provided in the form of a phosphate — not the bubbly fruit-drink kind but the stodgy compound P_2O_5; and potassium (symbol K — for "kalium," an old term meaning "alkali"), which is usually in fertilizer in the form of potash, or potassium oxide (K_2O). These three elements are vital components of a healthy plant. Without all of them, in proper balance, a plant can't repair itself or build new cells.

SYMPTOMS/
NITROGEN
DEFICIENCY

Older (lower) leaves turn yellow or light green, dry, and drop off; some leaves become orange or red; others fade

New growth is stunted, pale, possibly curled or otherwise distorted

---

Nitrogen encourages the growth of green leaves and sturdy stems. Chlorophyll, the green substance in most plants that allows them to produce their own food internally, contains a good deal of nitrogen; thus, a plant not receiving adequate nitrogen supplies turns yellowish and growth slows. A plant getting an overdose of nitrogen (from too much enthusiasm about feeding on your part) puts out a superabundance of leaves — seemingly a treat, but actually bad for a foliage plant, because its stems become unable to keep up with leaf growth and grow too weak to support the plant; and a tragedy for flowering plants, because they are so busy leafing that they can't produce flowers.

<table>
<tr><td>SYMPTOMS/
PHOSPHORUS
DEFICIENCY</td><td>Leaf tips, edges, and veins turn reddish or bronze,
    beginning with older (lower) leaves
New growth is stunted, perhaps stopped entirely on side
    shoots
Leaves turn bluish green, then purple, perhaps brown or
    mottled, beginning with older leaves
Leaves drop off, beginning with older ones</td></tr>
</table>

Phosphorus is important to the growth of healthy, bright-colored flowers and sturdy roots. It brings out good color contrasts in variegated plants. Without sufficient phosphorus, a plant stops growing; its leaves turn a garish blue-green and then change to purple, perhaps becoming mottled. Leaves fall, starting with the older (lower) ones first. Leaf stems and veins become purplish or bronzed, too. Phosphorus in plant foods is in the form of phosphate. Bone meal is a good organic source of phosphorus. If you ever need to keep plants in less than optimum light and bad color results, try using a high-phosphorus-content fertilizer; the color will be improved.

<table>
<tr><td>SYMPTOMS/
POTASSIUM
DEFICIENCY</td><td>Leaf tips and edges turn tan or bronze (or even red),
    beginning with older (lower) leaves
Leaf blades turn yellow, beginning with older leaves,
    after tips and edges "burn"
New growth is stunted, with distances between leaves
    shorter than normal</td></tr>
</table>

Potassium is also important — for good flowers, strong stems, and healthy roots, and for the additional vital task of helping the plant resist disease. A plant not getting enough potassium will develop brown ("burned") leaf tips and margins, and then the leaf blades will gradually turn yellow, from the older, lower leaves upward; the leaves may also curl slightly along the edges; and new growth may be stunted.

These three *primary elements* — nitrogen, phosphorus, potassium — are present in all commercial inorganic fertilizers, which are called *chemical fertilizers*. Such fertilizers bear on the container an analysis of the content in percentages, always in the order just given; for example, a typical formula is 5 percent N, 10 percent P, 5 percent K, written "5-10-5." That means that a total of 20 percent of the material in the container is made up of the three primary elements. The mixture's 1:2:1 ratio makes it a well-balanced food for young, busily growing plants. Older plants, with roots already well-established, should be given a fertilizer with a formula in the ratio of about 1:1:3 when you want to strengthen the flowers and guarantee resistance to disease. A plant that needs to be encouraged to bloom (and consequently to have leaf growth temporarily suspended) will be helped by a food with approximately equal parts of the three main elements: a ratio of 1:1:1. Orchids, for example, like an evenly balanced formula such as 18-18-18. Such food is typically called African-violet food because of the ubiquity of African violets in our society (they're not to be confused with shrinking violets, which are now few and far between). A food with low numbers — for instance, 2-5-2 — can be used frequently, even once a week. The higher-number foods, such as 10-20-10, are quite concentrated and should be used only every three or four weeks.

Three additional elements — calcium (Ca), magnesium (Mg), and sulfur (S) — are needed by plants to a greater extent than the so-called *trace elements*, which we'll discuss in a minute. These three, often called *secondary elements*, are not represented in the fertilizer identification formula, but that fact doesn't make them less important. The way a plant uses these three elements is tied to the pH (acid/base balance) of the soil.

SYMPTOMS/
CALCIUM
DEFICIENCY

Leaf tips and edges turn yellow, then brown or spotted, and curly

Growing tips on stems die

Calcium generally assists flower, stem, and root development; it is important to the structure of cell walls. Without enough calcium — perhaps a result of underfeeding, or because soil that gets too acidic doesn't release its calcium — the growing tips of the stems don't develop fully and may die back easily. Leaf margins may turn yellow, then brown or spotted. Even the main stem may lose its "backbone" and collapse. To correct the situation, use a fertilizer containing calcium nitrate, or mix dolomite limestone into the soil.

SYMPTOMS/
MAGNESIUM
DEFICIENCY

Leaves turn yellow except at the veins (which remain green), beginning with older (lower) leaves

Leaves suddenly drop off plant in large numbers without wilting first

Magnesium use by a plant is blocked when the soil pH is too basic, or alkaline. Magnesium is an important ingredient in chlorophyll. The older leaves of plants

Chrysanthemum
with chlorosis

without enough magnesium turn yellow first. But unlike leaves suffering nitrogen deficiency, the veins remain green; this condition is called *chlorosis*. Leaves may also develop white edges or an overall purplish hue in response to a lack of magnesium. Leaves may fall rapidly without withering first. Dissolve a little — very little! — magnesium sulfate (Epsom salts) in water for use on the hungry plant.

SYMPTOMS/
SULFUR DEFICIENCY

Newer (upper) leaves turn yellow
Older (lower) leaves curl upward
Stems turn hard and inflexible
Growth slows or stops
Leaves suddenly drop off plant in large numbers

The third secondary element, *sulfur,* is vital for the plant to build proteins. Its lack shows first in younger leaves, which turn yellow (nitrogen deficiency causes older leaves to turn yellow first). Older leaves curl upward and leaves may drop off. The stems may turn hard and inflexible and growth tips may die. Use a fertilizer that includes ammonium sulfate.

At least seven other elements are required by plants for good health. These trace, or *micro,* elements are needed in only tiny amounts, but they play important roles, usually in the activation of various processes or in the use of other, major elements. A *full-formula fertilizer* contains all the traces needed; don't try to give the plants any additional ones separately — excess can be dangerous! Although even an occasional feeding supplies sufficient trace elements, you might someday need to consider a lack of one or more when evaluating possible causes of a plant's sickness.

Boron (B) aids the movement of sugars through the plant as well as its use of calcium. Without boron, leaves thicken and droop, starting at the base of the leaf instead of at the tip, which is more usual; no new leaves appear because growing tips die back. Look for a fertilizer that specifies a boron content and use it only according to directions: too much can be as bad as too little. You might also add just a tad of borax to the soil.

Chlorine (Cl) is more likely to reveal itself in its excess than in its deficiency, because of the element's presence in tap water. Chlorinated plants' leaves become thicker and their roots may burn. You can eliminate potential damage by letting the water sit out overnight before watering; chlorine will escape as a gas. Fertilizer labels often say that there is "no more than" a certain tiny amount of chlorine in the plant food.

Copper (Cu) starts the activity of other soil elements. Without copper, leaves turn brown, first from the tips and then along the margins; they grow alarmingly large and dark, though they may bleach out. Use a full-formula fertilizer.

Iron (Fe) plays an important role in chlorophyll synthesis but is not actually part of the chlorophyll molecule. Iron deficiency shows in yellow-but-still-green-veined young leaves (chlorosis). Leaves turn brown on the edges and curl; growth is stunted. Use a product called *chelated* or *sequestered* iron (which means that it's been treated to facilitate the plant's use of the element — iron's not imprisoned by the soil pH).

Manganese (Mn) serves as a catalyst in plant processes, especially nitrogen use. Without enough manganese, leaves turn yellow, beginning with the oldest, but even the smallest veins remain visibly green. Again, use fertilizer claiming that all plant requirements are included.

Molybdenum (Mo) is important to plant use of nitrogen and perhaps other elements. Without molybdenum, growth is stunted; leaves turn yellow, perhaps mottled; flower buds fall. Use a full-formula fertilizer.

Zinc (Zn) is a catalyst in several hormone and enzyme processes in plants. Without enough zinc, older leaves turn yellow between veins; they are smaller than normal and may be crinkly; new growth has insuffi-

cient space between leaves. Use a full-formula
or one that has zinc sulfate as a specified in

In trying to remedy a specific trace-element den-
ciency, keep in mind that overdoses of one element
may prohibit the plant's use of another element; such
is the delicate chemical balance of life. For example,
too much potassium induces a deficiency in magnesium; and too much magnesium, in turn, prompts a
calcium deficiency. Avoid this vicious circle by never
feeding a plant more nutrient than the package calls
for; and preferably — to be safe — feed it considerably
less. Stick to regular, judiciously light doses of one of
the many excellent foods on the market.

Choosing and Using Fertilizers

Commercial plant foods have proliferated in the last
few years, almost to the same extent as the plants for
which they are intended. We're given all sorts of
choices between organic and inorganic fertilizers (the
plants don't know the difference); and we are offered
liquids (to mix with water or use alone), powders (to
stir with soil or mix with water), tablets (which dissolve
bit by bit each time you water), special food for roots
and different ones for leaves — all to be dished out
with great quantities of love and friendly chatter. How
does one choose?

The best fertilizer for your plants is one that is suited
to *you* — one so uncomplicated that you find it simple
to use it regularly . . . but not *too* generously. That
perfect fertilizer may be a pretty colored liquid in an
attractive bottle: it can sit on your kitchen sink, where
it reminds you to use a few drops at least once a week
(such a frequent-use fertilizer must be very mild, with
a low total percentage of active ingredients). However,
if you are the organized type who can conveniently
recall every month or so that it is time to feed your
greedy green friends, use a stronger food. Just be sure
never to feed a plant that's in dry soil: its tender roots

have no protection against the strong chemicals. Water your plants first; then, a day or so later, feed them.

The main factor that determines your choice of plant food may be cost — especially if you have lots of plants. If two fertilizers cost about the same and one has 40 percent useful food, while the second has 15 percent useful food, the former is certainly a better value. You're paying for less inert filler, and you won't use it up as quickly as the weaker variety. Value-for-money is important these days.

But do you choose organic or inorganic plant food? In nature, a plant's nutrients will always be *organic* — composed of decaying plant and animal matter. Many growers swear by the results of using similar natural materials as plant food in their homes: fish emulsion for lots of nitrogen (and, yes, it does smell of fish!); bone meal (especially liked by cacti) for lots of phosphorus and more nitrogen; even wood ashes for potassium (if you try it in a fit of organic-only gardening, remember that ash is alkaline and will raise the pH of the soil). From a value-for-money viewpoint, organic fertilizers are probably a better value in general than inorganic ones because they last longer in the soil. The inorganic foods are easily washed out by watering and must be replaced more often.

A well-formulated *inorganic* food — one created synthetically in a chemical laboratory — does, however, provide all the nutrients your plants need "in one swell foop," in the percentages that horticultural scientists have found most reliable. Even among inorganics, however, you have choices.

Read the labels.

If the label does not list trace elements, don't assume that they are included (though they might be). Plan to give your plant friends a variety of different foods, including at least one that will provide the necessary trace elements. Manufacturers sometimes don't like to list trace elements on labels because of the numerous legal requirements involved. If you really want to know the exact ingredient proportions, write to the manufacturer.

If the label lists a selection of house plants for which the food is formulated and they are all foliage plants, don't assume that your flowering plants will also get the nutritional boost they need; you might in fact be preventing flowering if you use that food. And if the label says use with each watering, prepare to do just that. Your plants will be underfed otherwise.

Powders, crystals, and liquids are generally made to be mixed with water, although at least one exception is a product suitable for watering and feeding a terrarium at the same time. It comes already mixed and just squirts into the terrarium as nutritious rain (although, since you're trying to keep terrarium plants little, it strikes me as superfluous to feed them). Most products, however, require that you mix them. Always be certain that the solution is mixed and dissolved thoroughly so no "hot spots" of burning fertilizer go into the pot.

Follow the label directions exactly or — remembering that lots of food is not a wholesome meal for a plant — preferably use less than the amount of chemical called for on the package. Assume that fertilizer manufacturers are in the business of selling as much of their product as possible and might, therefore, be suggesting that you use more food than your plants can safely use in their specific light and watering conditions. To be on the safe side, use less than the strength of food called for. Your plants will thank you and you'll thank yourself when you realize that perhaps you're getting less fertilizer salt buildup on the pots than you were before (more on that subject later).

Time-release pellets or tablets are covered with a slowly dissolving coating of resin. They are popular because the consumer thinks plants are guaranteed a constant, adequate supply of fertilizer. Right. But time-release plant foods also almost guarantee that concentrated spots of chemicals will develop in the pot — spots that are certain to cause damage if the roots grow into them. Although it's probably far safer for you to be in constant control of the feeding situation, you certainly should feel free to try time-release fertilizers. Precise (12-6-6) is a 3M product that is mixed into the top of the soil about every four months. Osmocote (14-14-14) is a convenient time-release organic food often used in hanging-basket plants. Just remember: *do not* get impatient and feed a plant with another fertilizer before the time allotted to your time-release fertilizer is up. You'll burn the roots.

OVERFEEDING

The first sign that you are consistently overfeeding your plants will probably be the development of a white crust on the inside rim of the pot and perhaps on the soil surface, or a white powdery coating on the

Fertilizer salt buildup on a pot rim

outside of a clay pot. These are both buildups of salts from fertilizer — too much fertilizer for the plant to use. (If it weren't too much, there would be no residue left to show.) The white powdery material can be scrubbed off the outside of the pot with a stiff brush. The inside crust, however, can't be removed easily without removing the plant. Do so. The hard, burning crystals can injure the leaves or stems of a plant forced to lie down on the crust. African violets and other such delicate, succulent plants are particularly vulnerable to leaf or stem (petiole) rot from continuous contact with the rough incrustation.

SYMPTOMS/ OVERFEEDING (FERTILIZER ACCUMULATION)

White salt incrustation forms on inside of pot rim and a white, powdery coating forms on the outside of clay pots

Older (lower) leaves turn yellow, dry, and drop off; remaining leaves may wilt

Leaf tips and edges turn brown and dry

Leaves develop rusty spots, usually with brown edges (leaf rot from rubbing incrusted pot rim)

Excessive leaf growth weakens stems and few or no flowers form on a flowering plant (nitrogen overdose)

Flower petal tips turn brown

New growth is stunted, pale, possibly curled or otherwise distorted

Brown or black discoloration, possibly watery, creeps up stem from soil level and stem collapses (stem rot from rubbing incrusted pot rim)

When you suspect that you've been overfeeding your plants, first leach the soil. That means taking the pot to the sink and running water through it time after time. Excess food will wash out of the soil. Delicate plants may need a slightly safer way of leaching, though this method is not so thorough: Sink the pot to its rim in a tub or bucket of lukewarm water. Leave it for an hour or until water has visibly spread across the soil surface. Remove the pot from the container of water and let it drain.

Whichever leaching method you chose, you will probably not be able to entirely scrape off the crystal buildup that has formed on the pot rim. So it's a good idea to repot the plant in a fresh, clean pot.

You are most likely to develop excess-food incrustations when you've ignored a plant's natural resting period, usually in winter. The dormant plant is not going to take up all the food you give it; the surplus mixture will remain in the pot when the water has been used or has evaporated, leaving an unevaporable salt behind. Time after time the process is repeated until a dangerous buildup occurs. Remember, too, that just because it's less visible on plastic pots, that doesn't mean the buildup is not there. In fact, plastic-pot buildup is greater and forms quicker than clay-pot deposits, since clay pots absorb some of the salts into their porous walls. To be safe, it is perhaps wisest to cut your fertilizing in half if accumulations form, whether using plastic or glazed pots. And you can help protect sensitive plants such as African violets by smoothing pot rims with candle wax or paraffin.

Keep your eye tuned for browned leaf tips at times when the humidity has been kept adequately high — that and stunted growth of new stems are prime indicators of overfeeding. Another time to cut down on feeding is when plants are in soil containing a great deal of vermiculite — it retains nutrients longer than other soil materials, so the salt excess easily builds up.

Soil — The Medium Is the Message

The soil — or, actually, potting medium, since some varieties contain no soil at all — decrees, to a large extent, the health and growth of a house plant. Each plant, being an individual, demands its own soil characteristics.

Much of the way a plant uses the fertilizer you give it, for example, depends on a vital aspect of the soil itself — its acid/alkaline character, often referred to as *pH*. Yes, that is a lowercase *p* and a cap *H* — not a typo (but you probably know that from watching shampoo commercials). It's the standard symbol for a complex concept: the concentration of hydrogen ions in the soil. A strong acid contains lots of loose hydrogen ions ($H+$). Bases, or alkalis, contain lots of loose hydroxide ions ($OH-$). Neutral materials have a balanced ion content. An arbitrary symbol, pH indicates the relative acid or alkali value of a substance. A pH of 7 is neutral; a pH of 1 is the extreme of acidity, while a pH of 14 is extreme alkalinity. These numbers are logarithms; a soil with a pH of 6, for example, is *ten times* more acidic than one of 7. So when you add an ingredient to the soil to change its acidity from 5 to 6, you are making a very great change.

Why worry about pH? Because the soil acidity determines how the nutrients in the soil dissolve and thus

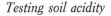

Testing soil acidity

whether growth slows or stops. Rainwater usually has a pH of 6.5 (there are more acidic rains but we'll ignore those), so plants have developed a preference for water with about the same pH value. Below pH 6, the solubility of fertilizers changes and must be compensated for in order to keep plants healthy. Above pH 8, the following elements are not absorbed by the plant and harmful deficiencies can occur: nitrogen, phosphorus, iron, manganese, copper, and zinc. When that happens, leaves are likely to show chlorosis to one extent or another. To correct the situation, *chelated* elements are often given. (That means that they aren't imprisoned in the soil by high alkalinity.)

Most plants grow in an acid/alkalinity range of 4 through 9, usually leaning toward acid. For example, some familiar house plants and their pH preferences are:

African violet	6–7	Boston fern	5.5–6.5
asparagus fern	5–6.5	English ivy	6–8
begonia	5.5–7	gardenia	5–5.5

In general, those plants that prefer moist soils also prefer slightly acidic soils, because humus (the moisture-holding decaying matter in soil) is acidic. Plants that like dry soils like some alkalinity, or at least neutrality.

Regular watering of soil week after week tends gradually to make it alkaline. If you're concerned about your house plants' soil, get one of the simple soil test kits now readily available. Follow the directions exactly as given. Then change the pH of the soil as recommended, or as you choose. To make a soil more acidic, you have several options:

· Add sulfur, such as in aluminum sulfate: two teaspoons in one gallon of water once a month.

· Water occasionally with cold tea.

· Water with vinegar: about one teaspoon in a gallon of water, perhaps once a month;

· Try watering with pickle juice (though the slight sugar content may attract flies).

· Stir in more peat moss, a naturally acidic soil material.

· Simplest of all, use an acidic fertilizer, such as Mir-Acid.

Though alkalinity is a greater danger than acidity, soils that are too acid sometimes occur and can be corrected by adding lime, usually in the form of crushed dolomite limestone, to the soil. Perlite, too, is alkaline and can be used to correct an overly acidic soil, as can the lowly eggshell — crushed, of course. Severe acidity makes leaves wilt and fall.

Just as important to the plant as the soil's pH value is its texture. As you've probably gathered from the discussion above, plants from different regions like soils with different water-holding characteristics. A loose, sandy medium dries quickly — a boon to a succulent that can't bear water held to its roots for any length of time. A soil with too much heavy material remains moist, but when it dries may harden and become compact, preventing new water from entering. Loose, sandy soil allows a great deal of air to reach the plant's roots; heavier mediums allow little, even none, to do so, unless allowed to dry partially between waterings.

Standard commercial potting soil contains a well-researched balance of various materials to provide the most satisfactory growing medium for the largest variety of plants. Such soil is usually a combination of humus, peat moss, vermiculite, and sand. Some plants prefer a bit of change from the standard for best growth; it's easy to vary the mixture. Next time you change the soil in your plants' pots, consider making some simple, healthful variations on standard, all-purpose soil. For example, switch from standard soil to African-violet soil for the following plants, which prefer the higher acidity: coffee plant *(Coffea arabica)*, ferns, begonias, citrus plants, impatience, gardenia, and pittosporum. Or add chopped peat and sharp sand, one part each, to two parts standard potting soil for geraniums, which will then thrive from the air reaching their roots but are protected from the possibility of the soil being allowed to dry out easily.

Some plants that may, surprisingly, do better in a cactus mix (buy one commercially or add three parts sharp sand and one part peat moss to one part standard potting soil) include: croton, rosary vine *(Ceropegia woodii)*, and most succulents, such as kalanchoe and jade plant.

Soilless potting mediums have become increasingly popular for many plants, especially those growing under artificial lights or for big plants that are just impossible to move when their pots are weighed down with earth. Soilless mixtures tend to be a combination of three ingredients: sphagnum peat moss (which would have turned into soil if it had been left alone for thousands of years), vermiculite, and perlite. Peat holds water — up to twenty times its own weight — and is antiseptic, thus preventing several diseases and soil-borne pests. Vermiculite is a sterile, expanded mineral that contains great air spaces, which hold water. Perlite is another expanded mineral that is used in place of heavier sand to allow air into the potting medium. Commercially, this soilless mix then has added to it lots of other materials to provide long-lasting nutrients, such as powdered superphosphates and lime, slow-release fertilizers, and even a wetting agent, which assists the materials in absorbing water again if they are allowed to dry out (dry peat, especially, normally repels water; it needs a wetting agent to get it working again).

One such soilless mix, called the Cornell Foliage Mix, is used by commercial growers for such constant-moisture lovers as zebra plant, *Cissus,* ferns, baby's tears, *Pilea,* and *Ficus.* When you get such plants home from the shop and prepare to repot them (after giving them a rest of several days to recover from shock, of course), you'll probably have to brush all the soilless medium off the roots before repotting in your standard potting soil. Otherwise, the plants' roots probably won't venture from a medium of one texture into a soil of another texture; its new *lebensraum* will be wasted. You can, of course, stick with the soilless medium. Some of the easily available soilless mixes that correspond to Cornell mix are Pro-Mix B, Redi-Earth, Metro Mix, and Jiffy Mix. Plants in soilless mediums must be fed sooner and more often than ones repotted into soil.

Whether you use a soilless medium or your favorite packaged potting soil (but, please, not unsterilized soil from your garden — that way lies death for tender, unadventurous house plants), you must be concerned with how water drains through the potting medium. When water doesn't drain through the soil quickly, it fills the air spaces in the soil, preventing oxygen from reaching the roots. It also, more seriously, cages water so that it surrounds the roots and stems. If they are already filled with water, as would be true with a succulent, the path is open for root rot; older leaves turn yellow and all leaves wilt, prompting you to supply dangerously more water. Soon death may come, if the soil isn't allowed to dry properly.

Rule number one for potting: Never put a plant in a pot without a drainage hole. That rule can make for some fancy scurrying on occasion — such as when I water the philodendron I keep in a bird cage suspended over a couch. When I water it, I have to stand underneath with a bucket until it finishes dripping (my own fault: I neglected to put a saucer in the cage).

**SYMPTOMS/
COMPACTED SOIL**

Water sits on soil surface
Soil separates from sides of pot and water runs down sides
Older (lower) leaves turn yellow, dry, and drop off
Leaves wilt, usually followed by withering and dropping
New growth is stunted and thicker than normal
Growth slows or stops

But at least the pot drains. Sometimes a plant will be in a soil that has been watered and dried so often that it compacts into a hard mass. The water either sits on top of the surface unable to seep through or the soil separates from the pot side and fresh water runs rampantly down the side, missing the roots it passes. These situations can be remedied by sinking the pot almost to its rim in a bucket or sink of lukewarm water. Let it sit for at least half an hour. Gradually, the water will seep in from the sides and up from the bottom, softening the soil as it goes. Be sure to stir the top soil with a gently wielded fork after it has softened. Even better, repot the plant in fresh soil.

Pay attention when a plant's growing instructions say to give it a loose soil (add sand or perlite) or a moisture-holding soil (usually regular potting soil will do, or add more vermiculite to absorb extra water; you can also add more premoistened peat moss, but that increases the soil acidity). If the instructions call for good drainage, add a layer of pebbles over the shards covering the drainage hole; such a plant is obviously vulnerable to root rot if the water is ever allowed to soak the soil.

Add Flavor to the Soup

All sorts of concoctions have been available at various times for giving your plants added oomph in some special way. One of the most recent popular soil additives is a homemade potion: an oral contraceptive for humans — The Pill — dissolved in water. I think perhaps plant growers hear the word *hormone* and assume that a hormone is a hormone is a hormone — and even stranger, it seems to work . . . sometimes. I've heard tales of plants in their death throes taking a new, hardy lease on life upon tasting Pill-doctored water; and there are stories about healthy plants that grew by leaps and bounds after going on The Pill — not to mention rumors of unexpected pregnancies resulting from contraceptives being used for purposes other than those originally intended. No one has yet seriously studied the subject to find the truth, but if you have *spare* birth-control pills and feel like experimenting, give them a try on house plants.

A hormone product about which considerably more is known is gibberellic acid, a plant growth hormone. Used for years in commercial greenhouses, the hormone was heralded as an almost magical substance when it first came on the market. If sprayed weekly with it, some plants doubled their size in a quarter of the time it normally took. Although it gradually became clear that gibberellic acid was not quite the Great Answer that it was first assumed to be, it is still often used, particularly with geraniums, which achieve spectacular growth as a result. But so what? You don't run a greenhouse; unlike a commercial grower, you don't need a plant to grow and move away quickly to make room for one more. But if you enjoy experimenting, just remember that a plant being forced to grow quickly needs considerably more food than it would normally, so double its fertilizer allotment.

Other hormones are given to plants as tonics, something to revive plants whose interest is flagging. These vitamin/hormone concentrates — similar to Rootone, Hormodin, Re-Root, or other transplanting aids — seem to concentrate the plants' energies on growing new roots and ever-important root hairs. If the base of a plant is strong and flourishing, the top is apt to be beautifully healthy. Just be sure to follow package directions exactly: an overdose of these strong chemicals can actually achieve opposite results — suppressed growth.

Other chemicals are available to *retard* growth, but these are of interest only to commercial greenhouses that, for instance, want to sell an Easter lily or a Christmas poinsettia with enormous flowers but not a great stem; one product reduces the elongation of the stem. You, as a home grower, may have similarly treated plants in your terrarium. The popularity of gardens-under-glass is dependent upon the ability of treated plants to stay small for a long time. A product called A-Rest, for example, keeps plants dwarfed for more than three months.

Lots of plant lovers are currently talking about a product called Restore. It's a combination plant food (3-4-4, all from organic sources such as bone meal) and soil rebuilder. It contains microorganisms so that, in the manufacturer's words, it "recreates in the pot Nature's own plant care system." The company recommends that Restore be used when soil has compacted and contends that it renews the soil so repotting is unnecessary unless the plant needs room for growth. In addition, it is claimed, water retention of the soil is increased, the soil is aerated, and salts are neutralized. That's a lot from one product. I've not yet tried Restore, but I have been informed by someone who has that any visitor to his home immediately knows from the aroma when he has watered with the product. But he certainly saves money on repotting plants — and big plants that can't be handled very easily get all the refreshment of a soil change.

As with Barbie dolls and skateboards, a fad brings all sorts of side products to the market. Hopefully, houseplant faddism is settling into a consistent new body of growers who care about their green friends and have discovered the joy of living with them. The best of the sideline products will stay with us and grow venerable, like you, the best of the house-plant growers.

~ 6. PESKY INSECTS

SOME OF THE LIVING CREATURES THAT MAY BE TROU-
blesome to your plants — besides enthusiastic but un-
knowledgeable human friends and greenery-chewing
cats and dogs — are just what the chapter title says:
pesky. Among the merely annoying pests are ants,
caterpillars, earthworms, slugs, and springtails. Other
pests, however, are death-dealing. Spider mites and the
other sucking insects — aphids, mealybugs, scales, and
whiteflies — can destroy a prized specimen almost before you know it's been attacked.

Fortunately, more plants lead a pest-free life than
are ever attacked. And more are attacked than die —
if you learn the symptoms and keep a constant eye out
for them. Become adept at using a magnifying glass.
Use it regularly to spot insect pests that are not readily
visible to the naked eye. You shouldn't have to wait
until the pests' effects are pronounced before treating
them.

In the last few years, as it became the "in" thing to
grow house plants, sellers have proliferated, perhaps far
beyond the realistic realm of their potential market —
as evidenced by the large number of shops that disap-

peared almost as quickly as they appeared. The stock many of these shops have been selling may have come from dubious sources — greenhouses that have been so busy trying to keep up with demand that they haven't been as attentive to possible pests as might be expected. Then, to make things worse, the plants are taken into shops that were, say, originally designed to sell shirts rather than scheffleras.

When you go to buy a plant at an unfamiliar shop, take a careful look around. Is the store clean? Does it have adequate light and ventilation for plants that may have to reside there for some weeks? Time spent in poor surroundings can lower the plants' resistance, leaving them vulnerable to attack by anything that ventures near.

Inspect a plant you're interested in — as well as its immediate neighbors — quite thoroughly. Are the backs of the leaves pristine? Are the axils of leaves (where they join the main stem) clear and dust-free? Does the foliage look healthy and perky? A "no" to any of these inspection queries should make you say no to the plant. Don't feel sorry for one with a cold and take it home to coddle: you'll endanger the rest of your plants.

On the opposite side of the coin, however, is the single yellow leaf. One yellowed leaf, especially an older (lower) leaf, may mean nothing by itself. But do let a lone yellowing leaf serve as a signal for you to inspect further.

When you get your purchase home, no matter how confident you are of its health, keep it in splendid isolation for at least ten days. Prepare a bath of soap and water. (You can have one too, but this one is for your new plant.) If you read straight through this chapter right now instead of waiting and running to it when tiny beasts are visible, you may tire of reading that the first thing to do when combatting insects is to try soap and water — the plant world's chicken soup — before reaching for the convenient pesticide can. But the repetition is warranted; the bathing process is simple, often effective, and it contributes to keeping both aerosol gases and chemical poisons out of our air.

Cover the top of the soil with plastic (or your hand, if the pot is small enough). Turn the plant upside down and swish it around in a pail or sink of warm, soapy water; use about two teaspoons of soap or detergent to a gallon of water. A big plant can be taken into the shower and carefully soaped with a soft sponge or sprayed with a mister. Be sure to wash up and down the stems completely — in the leaves' armpits and behind their ears, as it were. Just be sure no soap runs into the soil. Rinse the plant carefully. Let the cleaned plant dry in a nonsunny place, then return it to the isolation ward.

Bathing and isolation aren't punishments; if a plant stays pest-free, it can soon join new friends. This sort of treatment is the basic first step for fighting most insect pests. You're just employing it now as a preventive.

Keeping new plants isolated can be difficult. When I moved recently from Washington, D.C., to a Chicago suburb, I had to sell most of my plants (they sold as quickly as my stereo speakers at the garage sale I held). In my new home, I couldn't bear to be without lots of greenery, so my husband and I went on a plant-buying binge the likes of which I've never enjoyed before. Wonderful fun, but after the sixth greenhouse yielded up the sixth group of plants, we ran out of rooms in which to isolate each separate group. Purchasing stopped while the isolation siege went on.

If you run into a similar problem, you can, remember, isolate a new plant from others just by covering it with a plastic bag. The consequent increased humidity will help it recover from the shock of the move — an added benefit of the isolation.

The Pests in Particular   In the following pages, the major bugs that bother house plants are described, and an appropriate treatment is suggested. I almost always recommend that you work first with soapy water before using insecticides. Insecticides are meant to kill: *they are poisonous.* Think twice before using them in your home. And when an insecticide is suggested in the following pages, do not rush to use it. Instead, take time to read chapter 9 on chemicals, their uses, and their handling before you blithely start spraying or dunking your plants in poisons.

ANTS

SYMPTOM/ ANTS	Ants become visible on or near plants (a signal that other pests may be present)

Ants belong only on picnics. Their presence on a house plant may signal no picnic because they trail in the sugary wake of other, more serious pests. Aphids, scale insects, mealybugs, and whiteflies (all of which are described in this chapter) are sucking insects. They voraciously suck the juices out of plants, consuming more fluid than their bodies can use. The excess is given off as a sweet, sticky fluid called *honeydew.*

Ants love honeydew. So much so, in fact, that ants have been known to keep herds of aphids like herds of cows to guarantee a supply of the habit-forming fluid.

If you see ants on your plants, inspect meticulously with a magnifying glass for the presence of other insects — for the ones doing the damage to the plant instead of the more visible, but basically harmless, ants. Take care that the ants don't just move to another plant carrying their slave aphids along as precious baggage. You'll have to outwit the ants. Try picking them off (though that won't get their eggs). Wash the plant thoroughly and you may drown the ants. As a last resort, drench with malathion or a similar chemical solution. It's very strong, so avoid contact with your skin.

APHIDS

Leaves turn yellow and curled; some may drop off
Leaf surfaces become sticky and glossy (honeydew
  patches), perhaps with spreading patches of blackish or
  dark gray, powdery coating
New growth is stunted, pale, possibly curled or otherwise
  distorted

*Below: Aphids,
or plant lice*

*Right: Solanum
pseudo-capsicum
(Jerusalem cherry)
with aphids*

If you've ever known anyone with a rose garden, it's close to inevitable that you've heard about aphids. Almost every outdoor plant has a species of aphid, also called plant lice, peculiar to it. Only a few varieties of aphid move indoors, but they make up for their lack of relatives by sheer voraciousness. The identification of the particular kind of aphid doesn't matter except to an entomologist (and perhaps to other aphids). What does matter is that these rapidly multiplying

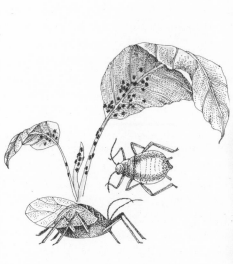

sucking insects must be eliminated immediately, before they can destroy your house plants.

Aphids are small (only up to about one-eighth inch long as adults), pear-shaped insects that may be green, black, red, whitish, or even pink. Some may be whitish with a waxy coating. If you use a magnifying glass to stare at your infestation (which usually occurs on new shoots and undersides of leaves), you'll note long antennae on the aphids. Some have wings and some don't; that's a sign of the troublesome fact that aphids may carry out their whole complicated life cycle — egg, wingless nymph and two forms of adult females (one that requires a male to reproduce and one that is self-sufficient, poor thing) — on your dieffenbachia.

Both nymphs and adults possess tubelike mouth parts that they use to drill holes in the tender tissue of young, juicy leaves and then suck the juices out. The final effect is that the leaf looks dull; it loses color because chlorophyll is removed. The whole plant begins to do less than well. Because the bugs congregate at tender growing tips, new growth is slow; and when growth does occur it may be distorted, both in leaves and flower buds. The misshapen buds are not likely to open. Old leaves turn yellow and pucker or curl. Even all that isn't the end:

Aphids, like other sucking insects, need to get rid of much of the moisture they suck (after using the sugars it contains). They excrete it as the sticky fluid called honeydew. You may first suspect something is wrong with a plant by feeling the sticky substance or seeing the gloss it gives to a normally unglossy leaf. The honeydew, in turn, causes at least three problems: (1) it draws ants if they're anywhere in your house; (2) it blocks the breathing pores on the leaf; and (3) it serves as the nutrient for the growth of an unattractive, though harmless, fungus called *sooty mold.* I said "harmless," and it is by itself — but sooty mold can prevent leaves from getting their proper amount of sunlight, adding to the factors that make the plant less than its glorious natural self.

Help! The first thing to do after discovering your plant has become an aphid's milkshake is to head for the kitchen sink. Give the plant a thorough soapy bath as described earlier in this chapter. Then place the plant in isolation. After three or four days, repeat the bath, wait a few days . . . and then repeat the process. It may take three or four such treatments to eliminate all the eggs that may be tucked away in hard-to-get-at places. If there's no sign of the critters ten days later, you've probably got the problem licked. Trim off damaged foliage before returning the plant to its friends, so that it won't be embarrassed.

Frankly, it's unlikely that you'll get rid of the aphids so easily. You see, some fly. And some probably leaped to the safety of other plants when you started "person-handling" their green home.

Aphids respond to contact pesticides, those that are applied directly to plant surfaces and kill on contact. The classic contacts are malathion, rotenone, pyrethrum, and nicotine sulfate (Black Flag–40). These are mixed with water, and the plant is dipped in the mixture or sprayed with it. Aphids, being sucking insects, also respond to systemic poisons — those that are added to soil as a solution, taken up by the whole plant system, and become part of the juice the bugs suck. Many people, including myself, see no reason to make a whole plant poisonous except as a last resort for a special plant such as a particularly lovely fern, which can't be sprayed with malathion.

BULB PESTS

<table>
<tr><td>SYMPTOMS/
BULB PESTS</td><td>Bulbs have soft, mushy parts
Growth is weak or stunted if bulb manages to grow at all</td></tr>
</table>

The main value of using bulbs to produce plants is that the indoor gardener can force them to bloom in winter — out of season, when they add color to a winter-weary mind. Most bulbs that you buy for that purpose are specially treated and can't be used again. Just discard them after enjoying the bloom.

Occasionally you may get a prepacked bulb which, when you open the package, turns out to have soft, squishy places in it. These spots may indicate that the bulb contains any of several pests, such as bulb-fly maggots or bulb mites. If the infestation is serious, discard the bulb. If not, cut out the spots with a sharp, sterile knife and dust the wounds and whole bulb with a product such as Bulb Saver.

CATERPILLARS AND CUTWORMS

SYMPTOMS/
CATERPILLARS

Fresh chew marks appear on leaves, stems, or buds
Dark excrement specks appear on leaves

Caterpillars are the larval stage of moths and butterflies but bear little physical resemblance to those flying insects. Instead, they are wormlike, with many short legs. Some, like the familiar woolly bear, are hairy; others are naked, with odd colors and knobby segments. Caterpillars are barely visible when they hatch from eggs (which may be inadvertently carried into the house), but they can quickly grow to one or two inches. The work of the caterpillar is to store up energy for the process of turning into an adult moth or butterfly. Energy means food. Food may mean the leaves and stems, and even the flower buds, of your house plants. Munch, munch.

Fortunately, caterpillars rarely congregate in numbers. If you note signs of your plants serving as meals (you may also see dark excrement drops on the leaves), hunt for the caterpillars and remove them by hand. Spray around the pots with malathion.

SYMPTOMS/
CUTWORMS

New shoots appear chewed off
Stems appear slashed
Leaves yellow and root-rot symptoms develop

Cutworm

Cutworms are caterpillars of one particular moth family. Not at all cute like woolly bears, cutworms are soft, dark, and rather repugnant. They develop from eggs of night-flying moths that may get into greenhouses, or even your house. Some like stems and will topple a plant in no time. Others burrow into the soil and feed on roots; root damage begins to show in the leaves. To see cutworms at work, you'll need to lie in wait at night. If damage continues and you haven't been able to catch the animals by stirring the soil and grabbing them before they disappear from sight again, drench the soil with a rotenone or malathion solution.

COCKROACHES

SYMPTOM/ COCKROACHES	Fresh chew marks appear on leaves (especially of humidity-loving plants)

Unfortunately, most of us know all too well when we have cockroaches in our homes. But the endeavor to keep the kitchen dry and spotless in order to eliminate their food sources may drive them elsewhere — such as to succulent leaves of humidity-loving house plants (roaches are particularly drawn to terrariums). These brown, beetlelike nuisances may well damage plants when you're not looking. First, try to eliminate them completely from your home. If you use one of the strong household poisons, be sure never to direct it at the leaves of your plants; that way lies death for the plants. If for some peculiar reason you've eliminated cockroaches generally from your home but have a few diehards on a plant, spray the plant with malathion (don't use it in the kitchen or anywhere near food). A good general cleanup of the growing area with an all-purpose disinfectant will also be helpful.

CUTWORMS

See *Caterpillars and Cutworms.*

CYCLAMEN MITES

**SYMPTOMS/
CYCLAMEN MITES**

Leaves turn grayish and dull, twisted or wrinkled, perhaps curled and brittle

African-violet leaves become twisted, hairy, perhaps with white swelling on top surface

Few or no flowers form on a flowering plant (especially African violets)

Buds turn black (especially on African violets)

Flower petals become streaked, wrinkly, and curled and fade quickly

---

Cyclamen mite

The good things you do for your plants to protect them from spider mites (discussed later in this chapter) are not terribly useful against their relatives the cyclamen mites. These critters go after — you guessed it — cyclamen (which is not usually recommended as a house plant but is popular in greenhouses), but they are also a nuisance to African violets and sometimes to other rosette-leaved plants. Cyclamen mites prevent such plants from flowering and turn buds black; or, if flowers are already open, cyclamen mites make them streaked, wrinkly, and curled, and they fade too quickly. Leaves become grayish and dull, perhaps curled and brittle. On African violets, leaves may become very, very hairy, twisted, and may bear white swellings on the top surface. Cyclamen mites themselves, visible only with a magnifying glass, are white or pale green. Generally they're a problem only during cool temperatures, unlike spider mites, which like hot, dry places.

In general, cyclamen mite–infested plants should be

quickly discarded. Be sure not to touch other plants until you've thoroughly washed your hands. Plants that you particularly treasure can be nonchemically treated: heat a pan of water to 115 degrees Fahrenheit (you must have a cooking thermometer to make sure this is just right); hold it at that temperature (not easy) for fifteen minutes while the sick plant — and its pot — are submerged in the water. An easier cure is to apply Kelthane three times, ten days apart. Some growers put sodium selenate in the soil, but it is very poisonous and not recommended for home use.

EARTHWORMS

Friends in the garden, worms are a nuisance in flowerpots because they disturb roots and can accidentally plug up the drainage hole. Never use garden soil for your house plants. Make complete root checks of all plants that have summered outdoors when you get ready to bring them in and remove any earthworms.

EARWIGS

SYMPTOM/ EARWIGS

Fresh chew marks appear in leaves overnight

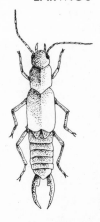

Earwig

Another rare intruder from the garden, especially in coastal areas, the earwig (named for the old wives' tale about one that crawled into the ear of a sleeping person) is almost an inch long, dark red-brown in color, and has quite obvious pincers at the back end. Earwigs, too, chew on leaves, leaving clear evidence of having dined well, and quickly, during the night. You'll need to be just as quick as they are to get them off the plant, because they're likely to run and hide in a closet or under a chair. You might lie in wait for them. Turn on a light — at random and widely spaced intervals — and hurriedly pinch the earwigs off when you see them.

Otherwise, spray with malathion. If you try to kill them with a household insecticide, do not spray the plants, just the area around them.

FUNGUS GNATS

If you keep conditions right (as described in the next chapter) for preventing the growth of fungus around your house plants, you'll usually prevent, at the same time, attack by fungus gnats. These small flies (also called mushroom flies) are gray, sometimes greenish, about one-eighth of an inch long; they swarm in a cloud over a plant whose soil has been kept too moist. However, one must beware of not only the flying gnats: they've laid eggs in the soil. The eggs develop into small (about one-fourth of an inch), whitish maggots that burrow into tender roots, making the plant puny and obviously off-color, and causing leaves to drop. Because they are attracted to rotting matter, you're most likely to find fungus gnats in plants growing in lots of peat — which is, of course, rotting vegetation.

So you've got two problems: the burrowing immature forms and the flying adults. Spray the adults — carefully, to avoid injuring the plant tissues — with a pyrethrum-based aerosol. Drench the pot, first in water (the maggots should drown), and if that's not sufficient, with malathion or nicotine sulfate. Diazinon, an organic phosphate, is often recommended for fungus gnats, but it is very toxic and better not used in a home.

GARDEN CENTIPEDES

Leaves wilt for no apparent reason
Growth slows or stops
Roots and underground stems appear damaged

*Garden centipede,
or symphylans*

Garden centipedes (not actually related to true centipedes, which are predators instead of plant munchers) are popularly supposed to have at least one hundred legs. They really have only twelve pairs (a true centipede has only fifteen pairs) — but that's still enough for an adventuresome pest to cling to someone going indoors and to set up housekeeping among your plants. All those legs are crowded onto a small (perhaps only one-fourth inch long), white, slightly flattened body. Symphylans (or symphilids), as garden centipedes are also called, like decaying organic matter, so you're more likely to find them in the soil of your humus-loving African violets than in cacti, especially if you are a compost-heap addict (compost heaps are heaped with symphylans). Trouble is, they don't just sit in the soil. They find their way to roots or underground stems and start chewing. Eventually the plant wilts, stops growing (to conserve energy), and may die if not cleaned of pests.

You'll have to catch sight of the small white insects scurrying into cover when the roots are disturbed to be sure what the trouble is. (The possibility of sighting these pests is an excellent reason for regular root checks — if you can't think of others.) Wash off all old soil; remove damaged roots. Repot the plant in fresh, symphylan-free soil. If necessary, drench the soil with malathion.

GROUND MEALYBUGS

See *Mealybugs.*

LEAF MINERS

Leaves develop raised, blisterlike, irregular elongated
   patches
Individual leaves die

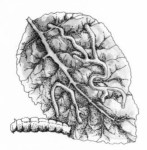

Leaf miner

If only leaf miners could be trained to work in coal
mines, our energy problems might be solved. Alas, they
stick to burrowing between the two thin outer surfaces
of plant leaves, particularly gesneriads such as gloxinias
and African violets. Actually the larval stage of beetles,
flies, or some other insects, leaf miners are, fortunately,
rare indoors. But they may come in on garden chrysanthemums, for example, or on azaleas or even eggplant.
They dig into a leaf, extracting the goodies from between the surfaces as they tunnel, and, of course, soon
kill the leaf. You can see them as raised pathways on
the leaves, like miniature moles. Spray the plant with
rotenone or malathion, and drench the soil with malathion. Remove all leaves with signs of damage. You
may need to consider using a systemic pesticide for a
serious infestation.

LEAF ROLLERS

Leaves curl
Tiny green eggs appear on plant
Growth slows or stops followed by gradual death of plant

Miners mine. Rollers roll. Such is the simplicity of the
insect world — once in a while. Leaf rollers really do
roll leaves; these caterpillars like to hide as leaf miners
do, but in addition to burrowing, they curl up in a
blanket of leaf. Probably the most common leaf roller
in greenhouses — and thus occasionally indoors — is
one called the oblique-banded roller, or rose-leaf tier.
It is light green with a dark head. It works as a miner

first and then rolls. Another, the omnivorous roller, is green with a dark stripe down its back. Both of these pests lay green eggs; look carefully for egg clusters on your plants. Remove all curled up leaves and inspect the plant fully for signs of incipient rolling. Spray the plant with malathion.

MEALYBUGS

Leaves turn yellow and wilt
White, waxy fluff forms on leaves
Leaves suddenly drop off plant in large numbers
Leaf surfaces become sticky and glossy (honeydew
    patches), perhaps with spreading patches of blackish or
    dark gray, powdery coating (sooty mold)
New growth is stunted, pale, possibly curled or otherwise
    distorted
Ants appear, attracted by honeydew

Mealybugs are tiny, soft-bodied, white creatures that look as if they were coated with white meal, because their bodies are covered with a waxy substance. Closely related to scale insects, mealybugs are like aphids, scales, and whiteflies in that they are sucking insects, capable of getting through great quantities of plant juices and excreting sticky honeydew. These four insects, along with spider mites, are the kings of pesthood. All other pests are rare and exotic by contrast.

If you look at mealybugs through a magnifying glass (which is not really necessary, because they may reach three-sixteenths of an inch long), you'll see an oval body, usually surrounded by a fringe of waxy filaments and occasionally long filaments at the tail end. They wander at will, albeit slowly, over a plant, seeking the juiciest protected places, such as in the axils of leaves. As they suck, leaves turn yellow and wilt, growth slows, and the plant dies. Unlike when you check spider mites, which form easily visible webs, you must look carefully to see mealybugs, probably noticeable as

Above: *Mealybugs*

Right: Ctenanthe
*with cottonlike
mealybugs*

white, cottony clusters of "fluff" (actually the egg cases). Look often and if you see just an odd small patch, you can wipe it off with alcohol. If more is visible, wash the plant thoroughly in soap and water as described at the beginning of this chapter. Isolate the plant for several days; then repeat the washing. Mealybugs hatch in ten days, so if the plant is pest-free after ten days, you've destroyed all the eggs and have won the day. If not, try spraying with a last-resort dose of malathion. Mealybugs can be removed from ferns (which can't stand most common insecticide sprays) by using a paintbrush to douse them with nicotine sulfate (just mix one teaspoon Black Flag–40 with a gallon of water and stir together with a bit of soap flakes). You may also need to use a systemic poison on ferns if the nicotine sulfate doesn't work.

One variety of mealybug, called the ground (or soil) mealybug, lives, obviously, in the soil instead of up on the skyscraper structure of the plant. It finds the juices of roots tastier than other parts. The attacked plant wilts easily between waterings, so if you're getting wilting cacti or African violets although the soil is kept moist, suspect soil mealybug. Dilute malathion and sink the whole pot in the solution, so that no eggs are left untreated.

MITES

See *Cyclamen Mites, Spider Mites.*

MUSHROOM FLIES

See *Fungus Gnats.*

NEMATODES

See chapter 7. (These animals cause a disease rather than injury.)

OBLIQUE-BANDED ROLLERS

See *Leaf Rollers.*

OMNIVEROUS ROLLERS

See *Leaf Rollers.*

PILL BUGS

See *Sow Bugs and Pill Bugs.*

PLANT LICE

See *Aphids.*

RED SPIDER MITES

See *Spider Mites.*

ROSE-LEAF TIERS

See *Leaf Rollers.*

SCALE INSECTS

Small brown or gray lumps, usually hard, appear on
  stems and leaves
Leaves yellow and wilt
Leaf surfaces become sticky and glossy (honeydew
  patches), perhaps with spreading patches of blackish or
  dark gray, powdery coating (sooty mold)
New growth is stunted, pale, possibly curled or otherwise
  distorted

Below: *Scale insects*

Right: Polypodium
*with scale insects. The
darker, evenly spaced
spots are the fern's
spore cases.*

Scale insects are, in effect, mealybugs with coats on.
The coats, or scales, are usually hard and colored gray
or brown, though they can match a plant's color and
thus be undetected until almost too late to save the
plant. Like aphids (see entry in this chapter), scales
suck juices and produce honeydew, so plants develop
stunted growth and may be covered with stickiness, on
which sooty mold grows. For some reason, scale infestation is found primarily on plants with glossy foliage.
  One of the most common indoor scale insects is

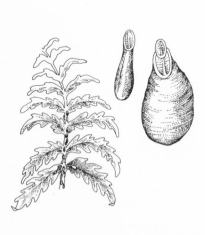

called soft brown scale. It can produce new offspring every day for weeks, so the washing of the plant in warm, soapy water may consequently have to go on for several weeks to be sure all eggs are eliminated. A more serious infestation may require treatment with malathion. At first, it may seem as if you've done no death-dealing at all, because scales seem to continue to cling to the leaf or stem for a month or more. You can tell if they are dead or not by removing and mashing a couple: dead ones will be crumbly dry; live ones won't — they squish.

Another specific scale insect is called hemispherical scale. It is, clearly, hemispherical in shape. Smooth and shiny brown, it is about one-eighth of an inch in diameter and is particularly attracted to fern fronds where, to the undiscerning eye, it can resemble the reproductive spore cases that develop there. The spores, fortunately, grow in evenly spaced rows; so any brown lumps that don't line up properly on the backs of fern fronds should be presumed to be scales.

If there are only a few scale insects present on a plant, flick them off with your fingernail or a knife tip onto a piece of paper. Then burn the paper or flush it down the toilet. A plant with leathery leaves can probably take having the scales scrubbed off with a soft-bristle toothbrush. A larger infestation may require spraying with an insecticide such as rotenone, pyrethrum, or malathion. As usual, ferns should not be sprayed with the common insecticides; instead, dip them in a solution of nicotine sulfate (see *Mealybugs* section).

SLUGS AND SNAILS

SYMPTOMS/ SLUGS AND SNAILS	Fresh chew marks and holes appear in leaves overnight Slime trails appear on leaves, pots, and trays

Visitors from the garden, snails and their shell-less relatives the slugs, are most often brought indoors

Slug (bottom) *and snail*

when plants that have summered outside are taken back inside. They take up residence (usually in a greenhouse) among pots during the day and venture out at night to feed on plants, usually by rasping the leaf surface but often by actually munching large holes in the leaves and young shoots. They exude slime that forms a telltale trail showing where they've been. If you're a good detective perhaps you can tell where they've gone so that you can find and destroy.

Commercial snail baits usually contain a chemical called metaldehyde. Be certain that the bait, a liquid or perhaps pellets, is used only according to instructions and is never allowed to touch the plants: metaldehyde is highly poisonous. Better yet, look for a bait with a different ingredient or — safer and more fun — use beer. Yup, beer. Just put a couple of shallow saucers of beer, fresh each night, near the plants where a snail or slug is feeding. The culprit will be attracted to the beer, crawl in for a nightcap, and drown. (Beer drinkers may be offended by this use of their beverage and sympathize with the pest, but they should look at it this way: for a beer lover, is there a better way to go?) You can also add beer to the commercial bait to increase its drawing power.

SOIL MEALYBUGS

See *Mealybugs*.

SOW BUGS AND PILL BUGS

SYMPTOMS/ SOW BUGS AND PILL BUGS	Leaves turn yellow and wilt Fresh chew marks appear on roots, stems, and young growth overnight

These bugs are tiny crustaceans (relatives of lobsters but certainly not as nice) that occasionally infest greenhouses and may take up habitation in house plants, especially in pots that are kept very moist. They have

Sow Bug

oval, segmented bodies, are brownish or grayish in color, and are less than half an inch long. The pill bug is a type of sow bug that can curl up in a tiny ball when disturbed, so don't mistake it for a bit of soil.

Sow bugs are drawn to humid places, where they prefer rotting vegetation (so keep your plant-growing areas clean). They burrow slightly under the soil during the day and emerge at night. Sow bugs don't turn up their noses at a good chance to munch on roots, stems, and tender young growth, especially seedlings.

To eliminate them, first pick off the critters you see, then clean up all waste. Spray soil and other surfaces with malathion. Even better, remove the plant from the pot. Wash off all old soil and repot the plant in fresh potting soil.

SPIDER MITES

**SYMPTOMS/
SPIDER MITES**

Leaves bleach and become mottled with grayish yellow tinge; close inspection reveals cobwebs
Leaves dry up and crumble
Growth is stunted, slow, or stops followed by death of plant

Spider mite and its webs

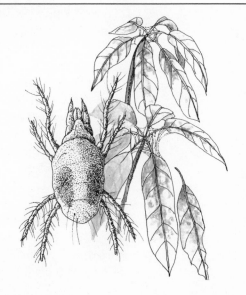

Spider mites are the real stinkers of the plant-pest kingdom. I know very few people who have grown plants for any length of time without discovering attacks by the ubiquitous spider mites — often called red spider mites (though they aren't necessarily red) or two-spotted mites. Even the most conscientious plant growers are prone to spider mite attack, generally on thin-leaved plants, when winter heating is first turned on and the humidity is not yet adjusted to compensate for the hot dryness.

Purists would not list mites in a chapter on insects, because technically they aren't insects. They are members of the spider family and thus have eight legs rather than the six required for insecthood. (The better to crawl over your plants, my dear.) Mites are tiny (about one-fiftieth of an inch long), barely visible, oval creatures that come in various shades of green, yellow, and red-brown. You'll probably not get a chance to see them closely (even with a magnifying glass) until after the plant is so thoroughly infested as to make their webs visible. About that same time, you may notice some mottling of the leaves — a sickly grayish yellow tinge appears, especially from the center outward as the pests suck out juices. If left untreated, the foliage may develop red or brown spots and then dry and die — sometimes very, very quickly.

The minute you perceive spider mites on a plant, abscond with it to a place securely distant from your other plants, because spider mites are dreadfully contagious. Create an isolation ward where the sickly plant will live for the next few weeks — where you *hope* it will live, that is. Never touch your other plants after ministering to the sick one until you have washed your hands completely.

If the infestation is limited to one part of the plant, you may be able to eliminate it by administering a hard, cold shower in the sink. Or, better yet, prepare a sink of water with a couple of teaspoons of soap stirred in. Soap makes water "wetter," thus allowing it to more thoroughly cover the plant and wash away the

Miniature rose with spider mite (photo by author)

bugs and their eggs. Cover the soil with plastic (or your hand), both to keep in the soil and keep out the soap and cascading spider mites. Turn the plant upside down and swish the stems and leaves through the soapy water. Then repeat in clean water to wash away the loosened critters and soap. A large plant can be sprayed with soapy water or given a sponge bath, but try to get it into the shower or even outdoors to spray with a hose. Be sure to rinse all plants thoroughly, no matter what the method.

Keep the plant in isolation and check it closely every few days. If there is no sign of a returned bug after ten days, you can replace the plant with its fellows. But frankly, such freedom is unlikely. Spider mites are considerably more determined than to allow a mere bath to destroy them. You will probably, after giving several soapy baths, be forced to use an insecticide, or more specifically, a miticide, such as Kelthane, Omite, or Dimite. Most commercial house-plant sprays, such as those based on malathion, pyrethrum, or rotenone, are effective against mites if used conscientiously several times, three or four days apart. Be sure you are spraying every square inch of the plant (but not so closely as to damage tissue with the harsh aerosol gases), leaving the mites no clear place from which to launch a new attack. Some plants, though, just seem to be vulnerable, and you may be forced to use a systemic. Mites easily develop an immunity to any specific insecticide that's used repeatedly, so change your spray often.

Prevention is the best way to eliminate red spider mites from your plant collection. They proliferate in the hot, dry climates common in winter in our heated houses. Therefore, keep the humidity up in every way possible: spray with water (especially the undersides of leaves), keep plants on pebble trays, set pots of water around, or — best of all — install a humidifier. Lowering the temperature is a great help, too. Not only does it raise the humidity but a lower temperature forces an increase in the period of time it takes for a generation of spider mites to reach egg-laying maturity. At a warm 75 degrees, adults may start new generations every five days. At only ten degrees cooler, the time required may double or triple, slowing the nuisance-making spread of these pests.

SPRINGTAILS

SYMPTOM/ SPRINGTAILS

Fresh chew marks and holes appear on leaves

Springtail

These little pests have, of course, springs in their tails. Perhaps a person with spring in his or her tail can be a delight, but the springtail uses its spring to move great distances among your plants. This insect is rarely just an "it": thousands of the one-sixteenth-inch-long pests can gather in one pot so that the small, rounded, dark bodies litter the soil, where they chew on ground-level plant parts. Spray the plants, pots, surfaces, and your plant tools with malathion. Cut down on watering — the presence of springtails in your plants means you are watering too much.

SYMPHYLANS (SYMPHILIDS)

See *Garden Centipedes.*

THRIPS

SYMPTOMS/
THRIPS

Leaves develop silvery streaks or transparent spots on top
  surface; rusty or whitish spots form on back
Dark excrement specks appear around holes in leaves
Leaves and stems become rusty
Leaves suddenly drop off plant in large numbers
Flower buds drop off
Flowers become distorted and streaked

No, you can't have *a* thrip — at least not in the United
States. Only the British call just one of these slender,
flying beasties "a thrip." Americans call it "a thrips."
Generally, thrips is, or are, almost microscopic, dark
brown in color, with perhaps the rear end slightly
lighter in color. Their wings are brushlike.

Thrips rasp the leaf surface, then suck the juices.
You'll probably first notice a silvery sheen on infested
plants, with little tiny dots that are specks of excrement. Flowers (thrips particularly like blossoms and
find gloxinias a treat) will become distorted and possi-

Thrips

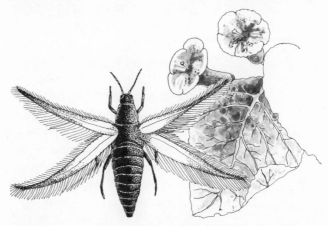

bly streaked. Leaves and stems get rusty looking, and the leaves soon fall. You'll probably have to use a malathion spray to eliminate the thrips.

TWO-SPOTTED MITES

See *Spider Mites.*

WHITEFLIES

SYMPTOMS/
WHITEFLIES

Leaves turn yellow and wilted or become bleached and mottled with yellow

Clouds of flying insects appear when plant is disturbed

Leaf surfaces become sticky and glossy (honeydew patches), perhaps with spreading patches of blackish or dark gray, powdery coating (sooty mold)

Whiteflies are the last of the "big five" juice-sucking pests — aphids, mealybugs, scales, spider mites, and whiteflies. (See *Aphids* for a description of the sucking process and its effects.) Unlike some of the others, though, whiteflies have the terrible talent of swift flight. The tiny, white, mothlike pests can just flutter away when attacked with a spray from an insecticide can. (It has been suggested that you can prevent their fluttering away by turning the suction hose of a vacuum cleaner on them, but watch out that you don't suck up the plant.)

If you disturb a plant and a cloud of tiny white flying insects forms, you'll know that you must contend with both the eggs and adults of the whitefly. Washing won't be adequate because of the adults' flying ability. You'll probably need to use a malathion spray; if the flies spread around to other plants, a short-term treatment of all your plants with a systemic — usually not recommended — may be necessary. A systemic will handle both the adults and the eggs as they develop.

For ease of handling, I suggest that you keep all

Whiteflies

plants that are particularly vulnerable to whitefly grouped together. Wash each one regularly to remove eggs, even if you tend to let your other plants get grubby. Get rid of lantana and fuchsia, both of which seem to be unable to live without whitefly, in order to protect your other plants.

ᴔ 7. DREADFUL DISEASES

Mold, Mildew,
and Rot
There are certain "plants" that don't like their fellow plants. Given the opportunity — generally by you — these harmful plants work their insidious damage until your house plants may be beyond saving. These not-nice plants that you must work at *not* growing are fungi (or, if you doubt your pronunciation, "fun-guses"). House-plant diseases can also be caused by bacteria and viruses, but bacteria are not very threatening to indoor plants, and viruses, which generally demand that an affected plant be discarded (though not all are harmful), are, fortunately, quite rare.

The outdoor world is subject to a great three-ring circus of fungal diseases. Grasses, to the dismay of lawn fanatics, may play host to as many as fifty different fungi. Pity the poor outdoor gardener. Not many outdoor fungi, however, survive the transfer to indoors — though others breed in the close, humid confines of a terrarium.

What is a fungus? Well, it is a plant, but it isn't recognizably green because it is so primitive that it has no chlorophyll, a development that came late in evolution. A fungus usually reproduces by spreading tiny bodies called spores — and they are in the air at all times, making up part of our ever-present dust in the air. In general, fungi thrive when the air is still and muggy. If you've kept your plants just a hair too damp, especially in too little light, lack of circulation of the air gives fungal spores a chance to settle and set up housekeeping on vulnerable plant tissues.

If you have ever sprinkled garments while ironing (probably in the old pre-drip-dry days) and then left them damp and rolled up, you may have returned later to discover that the clothes had a peculiar odor and perhaps gray spots in the damp folds: the clothes had mildewed. Mildew is a fungus that may attack plants in stagnant air. Mushrooms, too, are fungi — nice ones when picked correctly for eating, unpleasant ones when found growing in the pot of a tree, perhaps indicating that the roots of the tree have rotted. Rot, too, is a fungus disease.

ANTHRACNOSE

SYMPTOMS/ ANTHRACNOSE	Leaves and stems develop dry, brown or black, sunken spots, possibly rimmed by dark rings Leaf tips and edges turn brown and wither away; untended leaves may form bars of dark tan color

To a grower whose plants have developed strange spots on their leaves, it's logical to call the problem "leaf spot." But — nothing being simple — there are spots . . . and then there are spots! Spots of dead, often sunken, tissues on leaves, stems, or even fruit, indicate *anthracnose* — a miserable word developed by a Frenchman from the Greek for "carbuncle disease," but these spots don't have the enlarged, hardened tissue of a true carbuncle. The spots usually have dark rims. Tomatoes or other vegetables in the garden often have anthracnose spots.

The fungus infection anthracnose usually means that there has been too much water in the pot much

Ficus elastica
(rubber plant)
with anthracnose

too often. The humidity has been too high (an unusual problem except in greenhouses, but possible among plants grouped together or during long periods of muggy, dark days). The spots of anthracnose may also develop after a plant has been chilled abruptly, such as if the heat goes off in winter or a window is accidentally left open.

If left untended, the leaf tips of the infected plant may acquire bars of dark tan color across them. Leaf edges die, turn dark, and wither away. The spots won't repair themselves, so you must remove the infected leaves — a real hardship for a rubber plant or a gracious palm. Cut way back on watering for quite some days, watering only enough to prevent wilting. Don't mist the plant, either, and be sure that the air circulates well around all your plants. Spray or dust so-far-undamaged leaves with a mild fungicide, such as Maneb, Captan, or Zineb. When no more leaves develop dry-centered spots, consider that you've conquered the disease, but *do not* return to giving the full watering you had before: keep the plant slightly drier.

BACTERIAL LEAF SPOTS

See *Leaf Spots.*

BLACKLEG

See *Rot.*

BOTRYTIS

Leaves develop a gray-tan coating; light or dark brownish
spots form on leaves, turning grayish black, perhaps
watery

Flowers or stems develop a gray-tan coating or brownish
spots; buds become distorted

Botrytis is a blight — a spreading grayish mold that
sneaks in when you're not looking, especially in areas
where the moisture level is high and air is stagnant, and
wreaks havoc on African violets, begonias, and geraniums, plus, occasionally, some other plants that may
already be weakened by some other problem. Keep
plants healthy and sturdy and you won't be bothered
by botrytis, because they have natural defenses against
it.

Botrytis symptoms vary with the plant, but in general, it shows as brownish (light or dark) spots on
leaves, stems, or flowers. The plant parts may be coated
with a gray-tan mold.

Remove the infected plant parts (discarding seriously infested plants) and separate attacked ones from
the rest. Spread all plants apart so that air can circulate
among them; increase ventilation without creating
drafts. Spray the vulnerable plants with a fungicide
such as Captan or Zineb.

CROWN ROT

See *Rot.*

DAMPING-OFF DISEASE

Seedlings suddenly turn watery and wilt, collapse at the
soil line, or die overnight

Damping-off, a destructive disease caused by fungi in
soil, has not been of major importance to indoor-plant
growers . . . until recently. With the urge to get more
and more back to nature has come the availability of
seeds for starting familiar house plants. Now house-
plant growers can join their outdoor-plant kin in the
shock of losing an entire batch of seedlings to a sudden
mysterious fungus that seems to nip them off at the soil
line — *if* you don't use sterilized soil. But because you
do, you probably need not concern yourself that tiny
seedlings may turn watery and wilt while, underground, tender new roots rot. Sphagnum moss, too, is
safe to use for starting seedlings; in fact, one brand
proudly calls itself Nodampoff.

If you do get into large-scale seedling growing and
use garden soil for it, find a chemical product called
Anti-Damp (oxyquinoline benzoate) and use it according to the directions. At the least sign of a problem,
cut down on watering, heat, and humidity, and dust
the seedlings with fungicide.

LEAF SPOTS

**SYMPTOM/
LEAF SPOTS**
Leaves develop light-colored, usually circular spots; or
spots, different from rest of leaf in color and texture,
that are rimmed with light-colored rings

Anything — from bacteria to insects to a child with
scissors or paintbrush — can spot a leaf. Spots are very
common, even indoors, so even the most valiant of us
can be forgiven for ignoring spots, at least for a time.

But eventually, spots indicating disease — usually spots with a definite margin — will destroy a plant. Spots that are dryish or of normal leaf texture tend to be fungal in origin; those that are moist are probably bacterial spots. Spots that multiply into a large spot are called blight, or scorch.

Like anthracnose (see separate entry in this chapter), most leaf spots mean a superabundance of moisture — a damp atmosphere in which always-present fungi are free to grow. Generally, keeping plants spread apart, the air circulating, and the surroundings clean will be enough to prevent the spots. (Thank heaven, because otherwise you'd spend all your days growing spots instead of plants.)

Black spot, the rose-grower's nightmare, can occur indoors. It's easily identifiable: you have a rose, some

Coffea arabica
(coffee plant)
with leaf spots

leaves have black spots with blurry edges on them, the remaining leaf tissue is turning yellow, and soon the leaves fall — ergo, you have black-spot fungus. It is activated by water on the plant that doesn't get a chance to dry, such as when you water late in the day. Remove spotted leaves from *dry* plants so that the fungus can't be spread by moisture. Spray with a fungicide.

Basically, when spots develop on your plants, worry about surroundings rather than individual spots. Trim off damaged leaves and dust with a fungicide. Use the presence of spots as a signal to review all your plant-growing habits.

MOLDY SOIL

SYMPTOMS/ MOLDY SOIL

Grayish or sickly white growth like bread mold forms on soil surface

Root and stem rot symptoms develop

Soil that is consistently kept too wet — perhaps in an overenthusiastically watered terrarium or a wick-watered plastic pot — easily grows a gray or whitish mold on the surface. Plants show all the symptoms of root and stem rot (see *Rot*) because those horrid diseases occur in soil that's too wet. Scrape off the mold. Stir a fungicide into the remaining soil, add fresh soil to replace what was removed, and quit overwatering! A terrarium, because it offers a humid, closed atmosphere, may need to be cleaned out and restarted in order to cure the problem; be certain that bowl and all utensils are sterilized before starting again.

NEMATODES

**SYMPTOMS/
NEMATODES**

Roots become stunted, gnarled, distorted, covered with
  galls, and diminish in number
New growth is stunted, pale, possibly curled or otherwise
  distorted
Growth slows or stops
Leaves wilt, wither, and drop off plant
Leaves develop black streaks
Buds are distorted

Cynthia Westcott, the prominent expert on plant
pests and diseases, has recently moved nematodes from
"pests" to "disease" classification because, though
they are animals (small, wormlike critters), they actually cause disease symptoms instead of physical injury
to the plant. I'll go along with that reasoning and
include nematodes under diseases.

Nematodes are worms that reside in unsterilized
soil. You'll never have to fret about them if you use
only commercial potting soil, but if you get carried
away with making your own soil, especially from your
own compost heap, nematodes may be inevitable.
They work their damage quietly, making roots gnarled
and covered with lumpy galls. The wounds in the roots
open them to all sorts of other infections. Usually not
until nematode damage is far advanced does evidence
of their presence show up, in the form of the plant just
not doing well — no growth, unexplained droopiness,
perhaps streaks on leaves, followed by everything going
wrong.

Your regular root check — especially if the plant has
been outside for a time or is a gift and its origin is
unknown — should include a close inspection for the
thick gnarled and stunted roots indicative of nematode
damage. It's best to discard the plant if you find such
damage — and *don't don't don't* touch your other
plants until you have almost scrubbed the skin off your
hands. There are nematocides, such as V-C-13, availa-

ble to tackle minor infestations outdoors, but I can't ever regard the presence of nematodes in the house as minor.

POWDERY MILDEW

Leaves or flowers develop a whitish, dustlike coating
Leaves turn yellow and curled
New growth is stunted, pale, possibly curled or otherwise distorted
Buds are distorted

Most fungi do their damage internally, but the mildews are right out in front where they're highly visible, though not necessarily harmful (see *Sooty Mold*). If you see a whitish dustlike covering on leaves, and it's not residue from watering or feeding, be concerned: it may be the destructive nuisance powdery mildew. Left to work its will on your plants, it turns leaves yellow and distorted. If you look at the mildew through a magnifying glass, you'll see threadlike structures called mycelia crisscrossing the patch. If it's botrytis (see *Botrytis* entry) instead of powdery mildew, the patch will be distinctly gray, because part of the structures are dark instead of white. Like botrytis, powdery mildew can best be prevented by ensuring cleanliness, lowering the humidity, and maintaining good air circulation. Fortunately for the normal house-plant grower, both powdery mildew and botrytis are more common in stuffy greenhouses than in living rooms. But terrarium growers (and please forgive the implication that terrarium growers are not "normal") need to beware.

To treat powdery mildew, separate infected plants, clean up all around, remove infected leaves, and use a fungicide. Powdery mildew can actually be one of a variety of species of fungus, so you may need to try several products to hit on the effective one for your variety. Common chemical cures are Benlate, Benomyl, Mildex, Karathane, and Acti-dione PM. (Benlate is a fairly new systemic fungicide that will attack from the inside as well as the outside; use about one teaspoon per gallon of water.) Powdery mildew has a very short life cycle (about seventy-two hours), so you'll need to treat plants several times, three or four days apart, to get all the spores.

Left alone, or if you fail to eliminate all mycelia, mildew can rest awhile and later cause problems: new growth can be stunted and distorted, leaves may curl (in fact, you may notice leaf curl before you discover the mildew patches), and flower buds may be deformed.

ROT

SYMPTOMS/ CROWN AND STEM ROT	Soft, squishy sponginess, often a brown or black decaying discoloration, creeps through plant parts, causing collapse and death of those parts

Rot is the name of a disease, not a comment. Any part of a plant may decay, or rot, with the decomposition visible as dark, soft, squishy areas in parts above the ground; when occurring below soil level in the roots, rot is apparent by its effect on leaves.

Along with the other fungal diseases, rots are encouraged by high moisture levels — usually a polite way of saying you overwatered. *Crown rot* occurs particularly in plants such as African violets, bird's-nest fern, or others that have a dense collection of leaves or stems at soil level. The thickness of plant structures prevents water that was accidentally (I'm giving you the benefit of the doubt by assuming it was accidental) put into the crown from drying. The moisture sits and soon the tender tissues start to rot. If allowed to continue, damaged tissue may kill the whole plant before surgery can save it. Remove diseased tissue with a clean, sharp knife and powder the wound with fungicide. Decree that henceforth care shall be taken to

*Cactus with stem rot,
or blackleg*

keep water out of the crown. Extensive damage may
require that you take cuttings of any healthy tissue and
start over again.

Stem rot — sometimes called *blackleg,* because the
stem often turns dark and mushy — shows as discolored tissue (usually black and squishy or brown and
dryish) moving upward from the soil level. Cacti, especially, succumb to stem rot when the soil that touches
the thick plant is allowed to be soggy for any length of
time. After cutting out diseased portions, rebuild the
pot's soil so that pebbles rather than soil touch the
plant itself. Cacti and other succulents often don't
change color with stem rot, so there's no telltale blackleg — just sponginess and perhaps death; touch your
plants gently from time to time (watch out for prickles)
to be sure they are still crisp.

African violets and some other plants with leaves rising straight from the soil may develop stem rot (more properly called *petiole rot* on these plants) if the leaf stems continually rub on the pot rim. This danger can be alleviated by coating the pot edge with candle wax or paraffin, making a smooth rim and discouraging fertilizer salt buildup.

SYMPTOMS/ ROOT ROT

Roots lack holding power, plant easily uproots; roots appear dark and mushy when checked and give off a pungent odor

Older (lower) leaves turn yellow, dry, and drop off; remaining leaves may wilt

Leaf tips and edges turn brown and dry

Growth slows or stops

Other overwatering symptoms develop (see chapter 4)

Root rot is the most serious of the structural rots. It works its will, generally on succulent plants, while you gaily carry on as if something else were wrong and inadvertently do just the wrong thing. You are the culprit, both in starting the disease and in compounding it. First, you overwater; then, when your plant wilts and looks to be suffering from dryness, you water again — just when the sickly plant is least able to handle the excess.

Aglaonema *(Chinese evergreen) with severe root rot from overwatering*

You know yourself best. If you deliberately always underwater (on the expectation that what for you is underwatering is just right for the plant), then when the youngest growth on a plant dies off and the other leaves wilt, you are probably safe in assuming that the plant needs watering. *But,* if yours is a generous nature and you know that you tread a fine watery line between enough and surfeit, *do not water* a wilted plant until you have unpotted the plant and inspected its roots. This may sound funny . . . but smell the plant — closely. You may actually be able to detect a pungent rotting odor coming from the soil. You may also notice mold on the soil; it thrives in the same conditions as root rot, so you may use its presence as a clue.

A healthy plant has roots that are firm and whitish or yellowish beneath the soil line. If you disrobe the roots and find that even the smallest rootlets have gone dark and have a mushy consistency, you've been over-watering. Water has forced air out of the soil, encouraging fungus growth. The roots lose their ability to take up nutrients and water.

Wash the roots off. Using a sharp knife, cut off all root tissue that has gone dark and soft; it can't repair itself. Dust the roots with a fungicide to help prevent return of the problem. Repot the plant in fresh soil, using an extra-thick bed of sterile pebbles in the bottom as a drainage layer. Preferably use a clay pot rather than a moisture-holding plastic one, and be sure it isn't too big; with root gone, the plant should probably be in a smaller pot than it was in before. You may want to use soil with a bit more sand in it than you used before, to guarantee that water drains out rather than sits sogging in wait for more fungus spores. Give the newly repotted plant a real rest by letting it have several weeks of just enough water to prevent wilting — not enough for growth, because the plant is too busy recovering from the shock of near-death to be bothered with something as positive as growth.

You may have waited until the plant is in its last

throes before checking the roots and discovering root rot. If that is the case, you may find more root damage than the plant might reasonably be expected to recover from. There will probably be some shoots that have remained in good condition owing to the plant's effort to channel its waning strength toward what can be saved. Take cuttings of those and start fresh plants.

Remember, all rots can be contagious if your plants aren't sturdy enough to fight them. After handling a diseased plant, disinfect all equipment — with liquid laundry bleach, for instance — and wash your hands well, even under the fingernails, before touching another plant.

SOOTY MOLD

| SYMPTOMS/ SOOTY MOLD | Leaves and other plant surfaces develop spreading patches of blackish or dark gray, powdery coating over sticky, glossy patches of honeydew
Symptoms of too little light may develop (see chapter 3) |

Sooty mold isn't really a disease of the plants so much as it is a nuisance and a sign that your plants are infested by sucking insects such as aphids, mealybugs, scale, or whitefly. These pests exude a sweet fluid called honeydew onto the plant surfaces. A dark sooty mold proliferates on the sweet stickiness, usually not really harming the plant, but warning you to get rid of the bugs (see chapter 6). This mold does not feed off the host plant but can still damage it by blocking the chlorophyll in the leaves from its fair share of sunlight.

Work to eliminate the honeydew-making pests. Scrub the leaves in soapy water and rinse thoroughly to remove the sooty mold.

STEM ROT

See *Rot.*

~~& 8. CHEMICALS — READ THE LABEL

READ THE LABEL AND FOLLOW ALL IN-
STRUCTIONS TO THE LETTER.

A typical label on an insecticide container includes
such words and phrases as: *Use strictly in accor-
dance . . . , Do not use on . . . , Warning: May Be Fatal . . . , Hazardous . . . , Keep Away . . . , Toxic to fish
and wildlife . . . , Remove foods . . . , Wash hands
thoroughly . . .* and more.

Now, do you really want such a chemical in your
home?

If a badly infested plant is a duplicate, a small recent
purchase, or a variety readily propagated from cuttings,
just get rid of it. Don't bother to go beyond the initial
soap-and-water treatment described in chapter 6.

But we probably each have a few plants that are
special friends: inheritances from grandmother, large
decorator plants whose absence would completely spoil
our decor, rare specimens hybridized by an Indian fakir
by the light of a blue moon. When one of these special
plants is attacked by pests and the soap-and-water
treatment doesn't make a dent in the problem, you

must make a choice about using the poisonous insecticides.

There was a time, not so long ago, when people sought avidly for broad-spectrum chemicals that could be freely used in a wide protective swath. Rachel Carson and her book *Silent Spring* changed all that.

An insecticide is meant to kill. Chemical by chemical, the Food and Drug Administration, the U.S. Department of Agriculture, and the Environmental Protection Agency are investigating some of the old standard insecticides and finding them beyond the realm of safe use. Chlordane, for example, was listed as the preferred treatment for several house-plant pests in the 1972 edition of the U.S. Department of Agriculture's bulletin, "Insects and Related Pests of House Plants." The next edition omitted it because, even though chlordane was relatively safe to use, it lingered longer in the soil or on surfaces than is now regarded as safe. Lindane, also often suggested for use, is being phased out of use, too.

So products that you now regard as safe to use may, at any time, become one of those chemicals proscribed by the government.

In recent years, all chemicals meant to kill plant enemies have been rated for toxicity (in addition to their residual effects). One rating is shown as LD_{50}, which indicates the lethal dosage necessary to kill 50 percent of the test animals used in evaluating the chemical. The dose is related to weight, and the lower the LD_{50} number, the more toxic the chemical. The most toxic of the chemicals commonly used these days around house plants is Vapona, with an LD_{50} that varies from 56 to 80. Despite their convenience, especially when used on bits of strip put in a plastic bag with an infested plant, you'd better think twice before using such potent killers.

Some of the other common chemicals and their LD_{50} ratings are malathion, which varies from 885 to 2800; rotenone, which varies from 60 to 1500 (and is toxic to fish, so avoid using if you can); pyrethrum, which varies from 200 to 2600; nicotine sulfate, which varies from 50 to 60; Kelthane, 800; metaldehyde, 630; and the fungicide Karathane, 980. (Note that some fungicides need not be put in the same dangerous category as insecticides. A typical one, Ferbam, for example, has an LD_{50} rating of 17,000!)

When you consider that chemicals with a rating below 50 must by law be labeled DANGER and POISON, and that many require permits for their use, you'll recognize that chemicals with ratings anywhere near that level should be treated with the greatest respect and *CAUTION.*

Be Kind to Yourself and Others

If you decide to bring a toxic chemical into your home for use on your house plants — even a readily available aerosol-spray insecticide — you must take safety precautions:

· Store the chemicals in locked cupboards where they cannot be investigated by curious children or knocked over by rampaging pets.

· Do not remove chemicals from their original containers. If the label comes off, tape it back on securely. If the label is lost or destroyed, discard the chemical and its container — in a safe place — rather than wonder about an unmarked can six months later.

If you decide to keep a chemical around for its convenience, use it with respect:

· Spray only in a well-ventilated room, so that the chemical in the air cannot sit in a stagnant fog around your head. (But be sure there are no drafts that can carry the spray to other rooms.)

· Wear rubber gloves and scrub them thoroughly after using chemicals.

· In addition, wash your hands thoroughly with soap and water after using even the simplest spray (the nozzle might be dripping slightly).

· *Never* spray where food and drink are served (and certainly don't spray with a martini in one hand).

· Wash a chemically treated plant thoroughly after the poison has done its work before returning it to its friends.

· And use common sense: don't spray all around your plants and then move among them. (Even the "safest" sprays can get into your lungs and eventually do some damage.)

Dips, Drenches, and Sprays

The most common pesticides these days are packaged as aerosol sprays. But with the growing concern about the harmful effect of some aerosol-spray gases on our atmosphere, we are seeing a return to the sprayers of the old "Quick, Henry, the Flit!" variety — otherwise called hand atomizers. The chemical mixtures for these sprayers have to be mixed by you; they are mostly water — and should be mixed exactly in the proportions called for on the label! I'm not going to attempt to give any specific formulas for use of the various chemicals because you must always READ THE LABEL.

In picking a sprayer for use, be sure to select one you will use *only* for pesticides and for nothing else. Be sure it is rustproof and easy to clean. When you spray, be sure to get the backs as well as the fronts of leaves, and all up and down the stems. Spray enough to wet all the surfaces but not so much that they begin dripping. In general, it is safest to take a plant outdoors to spray it. But that may be impossible because of the weather, the size of the plant, or the fact that you live in an apartment. You can still avoid contaminating your home by covering the affected plant with a plastic bag while you spray it indoors. Keep the bag over the plant until the spray has had plenty of opportunity to settle. Never leave any insecticide in the sprayer when you're finished spraying — carefully dispose of excess and wash the apparatus thoroughly.

Battery-powered sprayers are now available, but I would reserve them for misting with plain water or for out-of-doors use; it's too easy to get poison where it isn't wanted, or to get too much of it on a delicate plant.

Frequently the liquid poisons are used in liquid form instead of as mists. A plant can be dipped in the liquid or its soil can be drenched. *Dips* are used for smaller plants, especially when you want to treat lots of them inexpensively and to be sure that you cover them completely. Put the formulated liquid into a pail (preferably plastic or enamel) and then cover the soil of the plant so it can't fall out, perhaps with a cardboard ring that fits around the stem and over the pot rim. Turn the plant upside down and swish it around in the chemical bath. Do not let your hands get into the solution (you should be wearing gloves). Pull the plant out and let it drip for a minute, then set it aside where it can dry — but *not* in the sun.

Drenches are used for soil-borne pests. The same poisonous liquid is used, but it is poured into the soil of the plant as if you were watering. Be certain that any excess is drained out and thrown away safely.

Another type of treatment available today is the *systemic* pesticide — one that works through the whole system of a plant. The plant absorbs the poison along with its water so that soon the entire plant becomes poisonous. Any pest foolish enough to come along and suck the plant's sap or nibble its greenery is in for trouble — but so too are curious children and pets. The poison lingers in the plant for weeks. *Don't use systemics if you don't have to.* You may feel forced to use a systemic with ferns, because chemical sprays can be so harmful to them. If so, take all precautions, READ AND FOLLOW THE LABEL, and keep the plants away from children and pets for a safe period . . . a *long* safe period.

Getting Down to Basics In essence, you probably should not need more than two basic chemicals around your house plants — perhaps malathion (Malathion) and dicofol (Kelthane) —

and never turn to them until after you've given soap and water a sporting chance to work.

Malathion, a thiophosphate, is a broad-spectrum contact (hit the pest: the pest dies) pesticide developed by American Cyanimid. Sometimes marketed as Cythion, it is an ingredient in most other commercial pesticide formulas. One note on its use: malathion vaporizes easily, so don't use it in the heat of the day — only in the morning, when the air is cool. Malathion is useful against aphids, caterpillars, mealybugs, scale, thrips, whitefly, fungus gnats, and even (when used as a drench) ants, symphylans, and springtails. The only common pest it doesn't have much truck with is spider mite, although sometimes malathion will even attack that problem. However, mites are nettlesome critters that generally prefer to die for a real miticide (sometimes called acaricide), such as Kelthane. Kelthane (chemically called dicofol) has an LD_{50} rating of 800 and is thus one of the safer chemicals to use in the home.

Some people looking for the organic route to pest control are attracted to pesticides of organic origin. Pyrethrum, for example, originally was made from the flowers of various kinds of mountain-grown daisies but is now usually synthetic. Unfortunately, pyrethrum and its derivative Resmethrin are quite toxic to fish, and there's no telling where the poison you throw away is going to end up. I'd avoid them.

Rotenone is derived from a variety of South American plants. It, too, is toxic to fish and has been found, when used outdoors, to occasionally kill ground-nesting birds. It can also temporarily paralyze the breathing organs of small mammals.

Nicotine sulfate is a classic material that has come back into popularity since *Silent Spring* because it's based on nicotine from tobacco. Organic, yes, but it has a very low LD_{50} rating and can be toxic if spilled on the skin.

A lot of work has been going into developing homemade organic pesticides. One that has a whole coterie of devotees calls for garlic — lots of it. Chop the garlic, soak it in mineral oil for several days, then stir with water and an oil-based soap. Strain the mixture and store it until you need it. Then use about one part garlic mixture to about twenty parts water as a spray that may well destroy aphids, mites, whitefly — and perhaps even vampires. Onion and red pepper cooked together may have the same effect (it certainly would on me). Some growers try a thin layer of all-purpose glue dissolved in water as a spray (but what does that do to the plant's breathing pores?). Ground-up tobacco soaked in water and then poured over foliage offers a mild form of nicotine poisoning.

Lots of fun to contemplate but probably not terribly useful as an indoor method of getting rid of insect pests is the use of natural predators — chameleons and ladybugs, for instance. To use such animals for pest control you need to group all your plants in one place, close together. Of course, you would always worry, especially if you hadn't seen the chameleon for a while: Am I about to step on it? And if the ladybugs started to multiply, you'd be in a fix — there's no way that the small number of problem pests that might inhabit your plants could adequately feed a growing ladybug colony. And if you have pets, you'd be likely to find your "pesticides" being turned into toys.

The best organic method of pest control is really *prevention:*

· Inspect each new plant thoroughly before you buy it. Then, when you get it home, isolate it for several weeks. If you haven't developed a particular fondness for it and pests show up, throw the plant out instead of trying to cure it.

· Keep all plants and their growing areas sparkling clean. Never let dead plant matter lie about where it can serve as food and cover for pests.

· Keep all plants as healthy as possible; the stronger the plant, the less likely that it will be attacked by pests.

· Since the Attila the Huns of pestdom are spider

mites, discourage them by keeping the humidity as high as possible at all times.

· And last, but hardly least: if you go the chemical route . . . READ THE LABEL AND FOLLOW ALL INSTRUCTIONS TO THE LETTER.

❦ 9. FAILING FLOWERS

T<small>HE</small> <small>NATURAL RESPONSE TO THIS CHAPTER'S TITLE</small> might be: "Failing flowers? Stick with foliage." Many people heroically declare their avid commitment to foliage plants because they have experienced disasters with flowers and have given up trying. But all the reasons for failure — except perhaps the occasional ornery plant that just takes a disliking to you (and you might ask yourself what you did to cause that) — are analyzable if you care to take the trouble.

One reason for giving up on failing flowers may be that you are basing your opinion of all flowering plants on the behavior of a few, such as African violets, which are natural disasters for some people and glorious bloomers for others. Or perhaps you're basing your views on the seasonal gift plants: poinsettia, cineraria, azalea, cyclamen. The sad truth is that these plants are basically greenhouse plants that begin the sometimes-slow, sometimes-fast slide toward death the moment they are removed from the greenhouse to be dressed in a pretty bow. If you've had trouble with these plants, you're in fine company.

Saintpaulia ionantha
(African violets)
blooming well (left),
and flowerless (right)
because of poor growing
conditions, especially
overwatering

In general, such seasonal gift plants should just be enjoyed indoors as long as possible — which may be several months in the case of a highly hybridized plant like the Christmas poinsettia. You can prolong the gift plant's beauty and color by keeping your home's temperature cool, the humidity high, and the soil moist. The most difficult of those requirements to meet is the cool temperature. Poinsettias across much of the nation thrived during recent winters because prolonged cold spells coincided with increasingly high home-heating-fuel costs, forcing homes to be kept cooler than usual. But even if you don't normally choose to keep the thermostat down, keep your plants in the coolest room you have — perhaps a guest room where you can close off the heat. Then bring the plants into the living room in the evening for their daily dose of admiration.

A second major source of disappointment in flowering plants is wishful thinking: "I wish I had a begonia," when all your windows face north or are blocked by trees; "I wish I had a geranium," when your house is kept above 75 degrees Fahrenheit at all times. A realistic approach as to what's possible is needed.

Few or no buds form on a flowering plant
Buds blast (wither) or drop off before opening; those that
  do open shrivel or drop off quickly

A flowering plant that does not get enough light just plain won't blossom well. The light needed to maintain the plant during most of the year is only enough for that — maintenance. Just think how much more energy is required by the plant to go through the process of building a bud, opening it, and keeping the flower crisp and beautiful for a decent period (one long enough to attract insects for pollination, at least in the wild). The plant needs extra food to burn for the energy needed — food that must be derived from light-initiated photosynthesis.

Too much light, on the other hand, can have serious consequences for some flowering plants. The problem, in addition to the threat of brown spots from sunburn, is that in lots of light, there's lots of heat. The plant is forced to yield much of its moisture to keep the humidity level around its leaves balanced. The roots can't absorb water from the soil and send it up the plant to the leaves fast enough. Something must give. Since flowering is a luxury for a plant, blossoms are often elected as expendable. Result: a plant with small flowers or one that sheds its flowers, if they ever bloomed at all, as soon as possible. To avoid the consequences of heat buildup behind south-facing windows, draw a sheer curtain, an openwork wicker screen, or a partially open venetian blind across the window for several hours at midday, perhaps from about 10:00 A.M. to 2:00 P.M., long enough for the worst of the sun to have passed but not enough to prevent light from reaching the plant.

Some plants have an even more specialized interest in light and thus so should you. Chrysanthemums, gloxinias, poinsettias, some orchids, kalanchoe, Christmas cactus, as well as quite a number of outdoor garden plants need days and nights of a certain length in order for blooming to be initiated. It's this knowledge that allows growers to make such plants bloom out of season, for Christmas or Easter. They dupe the plants into thinking that the seasons have changed because the day-night length has changed. This phenomenon, called photoperiodism, can also, though less conspicuously, affect leaf and stem growth and even leaf color, but flowering is more important.

Short-day plants, which include poinsettias and chrysanthemums, cattleya orchids, kalanchoe, and gardenias, sit placidly leading their lives most of the year, until coming winter brings short days and long nights. The change causes them to change their mode of growth from vegetative to flowering — that is, from asexual to sexual. Long-day plants, including gloxinias and hibiscus, are just the reverse: these normally summer-flowering plants may be forced to bloom in winter just by changing the length of their day.

Obviously, the short-day plants need to be put into darkness while it's still light out to convince them that winter is upon them. And even more important, *they must be kept in total darkness* — yes, *total* — for that required period, usually about fourteen hours. How you do that is up to you: move the plant into an unused closet, encase it in a light-tight box, whatever. Just be very, very sure that not even a street light reflecting upon the room wall is allowed to disturb it. That small amount of light can cause the plant to think its day is starting over again, and it will never bloom. Long-day plants wanted for winter bloom need to be kept under artificial light to extend their day to fourteen hours or more.

Of course, if you want to let all these plants bloom at their usual time of the year, they will probably do so beautifully without any extra guidance from you — their blooming will be triggered by the normal changes in daylight with the season.

WATER PROBLEMS

Few or no buds form on a flowering plant
Buds blast (wither) or drop off before opening; those that
   do open shrivel or drop off quickly
Flower petals develop brown spots

Flowers consist of a great deal of water and so, as with light, plants in flower must receive more water than they do just for foliage maintenance — otherwise, the flowers fade and shrivel too quickly. However, more flowering plants suffer from overwatering than from underwatering. The excess water that runs through the pot when you water must do just that — run through . . . and *out.* Be sure that your flowering plants — and all others! — are in pots with fairly porous soil atop a layer of pebbles covering a drainage hole. Never let the pot sit in drained water for more than a few minutes after watering. Remember, too, that overwatering can occur inadvertently (admittedly, I've never known anyone to confess to *advertent* overwatering) if the plant is in too big a pot. Most flowerers like crowded, thus slightly dryish roots before they'll bloom. Let them be slightly pot-bound.

Consistent underwatering reveals itself also in lack of buds, and in petal tips turning brown. There's a fairly fine line between underwatering and having a plant healthily pot-bound. Have you discovered that line?

Moisture needs to be in the air continuously for most flowering plants to be content. But many object to the usual practice of misting when they are in bloom. They don't like the water droplets on their petals because sunlight turns the droplets into tiny lenses that magnify the sunlight, charring the petals. Geranium flowers, especially, should not be sprayed, because rot sets in almost in the blink of an eye — or the spritz of a mister. Instead of misting, you can help to keep the humidity for your plants up by lowering the temperature in your home. Only African violets, which are exceptions to all sorts of rules, really like the heat that is common in winter in our residences (though it may not be common much longer, with the rising cost of home heating fuel).

SYMPTOMS/ **HUMIDITY TOO LOW**	Few or no buds form on a flowering plant Buds blast (wither) or drop off before opening; those that do open shrivel or drop off quickly Flower petal tips turn brown

One bad consequence of this required high humidity — though fortunately more problematic in greenhouses than in homes — is the development of fungal problems such as botrytis or powdery mildew. These diseases occur in the close, stuffy atmosphere of high humidity. Preventing them is really quite simple, however: just keep all surroundings clean, move plants apart from each other, and be sure that fresh air circulates easily among the plants. In other words, forego the temptation to mass flowering plants together for a great color effect.

TEMPERATURE PROBLEMS

SYMPTOMS/ **TEMPERATURE** **TOO HIGH**	Few or no buds form on a flowering plant Buds blast (wither) or drop off before opening; those that do open shrivel or drop off quickly

First, let me say that too high a temperature does not necessarily mean that the temperature is too high all day long. For the most part, it means that the temperature is *kept* too high at night — there is not a sufficient difference between night and day for a plant to be happy (and that applies to foliage plants as well as flowering plants). Daytime temperature can, of course, be critical to some plants, such as the coolness-loving ones that just fall apart when subjected to the bone-warming 75 and 80 degrees Fahrenheit that many people like. The most abundantly blooming plant can abruptly stop flowering if the temperature gets too warm during a hot spell; fortunately, air conditioning usually prevents that, but if the world's fuel problems persist, less will be heard from our air conditioners.

In that great natural world we keep talking about, tropical plants lead a quite comfortable existence. It can be very hot during the day, but the temperature drops considerably at night, giving plants a chance to sigh with relief. During a hot spell in the United States, on the other hand, the temperature may stay in the nineties even at night, so no such relief is forthcoming. To help your greenery survive a heat wave without air conditioning, keep air circulating with fans — not blowing directly on the plants, of course — and cut down a bit on water so that plants go into a half-dormant state. During winter, people who prefer to sleep with nothing on may never turn down their thermostats at night — a condition that is no good for plants or you. Plants need and expect a drop in temperature — at least ten degrees Fahrenheit — at night. Without it, they're not apt to make blossoms.

Flower Power If you've made all environmental factors appropriate for flowering plants and they still don't bloom, there are three things you might try: a dietary change, "tight shoes," and a pinch in time.

A diet appropriate for a sedentary secretary is hardly right for an athlete. Nor is the diet for a foliage plant maintaining itself in low light right for a flowering plant, in bright sunlight, that's trying to burst into bloom. A common diet change recommended for plants being encouraged to flower entails switching fertilizer from the standard 1:2:1 ratio formula to an evenly balanced 1:1:1 food, often called African-violet food. The mere change of fertilizer itself may be part of what encourages blossoms, although the increased proportion of potassium is particularly helpful in provoking flowering. Some growers switch to a food that is very high in potassium to give the plant a real jolt; you might try one that is about 1:1:3 ratio. Regardless, the plant also needs plenty of phosphorus, which is vital to the development of flower buds (and no buds means no flowers).

Some plants, such as hoya and kalanchoe, especially need the jolt of a change to a low-nitrogen food when they're getting ready to make buds. In fact, most all bloomers except gesneriads can benefit from such a change, because nitrogen encourages leaves — the plant is so busy making them it can't be bothered with flowers.

Keep in mind that all plants growing in soilless mixtures, which are commonly used under artificial lights and in hanging baskets, must be fed often and completely because there are no nutrients in the mixture.

"Tight shoes" refers to the plant, not you (your footwear won't do a thing for the plant). Many plants won't bloom until they are quite pot-bound. It's as if they need the signal of cramped quarters so they stop spreading out roots and leaves and start producing flowers. That means, of course, when you transplant one of your bloomers, never, never use a pot more than one inch larger than before or you'll just be increasing the time until it blooms again. Similarly, many plants just won't bloom until they reach a certain size (by that time most of them are pot-bound), so be patient and "keep the shoes tight."

A third condition that can make or break your blossoms is the amount of pinching that has gone on. First of all, you must recognize that if a plant is one that grows bushy when it has its growing tips pinched out periodically, you must sooner or later stop pinching and let buds form or the plant will never bloom. But the opposite condition is also significant: many plants will not bloom *unless* they are pinched back. Oleander and campanula, for example, will develop buds only on new growth. That means, then, that unless a plant is to be allowed to get raucously large, it must be pinched back when it has finished blooming in order for it to blossom the next time around. What you are actually doing is stunning the growing tips so that they can't put lots of plant energy into producing leaves; your pinching thus gives the plant a chance to convert energy into flowers. Some plants require a complete cutback, or pruning, almost to the soil level, in order for them to bloom again the next year. What you're getting is, in effect, whole new plants.

In addition to applying these three flower-power techniques, you might run through the following review when you have a flowering plant that is reluctant to do its floral duty:

· Check the entry dealing with the specific plant type in chapter 11 of this book for any special guidelines that you might need to know.

· If all other conditions seem right, you might try to shock a budded plant into blossoming: withhold water longer than usual, change its light — whatever you can do without harming the plant. The shock may convince the plant that its comfortable existence may end unless it sends forth blooms, guaranteeing a future generation.

· Once you begin to see buds, make a firm resolution not to move the plant until it has started blossoming. Movement can make a bud twist around to get back to the light and it can actually twist itself off at the neck.

· Above all, let a flowering plant know how much you appreciate its gift of beauty to your home.

ঙঽ 10. KEEPING HOUSE PLANTS BEAUTIFUL

To GROW BEAUTIFUL PLANTS AND KEEP THEM THAT way — that's the object of the whole house-plant-growing exercise. The runt puppy with a runny nose may have appeal, but the schefflera with falling leaves? Never.

So once you've cured your plants of their problems (although they probably won't stay cured — there's always something new arising among your plants to keep life interesting), you should be determined to keep them sparkling and beautiful so that people always exclaim, "My, your plants are so lovely and healthy looking!" (They used to just say, "My, your plants are so beautiful!" but when it became *the* thing to grow plants, one had to start sounding knowledgeable.)

The bulk of beautification comes in the daily work of treating your plants properly, inspecting them regularly, and acting quickly to overcome problems. But in addition to that, certain less frequent — though scarcely random — activities can be of great help: the annual preventive checkup, which is considerably more extensive than the daily peer, and the occasional pinching or careful pruning that keeps plants shapely and growing nicely. Add to that your own personal selection of such special treatment as talking to your plants, praying for them, and entertaining them with music, and you have the formula for continued beauty in your greenery.

The Yearly Preventive Checkup   Many of your plants — particularly the old faithfuls that just keep chugging along year after year repelling insects, failing to succumb to lack of humidity, and so on — will not have had an occasion, you hope, to have their roots looked at for some time. Taking an annual look at the underpinnings of all but your largest — and thus most difficult to handle — plants can often catch trouble before it begins.

Late winter is a good time for the checkup, just before the plant will start its period of burgeoning growth. It will then, in its eagerness to grow, have the best opportunity to overcome the shock of being handled and it will readily take advantage of any new growing room you provide as a result of the checkup and consequent repotting. So about the middle of February (it may still be gray and cold outside but plants have begun to think spring) begin to look at your plants individually with an eye toward seeing how each got through the long winter.

You will, of course, have fresh and *clean* pots ready for any plants that need repotting, so if you have limited space for pot storage, it is best to start with groups of the largest plants and work down to the smaller ones, taking time between each group to clean the old pots so you'll have new, larger ones ready as you go along for the plants that need them. Water any plants you plan to scrutinize the day before the annual checkup so that the soil will cling together in a ball but not be soggy.

First, carefully inspect the pot itself. (You may think you do some of the things I suggest here all the time — but take a fresh look, more conscious of what you are seeing than when you just glance at the plants each day or so.) Is it clean? (Probably not.) Do roots come out of the bottom holes? Do any roots bulge out of the top layer of soil? Does the soil firmly adhere to the sides of the pot?

Then, covering the soil with your hand, carefully knock the plant out of the pot by tapping it sharply on a counter edge or sink rim. Hold the freed plant over newspaper and gently brush soil off some roots. If the plant has been growing for a year or more, you will probably see plenty of root. The roots, in fact, may have completely formed a network around what soil is left in the pot and may seem to have eaten any pebbles or drainage-hole covers. Very carefully work the pebbles out of the clutch of the roots. You'll probably find an amazing amount of soil gone because it virtually gets used up by the plant.

Look at the roots as described for a root-rot check (see *Overwatering* in chapter 4). Look for firm, crisp, white or yellowish tissue. If what you find is mushy or turning black, you have the beginning of root rot. Trim it away, down into the good tissue. Then repot the plant in the same-size pot if the plant was pot-bound or in one slightly smaller if it was not, to compensate for the loss of root. If you find dry roots that are shrunken and sere, they've probably been sticking out of the bottom of the pot and have lost their water-holding capacity. Cut them off, too.

Repot a healthy plant in a pot one or two sizes larger than the one used before. If the plant has been repotted several times without its basic soil ball being changed (record-keeping on long-term plant residents comes in handy, if you feel that efficient), it is probably a good idea to brush off all soil and start completely over with fresh soil. Be sure to repot immediately, or, if briefly called away from your potting work for any reason, to wrap exposed roots in wet paper towels and cover them with plastic until you get back; never let roots dangle out in the open air for long.

Large plants can't easily — and, in fact, shouldn't

be — repotted regularly. Repotting only gives them encouragement to keep growing — an activity that is nice in small plants but alarming in ones that already have a better view of the ceiling than you have. Large plants do, however, need the regular attention that smaller plants get when you repot them.

Using a spoon and a gentle hand, take out as much soil from the top of the pot as you easily can without disturbing the roots. Replace it with new soil, patting it down firmly to join the old. Water well to let the two soils mix at their junction. The new soil should give your big plants and those in planters about the same relief as you may get from a well-mixed martini — and the effect is even longer lasting.

While you have the soil out take the opportunity for a quick — albeit incomplete — look at those roots that are visible. Are they firm? Beneath the normal dirt are they white or yellow? If so, breathe a sigh of relief and carry on. Unfortunately, developing root problems are much more apt to be occurring deep within the pot and may not be visible when only the "lid" is removed.

The other time of year when plants must be similarly inspected with rather more thoroughness than usual — though you might not need to turn them completely out of their pots — is when you bring them indoors after a summer in the sun (see *Vacations . . .*, chapter 4). At that time you might add — though *only* at that one time (at least per my recommendation) — a judicious spray of a general pesticide to be sure you're not bringing outdoor trouble into the house along with your newly invigorated plants.

Keeping Plants Shapely

Any time of year that your plants are growing well is a good time to pinch, prune, or trim.

The growth hormones within plants are controlled by sunlight, which never hits plants evenly, so growth is often uneven; or growth occurs along a couple of main shoots and the side shoots remain puny. You can

Trim brown tips off thin-leaved plants with a sharp scissors

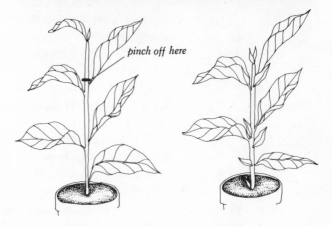

pinch off here

Pinch the growing tip off a leggy plant just above a leaf node. New growth will soon make the plant fuller (right).

correct these problems on many plants, mainly the many-stemmed ones with soft stems as opposed to woody ones, by pinching them back. If you deliberately remove, with your fingernails or with scissors, the end of a growing stem (just at a node where leaves grow), the hormones within the plant will concentrate their efforts elsewhere: on the side shoots. New little leaves will appear at leaf nodes, increasing the amount of foliage on individual stems. Side growth that had just been tiptoeing along suddenly begins to bound, and the whole plant gets rounder and fuller.

Such pinching should be repeated several times, especially after rooting cuttings from such plants as impatience, wandering Jew, coleus, aluminum plant, and iresine. These plants tend to keep growing tall (or long) unless you pinch them back to encourage them to grow along the sides. They certainly look better when wide and full.

Pinching is most effective when a plant is young and when it can result in filling out the plant all around, even down to the pot. If you wait until a plant is already fully grown and then start pinching, the new growth that forms as a result will all be at the top of long stems, making a top-heavy plant. The only answer then is genuine pruning: in effect, starting over.

Pruning is a rather more drastic process than pinching and really becomes surgery (see chapter 4). It can be most effective when a plant has seemingly been utterly destroyed by pests. Spider mites, for example, can strip a miniature rose naked almost overnight. First get rid of the pests. Then, when they haven't reappeared for several weeks (during which you've kept the soil just barely damp, because there are no leaves to use up the water), cut the stems back almost to soil level. Continue to water gently and then hope. Soon the plant should begin to put out tiny new sprouts, then stems, then flowers. An annual pruning, done after flowering is through, encourages renewed blossoming in roses and other woody-stemmed plants.

Pruning dead branches off other woody-stemmed plants, such as *Ficus* or other indoor trees, is also a good idea. Most plants gradually develop some dead branches as they live — it's one of the vicissitudes of life, in fact. They need to be pruned from the plant without harming the living matter. Follow each branch to its origin and make the cut in living tissue just above a leaf.

Pruning off healthy branches, as horrible as it seems, may well have a beneficial effect on a thickly branching plant — one branching so thickly, in fact, that little fresh air is allowed to circulate among the branches. The trapped air stagnates and then the slightest injury or weakness leaves the plant vulnerable to botrytis or other fungal diseases. Keep your busy-busy plants well pruned for their own safety. Remember, too, that most plants can have their roots pruned as a means of keeping them under control (see chapter 4).

AIR LAYERING

Then there are those rather ornery plants that have only a single stem and consistently drop lower leaves off them, no matter how good we think we've been to the plants. These plants can't be pinched or pruned (except as a last resort to save a plant). There's only one way to eliminate the top-heavy look of such plants as dracaenas (though some, such as *Dracaena marginata*, look good with their leaves all on the top), dieffenbachias, ti plants, India rubber plants, polyscias, even scheffleras — in fact, all the thick-stemmed plants that, if cut, will always leave a blunt exposed stem end: the process called *air layering.*

Decide where on the tall, bare stem you want the new bottom of the plant to be. Cut into it, halfway through, at a diagonal, or scrape away the outer layers of cells all around the stem. Cover the cut or scrapes with Rootone or another rooting hormone. A cut needs to be held open with a clean, wooden matchstick, otherwise it might repair itself. Completely wrap the cut areas in damp sphagnum moss. Then cover the moss with plastic wrap, preferably black, held tightly to the stem with tape. (Dark plastic is best because light is absorbed instead of reflected and heat is built up within the wrap; heat encourages the formation of roots.) Be sure that the moss ball is completely airtight so that there is no chance it will dry out during the long waiting process. You might unwrap it occasionally and check the moisture content. If it is drying, wet it with your mister, then wrap it tightly again. Sooner or later, new roots will be visible through the moss: you've got a new plant perched atop the old one (that's one reason air layering is often called a propagation process — you end up with two plants instead of one). Cut off the new plant just below the new roots. Pot it in a tight pot until it has a chance to feel secure and happy with its new feet. The old, leafless plant can be cut down to just above the scars from the bottom leaves. Keep it warm and humid and it may begin to put out new leaves to replace the old. But don't count on it — just be pleased that the plant is now able to shine with its new feet forward.

An Atmosphere of Good Feeling In 1966 Cleve Backster, a New York polygraph (lie detector) examiner initiated a new view of living things, and plants in particular, when he claimed to have discovered that his corn plant *(Dracaena fragrans massangeana)* could think — or at least that it could register electrical-resistance reactions on the polygraph that seemed to indicate fear when Backster threatened to burn its leaves (and was serious about the threat). He later observed plants going into "deep faints" in reaction to overwhelming stress. Soon he and others observed that plants established a "psychic" link with the particular people who care for them; a plant can follow its owner in its "mind's eye" and react to stress when the owner reacts, to joy when the owner is joyous.

This and similar work has gone on and on since then. Some people scoff; some thoroughly agree that plants are only one more segment — not quite understood — of sentient life. The news of such research has made widespread the belief that one should talk to one's plants, encourage them, soothe them, remind them of one's love. Even people who won't confess to accepting that plants have "minds" with which to perceive and emotions with which to react often talk to their plants "just in case." (And if it be true, a talking plant-stand just won't do the job; your plants won't be fooled into thinking its voice is yours.)

My own view is still one of "wait and see." Much more research, under strict scientific controls, needs to be done. In the meantime, house plants are thriving that might not otherwise because the newly attentive people who are convinced plants need chatter are also watering them, inspecting them, removing dead matter, and doing all the other things that lead to healthy plants. The plants benefit as they chat. (Wouldn't it be wonderful if the whole business was actually started by Backster's dracaena deliberately, part of its plan to guarantee that the forthcoming boom in house-plant growing attracted people who were willing to chat and consequently give good care to all the dracaena's plant friends?)

Even before Backster, a couple from England (the De La Warrs; he's a civil engineer and she's an osteopath) who were experimenting with irradiating plants to improve growth discovered that the plants with phenomenal growth were actually responding to the human attention and not the irradiation. They went on to discover that when plants were fertilized with material that the people doing the feeding *believed* contained nutrient (but which in reality didn't), the plants being fed grew better than those being fed the same material by people who knew there was no nutrient.

In similar research, the Reverend Franklin Loehr reported that plant growth could be greatly accelerated by praying for the plants while picturing them as having grown to ideal size. Neighboring plants that were not specifically prayed for reportedly did not grow so well.

Who knows? I certainly don't. The one basic belief I have so far is that plants are certainly part of the same life stream from which intelligent animals developed. It would seem extraordinary that there was no bare beginning of perception on the part of plants. But I find it hard to believe that plants understand English.

However, the ideas that turn on a plant grower are often those that will turn on his or her plants. I go along most heartily, for example, with playing music for my plants. Government research has shown that plants respond well to tones of certain frequencies, and manufacturers have marketed records incorporating lots of those frequencies. I, however, incessantly play classical music because it makes *me* thrive — and I just hope that my plants find the frequencies they like, too. They seem to.

But whatever personal touch you add, always be looking at the condition of the soil, inspecting the leaf backs and axils for pests, reacting to color change in a leaf, verifying the stiffness of a stem — all in all, making sure that your plants are healthy and that they will remain your friends for as long as possible.

❦ 11. MAJOR HOUSE PLANTS AND THEIR PROBLEMS

THERE ARE BASIC WAYS IN WHICH PLANTS GIVE THEIR owners hints that things are going wrong. Those basic symptoms are covered in the preceding chapters. Their possible causes as summarized in chapter 2 should be the first ones you consider when tackling the health care of your plants: the obvious answer is usually the right one. However, most varieties of plants have their own characteristic ways of reacting to environmental problems or to you and the care you give them; they have their own particular vulnerabilities. Such special reactions are treated in the following pages.

The plants are listed in alphabetical order by botanical name (or occasionally by type — for example, ferns). If in doubt about your green friend's botanical name, look for its common name in the index, which will send you to the correct name. When only the first part of a botanical name (the generic name) is given, the information that follows relates to all common house-plant species in the genus. A few listed plants behave just like a closely related one and are cross-referred in the text to their relative.

The "GROWING TIPS" given are by no means

meant to be complete. They are just random suggestions that have been accumulated through experience, reading, listening to friends, and so on. I hope they're useful.

Abutilon (Abutilon, flowering maple, bellflower)

SYMPTOMS *Some leaves become mottled and variegated with white or cream* — No problem: it's a natural virus that frequently attacks *Abutilon;* it's not contagious to other plants and does not harm the affected plant. Just enjoy the variety and be sure to give the plant good light. If the mottling or spotting turns brown, however, the virus has turned contagious; cut off the damaged leaves.

Leaves drop off — This quaint habit of the flowering maple almost finished its tenure as a house plant. However, new varieties have been developed that try to hang on to their leaves. You can help by keeping the humidity constantly high.

No buds or flowers form — Fertilizer tends to make the plant produce foliage instead of flowers. Don't feed the plant; just change its soil once a year, returning the pot-bound plant to the same tight-fitting pot. *Abutilon* needs coolness (never higher than 70° F.) for buds to set.

Buds form but don't open — *Abutilon*'s soil must never be allowed to dry completely. Keep the soil moist and the humidity high.

INSECT PESTS Scale, whitefly.

GROWING TIPS *Abutilon* reacts very quickly to light, so turn the plant daily to keep it growing evenly, except when buds have formed. Pinch back shoots in September for winter blooms.

Acalypha hispida (Chenille plant)

SYMPTOMS *Leaf tips turn brown and the plant is obviously un-happy* — Humidity too low. A large amount of moisture must be in the air at all times.

No buds form — Not enough sunlight. The fascinating flowers are the only real reason for growing *Acalypha;* be sure the plant has lots of sun but break up the light at midday. Buds may also delay in forming if you've pinched off the growing tips to make the plant bushy. Don't.

INSECT PESTS Mealybugs, spider mites.

GROWING TIPS *Acalypha* easily gets raggedy looking. Take fresh cuttings each autumn for new, healthier-looking plants.

Achimenes (Achimenes)

SYMPTOMS *Growth stops and the plant goes dormant* — That's normal once a year, in fall, for this rhizomatous plant. If it happens at other times, you've probably let the soil go dry.

No blossoms form — Ditto: the soil must be kept continually moist.

GROWING TIPS After the rhizome produces three sets of leaves in spring, pinch back the shoots to make the plant bushy. If the plant is growing in a hanging basket, pinch only twice; then let the stems start dangling over the sides.

SEE ALSO gesneriads (general)

Adiantum (Maidenhair fern)

SYMPTOMS *Leaflets turn yellow and drop off* — Lack of moisture. Maidenhairs are more difficult than other ferns in their water demands. For best results, keep the temperature below 65° F. to facilitate a relative humidity above 65 percent. If lots of leaves fall at once, the plant is probably going into dormancy for a brief period. The greenery will soon return if you don't let the soil dry out. Individual fronds yellowing and drying is a sign of normal aging; they last only a few months. Clip them off at the soil.

Leaves develop brown spots; general wilting occurs — Too much direct sun. Keep the plant in indirect light, with soil moist and humidity high.

Plant goes totally bad — Check your kitchen for gas leaks — they're lethal.

SEE ALSO   ferns (general)

Aechmea   (Living-vase plant, urn plant)

SEE   bromeliads (general)

Aeonium   (Saucer plant)

SYMPTOMS   *Leaves turn red* — That's normal, in good sun, for this succulent (but it does not require direct south light for growth).

Plant just up and dies — It probably bloomed. *Aeoniums* die after flowering. Just hope that the plant has branched and not all rosettes have bloomed; the rosettes that didn't will keep the plant alive.

GROWING TIPS   This is an African coastal plant and must always be kept warm.

SEE ALSO   *Crassula* (which is closely related)

Aeschynanthus   (Lipstick vine, lipstick plant)

SYMPTOMS   *Older (lower) leaves drop off* — Drafts; over- or under-watering; damaged roots. Review all the plant's living conditions, as well as your own habits.

Very few buds or flowers form — Too little light; and you probably did not let the soil dry in winter for a refreshing dormancy period, followed by a period in cool, even cold, temperatures.

Buds blast — Humidity too low; try to keep it at least 50 percent.

INSECT PESTS   Aphids.

This interesting plant will bloom almost all year round — without winter dormancy required — if grown under artificial light.

Unlike most hanging plants, the lipstick vine does not need continual pinching back to remain full and shapely.

SEE ALSO gesneriads (general)

Agave (Agave, century plant)

SYMPTOMS *Leaves turn yellowish and go limp; stems turn somewhat mushy near the base* — Root rot from overwatering, probably complicated by chilling. Let the soil dry completely and stay dry for several days. Then resume watering, but take it easy: rewater thoroughly only when the heart of the soil ball has dried.

Leaves shrivel and edges turn brown — You were too concerned about overwatering and managed to underwater. Soak through several times in the sink and rewater thoroughly each time you water, making sure the soil ball soaks through.

Leaves develop spots — *Agave* is subject to anthracnose and other leaf-spot diseases from too high humidity and chilling. Cut out the damaging spots, dust with fungicide, and make sure that air circulates.

Leaves develop gray, powdery splotches — Botrytis mold from overwatering and perhaps chilling. Treat for botrytis.

No blossoms form — Well, it doesn't take one hundred years to get one, but the plant does need to be at least ten years old — and it sometimes doesn't bloom until the ripe old age of fifty. Don't hold your breath, especially since the plant will die after blooming.

INSECT PESTS Generally pest-free, but keep a slight eye open when mealybugs and scale are in the vicinity.

GROWING TIPS Feed only when new growth is visible. Like most succulents, *Agave* doesn't produce new leaves with gay abandon and so does not need much food. Use a slightly acidic soil and keep it that way by using an acid fertilizer when you do feed the plant.

Aglaonema (Chinese evergreen)

SYMPTOMS
Leaf edges turn brown and curled — Too cold; but unlikely to happen unless your heat supply goes on the blink and the temperature drops below 60° F. Remove the damaged leaves and keep the plant warm.

Older (lower) leaves drop off — They generally do, although fortunately at a rather slow rate. If it happens too often, check for root rot from overwatering.

Plant grows too tall, with bare lower stem — This is the normal result of the problem just mentioned. Eventually you will probably want to do something about the naked lower stem, especially when the stem seems no longer sturdy enough to support top-heavy growth. Cut off the top at the point where you want new roots. Root the top in water or a peat-sand mixture. Cut the bare remaining stem to where you want the new top to be. If you don't keep watering as much as you did the old, big plant, it should produce new leaves, giving you two plants. Cut way back on water until new growth appears. Otherwise, the roots, with no work to do, will drown.

INSECT PESTS
Mealybugs, spider mites, scale.

GROWING TIPS
As it gets older, prop up the plant with a stake inserted in the pot. Feed only a couple of times a year, and only once if the plant is growing in dim light. Wash the big leaves often for best appearance and health.

A plant that just doesn't seem to be doing well may be getting too much sun.

Aloe arborescens (Candelabra plant)
A. variegata (Partridge breast)

A. vera (or barbadensis) (Burn plant, medicine plant, unguentine plant, aloe)

SYMPTOMS
Leaves turn brownish, possibly developing black spots — Too much light. Protect these succulents at midday in summer.

Leaves lose color — Too little light (especially *A. variegata*).

No flowers form — *Aloe* must have at least six hours of bright sun each day to bloom. Most people grow these succulents for their interesting leaves.

Stem cuttings rot before rooting — Let the cuttings dry for at least two days before inserting them in a rooting medium. Some growers actually touch the cut end with a hot iron to speed the formation of the protective callus.

INSECT PESTS
Mealybugs. Spider mites or scale rare but possible.

GROWING TIPS
If you use the burn plant for medicinal purposes (break off a leaf and rub the white fluid on burns, scrapes, and bad complexions), cut only the side leaves off. The young center leaves are required to keep the plant growing.

Alternanthera amoena (Parrot leaf)

SYMPTOMS
Leaves dry and drop off — The soil dried or the plant got in the way of cold drafts. It needs at least a combination of constant dampness and warm, fresh air for health.

Whole plant is straggly looking — Keep pinching back the shoots to help it maintain its shape.

INSECT PESTS
Aphids, mealybugs, spider mites, scale.

Ananas comosus (or sativus) (Pineapple)

SYMPTOMS
Leaves turn black and pull easily from the crown —

Ananas *(pineapple)*
crown cut from the fruit.
A plant grown from this
cutting will not be very
attractive, because
the leaves are too
bruised and dry.

Heart rot, a fungus disease. Discard, buy a new pineapple at the grocery store, and start over. But if you are determined to retrieve some part of the old one, perhaps for sentimental reasons (over a pineapple?), pull out all the loose leaves and pour fungicide into the heart. Eventually a side shoot will develop on the crown. Cut it off and start over with that.

Leaf edges turn brown — Cold drafts; low humidity. Check your growing conditions.

INSECT PESTS   Aphids, mealybugs, scale.

GROWING TIPS   To grow your own pineapple, trim the fruit off the crown, leaving the skin and some hard core attached to the leaves. Let the cutting dry for a couple of days to prevent it rotting while rooting. Plant in sandy soil in a deep container. Water only when the soil gets almost completely dry. Keep water in the cup formed by the rosette of leaves. New growth will eventually appear in the center. Don't count on getting a new edible fruit — although you might, particularly if you cut off and plant an offset (it seems that only alternating generations of pineapple plants develop fruit easily). Remember that the dwarf pineapple's fruit is not edible.

SEE ALSO   bromeliads (general)

Anthurium   (Anthurium, flamingo flower, tailflower)

SYMPTOMS   *Everything goes wrong, leading to gradual, heartbreaking demise* — You have probably let the roots that appear above the soil stay exposed, which is quite acceptable for some other plants, but not anthuriums. Keep them covered with damp sphagnum moss. In addition to protecting the aerial roots, the damp moss will help increase the general humidity, the other contributor to slow death.

Leaf tips and edges turn brown — Humidity too low.

Older (lower) leaves turn yellow, develop brown spots — Underwatering. It should be clear by now that anthuriums need almost excessive amounts of water in their soil (but the drainage must be absolutely perfect) and in the air around them. Run great amounts of water through the pot when watering. Water when the soil is still damp from the previous time.

Plant loses color generally; leaves develop white or tan spots — Too much sun. Here's the fortunate part of this plant: it doesn't require so much sun that it is impossible to keep the humidity up. North light in summer and east or west in winter are acceptable.

No flowers bloom, or those that do appear small and distorted — Again, humidity too low.

INSECT PESTS   Mealybugs, spider mites, scale, whitefly. If you must use an insecticide (do try to avoid it), nicotine sulfate is preferable. Dimethoate will probably harm the plant, as will Kelthane.

GROWING TIPS   Anthuriums need a brief rest each year so they can
continue putting out their spectacular flowers. For
about one month, give them less light, water, and food
than you usually do.

Aphelandra (Zebra plant)

SYMPTOMS   *Older (lower) leaves drop off* — They certainly do!
Woe unto all growers of this eye-catching plant outside
of humid greenhouses. Those bottom leaves are destined to fall because we're all human. It's almost impossible to maintain the humidity needed, and not
many people are willing to live in a temperature between 65° and 70° F., the range at which it's easiest to
keep the humidity up. Do the best you can and just
plan to take a cutting of the top each year to grow new
plants (you will probably have to keep the cutoff top
in a plastic bag to encourage it to root). Some people
find the long, bare stem attractive; you might.

Bottom leaves also drop if the soil is kept too soggy.
Check the roots and make sure that they have not been
sitting in water, turning diseased and mushy. Add perlite to the soil to hold water while increasing drainage.
Note, too, though, that underwatering can also cause
leaves to drop, though that condition is fairly unusual.

No flowers bloom — They usually don't until the plant
is fairly large and somewhat pot-bound.

Flowers don't last — Feed the plant every week while
it is in bloom; maintain regular watering to keep the
soil moist but draining well.

All leaves drop off — It can happen. Check the growing conditions. Cut the stem way down and be patient;
growth might return.

INSECT PESTS   Very attractive to spider mites, but if you've kept the
humidity high enough to prevent leaf fall, you've also
prevented mite infestation. Watch out, too, for mealybugs, aphids, and scale.

GROWING TIPS   The leaves will usually fall off after the plant blooms.

If you want to keep the same plant instead of taking cuttings, prune the stems back. For a period of about one month, let the soil get to "damp" between waterings instead of keeping it "moist."

Aporocactus flagelliformis (Rattail cactus)

SYMPTOMS *Stems become discolored and limp, with black mushiness near the stem base* — Root or stem rot from overwatering and chilling. Take tip cuttings of good tissue and let them dry for several days before inserting in sandy soil. Start fresh, promising not to water unless the cactus soil has dried completely.

INSECT PESTS Basically a pestless plant, but keep an eye out for mealybugs.

GROWING TIPS This is an unusual cactus in that it's a hanging plant. Make sure, however, that your rattail doesn't trail gracefully into another plant's pot; it can easily take root — probably in the wrong environment.

SEE ALSO cacti, desert

*Araucaria excelsa (*or *heterophylla)* (Araucaria, Norfolk Island pine)

SYMPTOMS *Needles turn brown and fall off; lower branches die* — Either too much or too little light; drying of the soil; lack of humidity. Araucarias want bright but not direct light. They also need a cool temperature, between 50° and 60° F. at night. Never let the soil dry out completely. If the damage isn't too severe, you can prune the harmed branches, although the graceful, symmetrical shape for which this tree is justly famed will never be the same. Basically, this plant really doesn't like indoor life, but if you give it a moisture-holding but well-draining soil, water it when the top has dried, and keep the humidity as high as you can (spray it often and perhaps keep the plant in a jardiniere with damp moss around the inner pot), it will be fairly happy for a long time. Keep the air circulating.

Plant grows lopsided — Needs to be turned more regularly. Take care, too, that nothing is crowding the tree; it should be free on all sides.

Branches droop — Probably overwatering. Let the soil dry. Check that the soil drains well. Water only when the top of the soil is dry.

INSECT PESTS Aphids, mealybugs, spider mites, scale — but all rare.

GROWING TIPS Keep this tree in a fairly good-sized pot. For example, a plant that has reached twenty inches tall should probably be in a ten-inch pot. But make sure that the drainage is good so that all that soil is never allowed to get soggy around the roots. Provide cool temperatures whenever possible to prolong the tree's life indoors.

Ardisia crispa (or crenata) (Ardisia, coralberry)

SYMPTOMS *Lower leaves drop off, leaving bare stem* — That's usual for this plant. Check that the soil is not allowed to get soggy. If the stem gets too ridiculously bare, air-layer the top of the plant.

No flowers bloom (followed by no berries forming) — Double-check all growing conditions. Ardisias don't like hot, dry rooms. Give them bright light and keep the sandy soil moist.

INSECT PESTS Very prone to scale. Wash the plant regularly under a hard spray of water to keep it clean.

GROWING TIPS Once flowers have started to form, encourage their staying around long enough to produce fruit by feeding the plant frequently with a low-concentration food.

Ardisias can be cut back to help them stay shapely.

Asparagus (Asparagus fern)

NOTE Asparagus ferns are not true ferns. Don't treat them as such.

SYMPTOMS *Needles turn yellow and drop off* — The soil is too dry;

the air is too dry; the temperature is too high; the sun is too bright; the plant has just been moved to a new environment; there's too little sun; the plant is pot-bound; the temperature has changed; the plant doesn't like you.

If you get the idea that asparagus ferns turn yellow and shed their leaves at the least provocation, you're right. I suspect that if you frown at the plants, their leaves turn yellow in chagrin. However, they also have a great deal of joie de vivre. So just cut back the yellow stems, all the way to the soil line; double-check everything you, and your environment, do to the plant, fix what you can, and wait for the stems to replace themselves. They do so readily. A forgiving plant.

Foliage turns vaguely yellow — not the yellow of environmental problems (sorry about that; it's hard to describe various yellows) — Plant needs nitrogen. Feed mildly and often with high-nitrogen-content food.

Newer (upper) leaves turn yellow (as opposed to older [lower] leaves and whole stems) — Plant needs iron. Feed occasionally with an acid fertilizer. If very severe, feed with chelated iron.

Plant sulks and looks generally unhappy — Probably age. Separate the plant into sections, with several tuberous roots in each clump. Pot the clumps separately and give each a fresh start on life.

Flowers of A. sprengeri (emerald feather) do not develop into berries — They probably won't. You have to have both male and female plants for fruit to develop.

INSECT PESTS   Very prone to spider mites and mealybugs, which makes asparagus ferns difficult to keep; also gets aphids, scale, and thrips. *Do not use* nicotine sulfate and preferably not Kelthane or malathion.

GROWING TIPS   Regularly fill the kitchen sink with water and immerse the plant to make sure that the soil ball never really gets to dry out. At the same time, take advantage of the opportunity to help prevent pests by washing down the plant in a hard spray of water.

Aspidistra (Aspidistra, cast-iron plant, "that plant
elatior Bea Lillie sings about")

NOTE   Aspidistra problems are rare; this plant seems literally cast-iron, with a rustproof constitution to match. However, just in case . . .

SYMPTOMS   *Leaves develop brown tips or spots* — Too little water in soil or in air. But never let the plant sit in soggy soil: mushy-looking brown marks will appear on the leaves.

Leaves are healthy but just kind of sad-looking — Age; trim them off at the base.

Leaves turn yellow — Too much light; aspidistra needs no more light than that from an unobstructed north window. It can also live in fluorescent light.

Leaves develop dampish, light-colored spots — Leaf-spot disease. Evaluate conditions and treat plant with a fungicide. Remove damaged leaves.

INSECT PESTS   Basically pestless, but might get spider mites if you don't keep the humidity pleasantly high. Wash off the leaves regularly with a soft cloth (don't be harsh with the cloth or sponge — the leaves can be permanently marked). May also be subject to scale on rare occasions.

GROWING TIPS   Aspidistras like to be somewhat pot-bound, so repot only every three or four years. Do, however, give them a root check for overwatering and refresh the topsoil occasionally.

Asplenium
bulbiferum (Mother fern, hen-and-chicken fern)
A. nidus (Bird's-nest fern)

SYMPTOMS   *Plant wilts* — It needs water. Unlike most other ferns, it probably won't lose its leaves as a result of being underwatered.

New growth is stunted — Temperature too low, or the plant intercepted cold drafts. Check the environment.

Leaf edges turn brown — Humidity too low; almost

inevitable unless you grow the plant in the bathroom. Feel free to trim the leaves with scissors.

Whole fronds turn brown — The cause, believe it or not: too high a humidity — something that would seem to be impossible for most ferns. The *Asplenium* ferns can't take a room humidity higher than about 60 percent. I wouldn't fret about that; few homes reach that humidity level except during summer storms.

Frond margins turn wavy and brown-spotted — Inconsistency in watering. Check your behavior. The soil should be kept moist. Never let it dry, then drown it in dismay: that may soothe your own conscience but will harm the plant.

Translucent spots form on fronds, and usually get larger and larger — A bacterial leaf blight. Destroy the plant and keep everything near it absolutely sterile. Lower the humidity and reduce the water supply if you try again.

Center turns mushy and black; whole plant does badly — Crown rot. You have carelessly let water accumulate in the center of the plant. You can try cutting the plant way back to see what happens, but you'll probably have to throw it away because the growing area has been destroyed. Next time, be careful when you water.

SEE ALSO   ferns (general)

Aucuba japonica (Aucuba, gold-dust plant)

SYMPTOM   *Leaves develop spots (other than natural markings); lower leaves turn yellower than normal and drop off* — Underwatering. Drench the soil and thereafter keep it moist but draining well. (Also, since aucubas are subject to leaf-spot diseases, keep the air circulating well so that the required high humidity doesn't let fungus get started.)

Growth becomes tall and straggly — That's normal with age; prune back to desired size and shape in the spring.

Aphids, mealybugs, spider mites, scale.

Grows best when nighttime temperature is cool.

Azalea (Azalea)

SEE *Rhododendron Simsii*

Beaucarnea recurvata (Ponytail palm, bottle palm, elephant's foot)

SYMPTOMS *Plant's "bottle" feels slightly soft* — Great! That's just the clue you need to know when to rewater (which won't be very often).

Leaf tips turn brown — Yes, they do — quite easily.

Beaucarnea recurvata *(ponytail palm) with crown rot. The plant is also pot-bound.*

Just trim the damage off and keep the humidity reasonably high.

Fronds wilt, change color, and collapse around "bottle" — Crown rot. You probably watered heavily and allowed some water to sit in the crown. If the damage isn't extensive, cut out the diseased parts, dust with fungicide, and hope.

New growth is puny — Plant needs better light and perhaps more warmth (although if the plant is grown in full sun, the temperature should be kept as low as possible).

"Bottle" feels very soft and mushy — Stem rot disease. You have overwatered. Remember that the "bottle" (stem) is a reservoir holding a great deal of water; like succulents, this plant can't handle excess water in the soil around it, too. Spray with fungicide. Make sure the air circulation around the plant is good. Withhold water until you think the whole plant may shrivel away. Then water again and let the soil get quite dry before being generous again. You may yet lose the plant, however. Weep and learn.

INSECT PESTS   Mealybugs, scale.

GROWING TIPS   This plant (which is not a true palm) is basically indestructible once it gets past "childhood." Feed only once a year, in spring.

Begonia (general)

SYMPTOMS   *Leaf edges dry out and leaves soon drop off* — The temperature is too high and the humidity is too low. Begonias generally can't take humidity below about 40 percent; the temperature shouldn't be allowed above about 72° F., and a drop of about ten degrees at night is recommended. (Occasionally, too much nitrogen in the soil can also cause leaf-tip burn; run water through the soil several times and don't feed the plant for several months.)

Leaves and flower buds develop a whitish, dustlike coating, turn dry and curl — Powdery mildew. Treat with fungicide. Avoid getting the leaves wet from now on. Don't mist them; just use pebble trays to increase humidity. Keep the air circulating well.

Leaves turn yellow and drop off; stems turn brownish and squishy at the soil line — Probably overwatering. Begonias are very sensitive to soggy soil. They don't have extensive root systems, so they need shallow pots, which will help keep you from overwatering. When potting, do not press the soil very firmly against the roots; they need some air. Do not use plastic pots with begonias. Begonias are somewhat succulent, so let their soil dry out a bit between waterings.

Entire plant collapses — Overfeeding; buildup of fertilizer and water salts in the soil. Soak the pot in lukewarm water for half an hour. At least once a month drench the soil by running water through it thoroughly six or seven times.

Leaves develop soft brown spots — Leaf spots from moisture on the foliage. Be sure not to water your begonias on damp, dark days or in the evening, when leaves won't have a chance to dry quickly. Do not spray with a mister.

Leaves develop watery blisters — Edema from overwatering. Let the soil dry between inundations with more water.

Lots of gray-tan mold forms on leaves and stems; leaves turn black; base of stems develop brown spots — Botrytis blight. Spray with a good, safe fungicide; keep air circulating around the plants.

INSECT PESTS   Aphids, mealybugs, leaf rollers, spider mites, whitefly, thrips. Preferably *do not use* dimethoate (Cygon) on begonias; it might distort new growth.

GROWING TIPS   Like African violets, begonias just cause trouble for some people. The temperamental plants seem to know who likes them and who doesn't. The most congenial are probably the Lucerne angel-wing begonias, such as

Corallina de Lucerna *(B. corallina)*, which has attractive silver-spotted leaves. The beefsteak begonia *(B. feastii)* is also considerably hardier than most.

SEE ALSO   *Begonia rex, Begonia semperflorens, Begonia* (tuberous)

Begonia rex   (Rex begonia, painted-leaf begonia)

SYMPTOMS   *Leaves lose their general attractiveness and stop growing* — The plant's energy will be diverted to growth of flowers instead of leaves unless you pinch off the flower buds when they appear. Decide in advance if you want flowers or leaves as your plant's main feature.

Leaves drop off and the plant goes dormant — *Begonia rex* is a rhizomatous plant and may go dormant with little provocation. Put it in a cool, dim place, and water it only enough to keep the rhizome from shriveling. (You will be able to see the rhizome; it should never be potted below the soil, but rather at the surface — otherwise, it easily rots.)

GROWING TIPS   Rex begonia leaves are spectacular; keep them clean by dusting them with a small, soft brush (a cloth can bruise the metallic-looking surface). Wash them occasionally to prevent pests.

SEE ALSO   *Begonia* (general)

Begonia semperflorens   (Wax begonia)

SYMPTOMS   *Plant grows lopsided and has few flowers; new growth is stringy* — Needs more light. Move the plant gradually to a brighter location. Avoid direct noonday sun in summer.

Plant loses leaves and generally collapses — You've probably just brought it indoors after a summer in the garden and your house's central heating has already been turned on. Don't let the wax begonias stay outdoors after the cool temperatures of approaching autumn have begun; take them back inside early or the shock of the move will be too much for them.

GROWING TIPS   After blooming occurs, cut back the stems to just above the lowest leaf nodes. Cut down on watering until fresh growth appears. (Root the cuttings to get more plants.) Be sure to keep old blossoms and leaves picked off the plants, both for appearance sake and to prevent disease.

SEE ALSO   *Begonia* (general)

Begonia (tuberous)

NOTE   Tuberous begonias are basically flowering gift plants and grow best only in greenhouses. However, you can work at keeping them as long as possible by putting them in a cool place at night (below 60° F.) and showing them off only in the daytime.

SYMPTOMS   *Buds blast (wither); flowers drop off; entire plant looks unhappy* — Temperature is too high.

Open flowers develop brownish spots — Probably caused by insecticide spray. If spraying is unavoidable, remove blossoms first and show them off as cut flowers in water.

Leaves develop whitish blotches — Powdery mildew, a very active enemy. Spray with Karathane or Captan.

No blossoms form — This is a long-day plant; to set blossoms it needs several weeks of days each consisting of well over twelve hours of daylight.

No plant growth occurs — Tuber was put too deep in the pot. Don't cover it completely with soil or it will rot.

INSECT PESTS   See those listed under *"Begonia* (general)." Also, tuberous begonias' fleshy leaves and stems will attract slugs and snails that enter the house.

GROWING TIPS   You must decide if you want flowers or a bushy, leafy plant: a tuber with one eye will produce one tall stem and spectacular flowers; tubers with more than one eye can be pinched as the stems grow for a full plant.

Too much water is at the heart of most tuberous-begonia problems. Also, these plants are very weak-stemmed, so you must stake them when they reach about twelve inches high.

SEE ALSO *Begonia* (general)

Beloperone guttata (Shrimp plant)

SYMPTOMS *Older (lower) leaves turn yellow* — Too much water. Shrimp plants should be rewatered only when their soil has dried in the top half of the pot. Yellow leaves can also mean, however, that a plant has just bloomed and it wants a rest; cut way back on watering for a while until new growth appears.

Newer (upper) leaves turn yellow — Iron deficiency. This is an acid-loving plant; pot it in acidic soil and occasionally feed with acid to keep it happy.

Plant gets leggy — The shrimp plant usually grows straggly naturally, so take stem cuttings each year for new plants. Pinch some stems back frequently to keep the plant bushy as it grows — but not all stems, because that just delays flowering.

Flowers drop off before changing color — Humidity too high. Do not mist, and be sure to let the soil dry on top before rewatering.

INSECT PESTS Aphids, mealybugs, spider mites, whitefly.

GROWING TIPS The shrimp plant needs all the sun it can get, which may cause problems in keeping the temperature cool. Use only stems that did not bear flowers for cuttings to grow new plants.

Billbergia (Living-vase plant, billbergia, queen's tears)

SYMPTOMS *Leaves turn reddish* — That's normal in bright sun.

SEE ALSO bromeliads (general)

Bougainvillea (Paper flower, bougainvillea)

SYMPTOMS *Leaves and flowers drop off* — You've probably let the roots dry out. Keep the soil damp but well drained when the plant is blooming; let it dry slightly between waterings when the vine is not blooming. However, if just the leaves fall off and the plant has bloomed, this tropical plant is probably going dormant for a brief period. Water only slightly until new growth is visible.

No buds or flowers form — Buds set on this plant on short days, so it must have at least twelve hours of darkness each day, for several weeks, preferably in late fall.

Leaf margins turn yellow — Plant wants an acidic soil in order to use its iron and magnesium properly.

Plant stops blooming — After blossoms fade, the stems must be pruned back to the main branches in order to encourage more flowers.

INSECT PESTS Mealybugs, spider mites.

GROWING TIPS This is the spectacular flowering vine that adorns houses in the tropics. Feel free to cut it back frequently to keep it a reasonable size.

Bouvardia longiflora (Sweet bouvardia)

GROWING TIPS This is basically an annual, but you can try to hold it over for a second show by pruning the stems way back after it has finished blooming. Keep the plant in a cool place (between 50° and 60° F.) for several weeks. New buds may form.

Brassaia actinophylla (Australian umbrella tree, umbrella tree)

SEE *Schefflera actinophylla*

bromeliads (general)

NOTE In addition to those listed under SEE ALSO, other popular bromeliads include *Aechmea, Guzmania, Nidularium, Tillandsia,* and *Vriesa.*

SYMPTOMS *No blossom forms* — Don't worry too soon about that, because the advent of a flower spells doom for bromeliads. However, if you are ready for a long-lasting, spectacularly colorful blossom (with color combinations found nowhere else in the plant world), first try changing the plant's environment in some harmless but significant fashion (for example, give it more light). If that doesn't prompt the plant to bloom, you can encourage a mature bromeliad to bloom by enclosing it for several days in a plastic bag containing a ripe apple. That sounds a bit like magic, I admit, but really it is the ethylene gas given off by the apple (a gas that is destructive to many other plants) that starts bud formation.

Leaves wither — They will eventually, six to twelve months after blooming, but the plant will have sent out an offset — a baby plant — first. For a new plant, detach the offset (sometimes called a pup) when it is about one-third the size of the mother plant. Throw away the old plant.

Plant looks generally disgusted with life — It probably needs more sun. Although these hardy beasts survive

Bromeliad (living vase plant) — pouring water into the "vase" formed by the crown of leaves will raise the humidity.

in dim light, they need good light for best perform-ance. Also, make sure you have been keeping the "vase," if the leaves have formed one, filled with water — preferably rainwater, if your tap water is hard or contains much chlorine. Dump out the old water that has been sitting in the "vase" and pour in fresh water once a week.

INSECT PESTS   Very rare, though bromeliads may get occasional light scale. *Do not use insecticide.* Wash the plant thoroughly each week, and you will probably never have pests. Soap and water should get off any scale that shows up; if not, throw the plant away.

GROWING TIPS   Bromeliads have almost no root system, because in the wild they live perched on trees or among rocks where little soil is available. If you use a pot, make it a shallow one, with very loose soil, or even just Osmunda fiber. You can also mount the plant on driftwood by wrap-ping the roots in sphagnum moss and fastening the moss ball to the wood; take the moss down and soak it about once a week.

All bromeliads require lots of fresh, circulating air. Consider the daily use of a small fan to help them get it, but be sure not to make problems for your other, less breeze-loving plants.

SEE ALSO   *Ananas comosus (*or *sativus), Billbergia, Cryptanthus, Neoregelia*

Browallia speciosa (Browallia, bush violet)

NOTE   This is basically an annual that blooms all winter; don't try to keep it any longer.

INSECT PESTS   Fortunately, pests don't like this plant much — al-though you should keep an eye out for aphids, whitefly, and, just possibly, leaf miners. If placed outdoors or in a greenhouse, browallia can get root knot nematodes.

GROWING TIPS   Keep the temperature warm but not hot, the soil moist, and the humidity at about 50 percent. Browallia is very reactive to light and must be turned every day. Pinch the stems back often to keep the plant full.

cacti, desert

Plant's skin shrivels slightly — That's fine. The cactus is telling you that it's time to water again — but be sure to do so just slightly.

Skin develops yellow or brownish tinge — Sunburn. Even desert cacti can't take direct sun at midday in summer if the temperature around the plant rises higher than it would in the desert.

Plant grows misshapen — Not enough light. Move the plant to a brighter location. Don't flood with water until it gets thoroughly adjusted to its new location. You can repair a badly misshapen plant by cutting off any ugly protuberances with a clean, sharp knife. Let the cut form a callus for several days; then tuck the cut end in a soilless mixture and don't add water for at least one week.

Plant body turns squishy, black or brown, and watery at the soil line — Stem rot from overwatering (see photograph on page 154). Cut away the damaged tissue and dust with fungicide. Repot the plant so that coarse gravel or perlite forms a layer covering the wounds; no water must be allowed to stand against damaged tissue until it is thoroughly healed. Cacti that already have brown rotting areas on them may develop pinkish pustules on the rot: these are anthracnose spots. Cut them out and dust the plant with fungicide.

Skin develops spots with a damp texture — Leaf-spot disease, from too much moisture in the environment (see photograph on next page). Cut out damaged spots; dust with fungicide. Improve air circulation around the plants and lower the humidity. Make sure that the soil always dries before rewatering. Remember, too, that it is very easy for the cut-out spots to develop new rot. Take care: extra water won't help a sick plant.

Plant flesh develops a grayish tan, powdery covering,

Cereus *(cactus) with leaf-spot disease from too much moisture*

with brown spots — Botrytis mold; treat as suggested in chapter 7.

No blossoms form — Many desert cacti will never bloom indoors, but if you've been told that yours is a potential bloomer, give it special encouragement. Use a pot that seems ludicrously too small — one that seems to compress the roots. This "mistreatment" will persuade the plant to put some energy into blooming instead of just getting fat.

Buds drop off — Did you move the cactus? Don't, after buds start forming (even though ordinarily cacti should be turned every few days to ensure even growth).

Skin develops small white spots — Possibly a mealybug infestation. Clean off the spots with an alcohol-soaked cotton swab. (See INSECT PESTS.)

INSECT PESTS   Mealybugs (see above), ground mealybugs, scale, sow bugs, slugs, and snails. *Do not use phosphate insecticides!* If cleaning with alcohol or water does not remove the pests, use nicotine sulfate.

GROWING TIPS   Use only clay pots for cacti; all other types hold water in the soil and prevent air from reaching the roots. *When in doubt, do not water!*

SEE ALSO   *Aporocactus flagelliformis, Cephalocereus senilis, Lithops*

Caladium (Caladium)

SYMPTOMS   *Leaves start dying back after a long growing season* — That's normal: the plant is just going dormant (it grows from a tuber that needs a rest). Cut back gradually on water. When all stems have died, stop watering for two months and keep the tuber in a cool but not cold (about 60° F.) environment; then repot, resume watering, and return plant to normal temperature.

Leaves start dying back before the normal growing season is over — Probably the humidity has been too low or, occasionally, the temperature may have turned too cool. If the plant starts to go dormant as a result, there isn't much you can do. Assist by cutting back on water or the tuber will rot, since it isn't using up the water. Drafts can also startle the plant into losing leaves.

Colors lose their vividness — Caladiums need an acidic soil. Feed with acidic fertilizer, or water occasionally with weak tea; alternate acidic food with fish emulsion. Caladiums will develop green leaves — not what they're grown for — if they get too much nitrogen. Do not feed with a nitrogen-rich food; use one that is about 4-8-8. Colors will be best in bright light but not hot, noonday sun.

New leaves lack color — That's normal; they will acquire their famous reds as they age.

Seemingly healthy plant collapses around pot rim — A well-grown plant may develop leaves too heavy for its stems. Stake the plant.

INSECT PESTS   Basically pestless, but keep an eye out for aphids.

GROWING TIPS   If you like the spectacular leaf colors caladiums offer but don't want to be bothered with tubers and their annoying dormancy periods, try the miniature *Caladium humboldtii:* it doesn't require a rest period.

Calathea makoyana (Peacock plant, calathea)

SYMPTOMS   *Leaf edges turn brown* — Too little moisture (either as humidity or in the pot), although *Calathea* is not as bad in this regard as *Maranta.* Trim off the damage with scissors and increase the humidity. Don't mistakenly start overwatering to compensate. If low humidity continues (especially combined with dry soil), leaves may fall. Mist regularly and keep the plant on a pebble tray.

INSECT PESTS   Spider mites, scale.

GROWING TIPS   *Calathea* and its close relative *Maranta* have underground storage organs and so do not need as much water as their thin leaves would normally indicate. Also, they need a slight winter rest; when growth slows, for several weeks let the soil get a little drier than usual before rewatering.

SEE ALSO   *Maranta* (which is closely related)

Calathea zebrina (Zebra plant, calathea)

SYMPTOMS   *Plant grows too tall* — You can't pinch to control the plant's growth, so air-layer it in several places to get several new, short plants.

Calceolaria (Pocketbook plant, slipperwort)

NOTE This greenhouse or garden plant is sometimes given as a gift, but it doesn't react well to the change in environment; it will probably lose all of its pudgy flowers.

Camellia japonica (Camellia)

SYMPTOMS *Leaves develop light-colored (brownish or silvery brown) spots* — Scalding from too much sun.

Leaves turn yellow — Normal, if only a few are affected. If many leaves yellow, soil may be too dry or there's perhaps not enough food.

Top leaves yellow, but the veins still show green — Chlorosis. Camellia is an acid-loving plant and should be fed alternately with a regular fertilizer and an acidic fertilizer; or water the plant occasionally with weak tea (quite appropriate, since *Camellia* is in the tea family).

Leaves develop yellow-margined spots — Leaf-spot disease — a fungus growing in reaction to something else that's wrong. Check all the care you give the plant, remove spotted leaves, and dust the plant with fungicide.

Flower buds drop off — Like gardenias, these colorful plants are a real challenge indoors (where, frankly, they don't really belong). Buds can drop as a result of: the move to an indoor environment, humidity that's too low, dry soil, and temperature that's too high. (Temperature should always be below 60° F., and preferably even colder at night; if the air gets warmer, humidity *must* be kept high.)

Flowers or partly opened buds develop brown spots that grow; flowers drop off — These are symptoms of a prevalent flower blight carried by plants that have been shipped in soil. To be safe, burn the infected plant; spray others with Ferbam or Captan.

INSECT PESTS   Mealybugs, scale, possibly symphylans (if the plant has been outdoors).

GROWING TIPS   First suggestion: Don't try to grow this plant indoors. However . . . if you do, don't turn a plant once buds have formed; buds will always try to face the light and can literally twist themselves off the stem if the plant is turned in the wrong direction. Single-flowered camellias generally behave better indoors than double-flowered ones.

Campanula isophylla (Star of Bethlehem, bellflower, campanula)

SYMPTOMS   *Plant won't bloom again* — After blossoming ends, prune the stems way back. Move the plant out of the sun for the spring and let the soil dry somewhat between waterings. After two months, repot and return the plant gradually to sun and more abundant water.

Leaves develop grayish, dusty spots — Botrytis mold. Keep air circulating around the plant. The preferred high humidity is easier to maintain when the air temperature is kept down in the cool range.

Capsicum annuum (Christmas pepper, capsicum)

NOTE   This is basically a flowering gift plant — an annual. Enjoy it as long as possible by keeping the temperature cool and the soil moist while the plant bears fruit. Discard after the colorful fruits have fallen off. Or, if you're determined to get a repeat performance, cut the stems back to half their length and repot in fresh soil; give bright light and circulating air; keep the humidity high.

SYMPTOMS   *Fruit shrivels and drops off; flowers drop off; leaf tips turn brown* — Humidity too low. This plant needs a great deal of air moisture; keeping the temperature coolish will help.

INSECT PESTS Very vulnerable to whitefly; also attracts aphids and spider mites.

GROWING TIPS To make sure that fruit sets, never, never, never over-water during August and September. Water only after allowing the surface to become dry down to about an inch below the surface. The plant must also have good light — even full sun — in order to develop flowers (no flowers means no fruit, you know).

The fruits on this plant are edible when ripe, but be sure to keep your hands away from your eyes after handling them: the "pepper" can irritate and start a serious itching.

Caryota mitis (Fishtail palm)

SYMPTOMS *Fronds develop discoloring and gradually die* — Root rot. Cut down on watering when the temperature drops; be especially careful in winter. You might put a sign on the pot to remind yourself.

GROWING TIPS This palm can't stand air conditioning. It prefers its warmth — up to 80° F.

SEE ALSO palms (general)

Cattleya (Cattleya orchid)

SEE orchids (general)

Cephalocereus senilis (Old-man cactus)

SYMPTOMS *Plant looks dull and is obviously not happy* — Check the condition of its "beard." It can be fatal for the old man to have its white hairs tangled and clogged with dirt from the air. If the plant lives near your kitchen, wash it occasionally to prevent grease from coating the hair. If you prefer a tidy look to your old man, brush the hair with a soft brush. If the hair is turning dark, it can be gently "shampooed" with detergent and water. Be sure to rinse it well afterwards.

SEE ALSO   cacti, desert

Ceropegia woodii (Rosary vine, string of hearts, hearts entangled)

SYMPTOMS   *Leaves wilt even though you've been watering properly* — The rosary vine may want to rest from time to time. Let the soil dry between waterings more than you usually do, until new growth appears (it can even be completely dry for about thirty days). Most plants of this type, though, are willing to go on and on without a nap. Leaves that wilt from underwatering may not revive.

Stem and leaves near pot shrivel and dry — A normal reaction from continuous pressure against the pot rim. Just cut off the stem at the soil and use the good end for rooting a new plant, either separately or in the same pot.

Little tannish lumpy things form on the stem — That's normal: they're tubers. Break them off and insert them only partially into a sandy rooting medium. Both tubers and cuttings root very easily.

INSECT PESTS   Basically pest-free, but keep an eye out for mealybugs and spider mites if they're in the vicinity.

GROWING TIPS   This is a succulent plant, so it is particularly prone to overwatering troubles (as evidenced by leaves turning yellow and dropping off). It should be watered only when the soil has dried almost to the roots. The plant needs good light, even full sun, to grow best and to bloom, though many growers are content for it to be flowerless.

Chamaedorea
elegans bella (Neanthe bella, dwarf palm, parlor palm)

SYMPTOMS *Fronds turn brown* — Probably from cold drafts. Remove plant and check the air sources around the room. Also, too much direct sunlight can burn the fronds and eventually destroy the plant.

SEE ALSO palms (general)

Chamaerops
humilis (European fan palm)

SEE palms (general)

Chirita sinensis (Chirita)

NOTE This gesneriad has two forms — one plain green and one a lush dark green spotted with silver.

SYMPTOMS *No stolons form* — They won't unless the plant is terribly happy. Just enjoy the color and don't take the lack personally.

SEE ALSO gesneriads (general)

Chlorophytum
comosum (Spider plant)

SYMPTOMS *Leaf tips turn yellow-brown* — Happens easily when roots have been allowed to dry or if the air's humidity is too low (the most usual cause). Trim off the brown part (see photograph on page 179) and spray the plant often.

Older (lower) leaves die back — Soil too dry.

Green plant turns bleached and grayish — Too much light. The plain green spider plant can live quite happily in north light, while the more common green-and-white-striped variety needs better light.

No runners and little plantlets form — These stolons are what this plant is all about, so review the whole

Chlorophytum
*(spider plant) that
has been kept in too
much light* (right) *for it
to develop plantlets like
those on the healthy
plant* (left)

situation, considering each of the following as a possible cause:

· Soil is consistently kept too soggy or too dry.

· Plant is too young. It won't "pup" until it is at least a year old.

· Too much light. Some recent research has indicated that *Chlorophytum* is a short-day plant, needing at least twelve hours — preferably longer — of darkness (*total darkness*) to reproduce; otherwise, the long hours of light, even if household lights are the source, just make it keep growing. (I had two spider plants that refused to grow plantlets. I went away for three weeks, with someone coming in only briefly in the daytime to feed cats and water plants. When I returned, the cats were furious and the plants had begun to grow runners. Then I learned about this research.)

· Too little light. Often heralded as a plant for dark corners, *Chlorophytum* really does want some light.

INSECT PESTS   Spider mites, mealybugs.

GROWING TIPS   Spider plants, which develop tuberlike roots that may crowd their way out of the pot, need repotting more frequently than most plants — though there is one school of thought decreeing that the spider plant won't send out runners unless it is pot-bound. It might be best to let your plant grow to the size you want, changing pots as needed, and then let it get pot-bound while you hope for runners.

Chrysalidocarpus lutescens (Areca palm, butterfly palm)

SEE   palms (general)

Chrysanthemum (Chrysanthemum)

GROWING TIPS   These are basically flowering gift plants and they won't last indoors. To keep a chrysanthemum as long as possible, give it full sun during the day and cool temperatures at night. If you're determined to get it to bloom again (gift plants are usually forced, so you may be able to get them to bloom at their normal time), cut off the stems, put the pot in the ground in a sunny spot, pinch to six inches before July 15 and feed a couple of times. Buds, which need short days to form, should be set by late summer.

Cissus antarctica (Kangaroo vine)
C. rhombifolia (Grape ivy)

SYMPTOMS   *Leaves dry, turn brown, and drop off* — Underwatering. Let the soil dry just on the top before rewatering.

Leaves yellow and drop off in great numbers — Overwatering. Let the soil dry completely. Run a root check if the leaf fall is severe. You may need to repot and increase the drainage. Remember that the less light these useful "ivies" are in, the less water they can use.

INSECT PESTS   Quite prone to spider mite in dry air; also gets mealy-bugs, aphids, and scale. Do not use dimethoate (Cygon) or Kelthane.

GROWING TIPS   *Cissus* is one of the best hanging plants because of the fullness with which it grows. However, you can change the effect of the plant by letting the delicate tendrils that develop along the stems clutch a rough wall and make the plant climb.

Cissus discolor (Climbing begonia)

NOTE   Don't fool yourself into thinking that this *Cissus* is basically trouble-free, like the others in the genus. This colorful vine must have very high humidity and constant soil moisture — but the red and silver of the leaves make it worth the effort.

SEE ALSO   *Cissus antarctica, C. rhombifolia*

Citrus (Citrus)

NOTE   Citrus plants growing indoors always seem either to be in great shape, worthy of admiration — or doing absolutely nothing right. Just give them your best efforts and then hope.

SYMPTOMS   *Leaves change color and drop off; buds drop off before opening; no fruit forms* — These symptoms can occur for any of the following reasons:

· Not enough light. Your citrus plant needs bright, direct sun except in midsummer, when it should be shielded with a sheer curtain;

· Underwatering. *Citrus* must never be allowed to dry completely. Let the soil dry only on the top between waterings, except when the plant is flowering (it needs to be pot-bound in order to flower, so you must work to keep the soil moist then).

· Uneven temperature. A swift temperature change creates all sorts of miserable symptoms, especially when the change is ten Fahrenheit degrees or more. *Citrus* prefers to live in temperatures between 60° and 70° F.

· Humidity too low. This cause is easily recognized because it also causes the leaves to curl.

Leaves turn yellowish at edges and possibly spotted — Any of the above — especially too warm, humidity too low, too little light.

Leaves turn pale and mottled with yellow — Chlorosis. Feed with an acidic fertilizer or give the plant a dose of chelated iron.

Leaves develop spots — Anthracnose or other fungus leaf-spot disease, perhaps because air does not circulate enough to handle the needed air moisture. Sudden chilling may also produce spots. Improve the circulation; remove damaged leaves. Dust with fungicide.

No fruit forms on a seemingly healthy plant — It may need sexual therapy. Dust the yellow stigmas of one flower with a soft brush; then dust the stigmas on another flower with the same brush, and carry on pollinating from flower to flower. Your pretending to be a bee will make sure that all flowers are fertilized.

Fruit drops off before ripening — Changing temperature or humidity too low. Keep temperature stable and humidity as high as you can when fruit is forming. Don't move the plant.

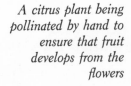

A citrus plant being pollinated by hand to ensure that fruit develops from the flowers

Fruit drops off although the humidity level is high —
That can easily happen indoors: all the smaller fruit
may fall off naturally so that the plant can put its
energies into one or two big fruits (which may get so
big as to look silly on the small plant). You'll probably
need to prop up the fruit-bearing branch.

Leaves develop a blackish, dusty covering — Sooty
mold forming on the honeydew left by any of several
insect pests. Get rid of the bugs themselves and wash
the leaves.

INSECT PESTS   Scale (citrus and scale are almost synonymous). You
may want to spray monthly with a Sevin-Kelthane
mixture, though I usually don't recommend preventive
spraying. Also watch out for aphids, mealybugs, spider
mites, nematodes, thrips, whitefly. Get the idea that
citrus is vulnerable? Right! Make sure you don't jeopar-
dize your other plants.

GROWING TIPS   If you want to grow plants from seeds found in fruit
you've eaten, you can . . . with patience. Just don't
expect them to flower and fruit for many years. Soak
the seeds for twenty-four hours to loosen their tough
overcoats. Plant them under a light covering of soil.
Keep the soil moist and the humidity high, and you
might get seedlings. Separate them into pots of their
own when they are three or four inches high.

Clerodendrum thomsoniae (Glory bower, bleeding-heart vine, clerodendrum, clerodendron)

SYMPTOMS   *No blooms form on new growth —* Prune the plant
only when it has just finished blooming; new growth
will not produce flowers.

Blossoms change color, from blue to purple — They
sure do — just before dying.

Old blooms don't drop off — They won't; you have to
pinch the tenacious flower stalks off the stem.

INSECT PESTS   Mealybugs, scale.

GROWING TIPS   To ensure new blooming, wait for old blossoms to die, then cut down on water (allowing the soil to dry some) and move the plant to a cooler place. When new growth is visible in the fall, resume watering and fertilizing in proper sunlight, cutting back the branches at least once.

Clivia miniata   (Kaffir lily, clivia)

SYMPTOMS   *Older (lower) leaves turn yellow; plant begins to fail —* Overwatering. Run a root check; make certain the soil drains well. Repot if necessary. It is safest to water *Clivia* from below.

Roots push above the soil — Unlike most plants, bulging roots are all right for a *Clivia.* The tighter the fit of the pot, the more apt the plant is to bloom. Don't consider repotting until the roots look as if they may get up and carry the pot away.

No flowers form — Clivia needs a period of dryness and coolness (preferably about 55° F. at night) during the winter for blooms to appear in the spring. Also, it needs to be very pot-bound. (*Clivia* won't bloom in any event until the plant is mature.) After two or three months of dormancy, increase the warmth and food supply (but not the water) until the flower stalks are several inches high. Then resume full watering.

Short flower stalks form (they should tower above the leaves) — Plant was too cool during dormancy; don't let the temperature get below 50° F.

INSECT PESTS   Basically a pest-free plant, but it may get mealybugs.

GROWING TIPS   You can plant the large seeds that form in the flower, but don't expect quick action: it takes seven years from germination to flowering. If you don't want the seeds, remove the flower stalk at the soil line immediately after the blossom loses its freshness so that energy can go back into its interesting leaves.

Clusia rosea   (Clusia)

SYMPTOMS   *Leaves drop off* — Too little light. This large-leaved tree tolerates poor light for only a while. It prefers some direct sun each day.

INSECT PESTS   Very susceptible to spider mites and mealybugs. Wash the tree regularly.

GROWING TIPS   The large, glossy leaves should be kept clean for this tree to appear at its best.

Codiaeum variegatum pictum   (Croton)

SYMPTOMS   *Lots of leaves drop off* — Too much or too little water. Crotons should have enough water to keep the soil just moist; let the surface barely begin to dry before re-watering. Cold drafts and spider mites will also cause severe leaf drop.

Leaves develop dull color — Probably not fed right. *Codiaeum* should have plenty of a food containing lots of phosphorus (the middle number), but only when actively growing. It also needs bright sun (not direct at midday in summer) for good color. The heat of noon-day summer sun will char and bleach the leaves.

Leaf tips turn brown — Humidity too low. Lack of air moisture can gradually cause the plant to die. Spray it regularly and keep it on a pebble tray.

INSECT PESTS   Very vulnerable to spider mites; also watch for mealy-bugs, scale, and thrips. *Do not use* Kelthane in warm weather; it can produce distorted growth.

GROWING TIPS   Prune croton well in early spring to get a bushy plant.

Coffea arabica   (Coffee plant, coffee tree)

SYMPTOMS   *Leaf tips or edges turn brown and leaves drop off* — Too cold. The temperature needs to be about 75° F., with high humidity and good air circulation. Brown

Codiaeum *(croton) with
severe leaf loss from
improper watering*

leaf edges may also indicate that the plant needs a
high-potassium-content fertilizer.

Plant looks graceless — That's the nature of this plant
when left to its own devices. It needs to be pruned and
shaped to be attractive. Feel free to play sculptor.

Lots of leaves drop off — Too little light or the plant
is pot-bound. It doesn't like either condition.

No flowers form — Coffee plants won't bloom until
quite mature.

INSECT PESTS Very prone to spider mites; be sure to spray the plant
often and keep the humidity high to prevent attack;
also gets mealybugs, scale, and whitefly.

GROWING TIPS   Feed with a low-nitrogen-content fertilizer to encourage flowering of mature plants.

Coleus blumei (Coleus, painted nettle, flame nettle, Jacob's coat)

SYMPTOMS   *Plant looks scrawny and dreary* — *Coleus* tends to look spent after a year of growing. Don't try to keep the same plant going for more than a year. Take strong cuttings and root them for new plants. *Coleus* also looks rather less than its best if the insignificant flowers are allowed to grow. Pinch off the buds when you see them to keep the plant full and maintain bright leaf color.

Leaves crinkle — An inherited but not dangerous trait that is often encouraged. However, if your smooth-leaved plant suddenly gets crinkled leaves, accompanied by spots, it may have acquired a virus: discard the plant.

Leaves are small and faded — Too little light. *Coleus* can take direct sun except at midday in summer. It should have direct light about six hours a day.

Leaves drop off — Underwatering. Keep the soil moist. Because of the need for good light, you may need to water daily in summer to keep the soil moist enough.

Older (lower) leaves develop brown spots and soon drop off — Overwatering. Check that the soil drains properly and that it is moist, not soggy. Do a root check; repot if necessary.

Stems become blackened, squishy near base — A fungus-caused rot called blackleg. Don't fight it. Just take clean cuttings and throw the plant away. Root the cuttings in a sterile medium such as perlite and keep the soil of the new plants slightly on the dry side.

Stems are limp during the day but crisp at night — Underwatering. You might want to let the plant have an extralarge pot so that the soil dries out less easily.

INSECT PESTS *Coleus* is a welcome friend to marauding mealybugs. It also attracts spider mites, aphids, and whitefly. Because *Coleus* grows so easily, discard all but clean cuttings when bugs are sighted and grow new plants.

GROWING TIPS Cuttings may rot with ease if not kept sparkling clean when you take them from an old plant. Use a hormone powder containing fungicide to protect them while they root.

Columnea (Columnea, goldfish plant, Costa Rican plant)

SYMPTOMS *Stems turn dark and squishy at base* — Stem rot from overwatering in cool temperatures. Let the soil dry thoroughly or repot the plant in fresh, well-draining soil. Keep the soil moist in summer; let it dry somewhat between waterings in winter.

Leaves closest to the soil turn yellow — Probably overwatering. Check the condition of the roots and the pot drainage.

Leaves develop spots — Something is wrong. Sorry to be so nebulous, but it could be almost any environmental cause. Check all aspects of your treatment. The plant needs good light, warm temperature, well-draining soil. Trim off the damaged leaves and dust the others with fungicide.

SEE ALSO gesneriads (general)

Cordyline terminalis (Ti plant, Hawaiian ti plant, cordyline)

SYMPTOMS *Older (lower) leaves drop off* — Too little light.

Leaf color is poor — Too little light. *Cordyline* needs full sun except at noon in summer. The reds that make this plant special will not be good except in good light.

INSECT PESTS Spider mites. *Do not use* Kelthane.

GROWING TIPS Stem sections of the ti plant are often sold in variety and grocery stores. The directions that come with them often do not mention the need to keep humidity up. The plants sold in this way are generally not very strong and often may rot before sprouting.

SEE ALSO *Dracaena* (general) — which is closely related.

Crassula (Jade plant, crassula)

SYMPTOMS *Leaves develop brown spots, go spongy, and drop off* — Overwatering, a grave danger with jade and other succulents. Let the soil dry between waterings and make sure it drains well (you may want to add extra sand to it). Water only when the leaves have gone slightly soft, as if they were about to wilt (they are, but the bigger danger is overwatering).

Leaves shrivel, starting at the tips; or older (lower) leaves turn yellow — Not enough water is reaching the leaf tips. It may not be that you've underwatered, but that overwatering is causing root rot, which prevents proper use of water. Remove the plant from its pot and check the roots. If they are firm and whitish, you probably really have been underwatering.

Plant just does poorly, though nothing specific seems to be wrong — Probably not enough light. A crassula should have at least six hours of direct sun each day, but be sure that the temperature isn't too warm. Prolonged exposure to high temperatures gives jade plants and other succulents spotted, weak leaves (see photograph on page 57) and makes older leaves drop. (If the sun's all right, run a root check.)

No blooms form on a blooming-type plant — A flowering jade plant needs good sun and full maturity to bloom (it may need to be all of eight years old). To encourage the plant to change its life-style, withhold all food and almost all water for a couple of months; then feed with a low-nitrogen food.

INSECT PESTS Jade plants are terribly vulnerable to mealybug attack. If the pests are around, they'll go after your succulent

— and if the plant gets them, it gets them bad. Plus, crassulas *can't take treatment with malathion.* You must patiently swab the entire plant with alcohol, try a nicotine-sulfate spray (which may also harm the plant), or use a nonmalathion systemic. Crassulas also may attract spider mites and scale.

GROWING TIPS Old plants develop quite heavy stems that snap at the snap of a finger. Be gentle with your plant.

Crassulas are often used in low-light situations. That's fine for a few months, as long as you don't overwater. However, the plants will best continue to tolerate low light if given several months' vacation in stronger light each year.

Crocus (Crocus)

NOTE These cormous (bulblike) plants are forced to bloom for early spring color indoors. There is no food supply in the corm to carry the plant on beyond its initial flowering. Discard crocuses after they bloom.

Crossandra infundibuliformis (Firecracker flower)

SYMPTOMS *Leaves turn yellow and drop off* — Overwatering. The soil must be kept moist but must drain very, very well. Don't go to the opposite extreme and underwater, however, because the plant will fail entirely if the roots are ever allowed to dry.

Almost any other common symptom appears — Humidity too low; it must be kept above 50 percent.

Leaves turn black and curl — Fungal blight from too much humidity. Rare; the main problem is keeping humidity high. Keep plant on a pebble tray and mist at least daily, preferably more often. Be sure the air circulates well.

Plant stops blooming after a prolonged period of good flowers — You probably allowed it to get too tall.

Prune quite severely (use cuttings for new plants). Always remove old flower spikes the instant they stop looking their best so that no energy is wasted on them.

INSECT PESTS   Aphids, mealybugs, spider mites, scale.

GROWING TIPS   Keep the stems pinched back for a bushy, attractive plant.

Cryptanthus (Earth star)

GROWING TIPS   Earth stars need more water than most bromeliads because they are naturally ground- rather than tree-growing.

SEE ALSO   bromeliads (general)

Ctenanthe (Ctenanthe)

SEE   *Maranta* (which is closely related)

Cyanotis somaliensis (Pussy ears)

SYMPTOMS   *Leaves turn brown* — Underwatering; should be watered when the soil has barely gone dry.

SEE ALSO   *Tradescantia* (which is closely related)

Cycas circinalis (Fern palm)
C. revoluta (Sago palm)

NOTE   These are not true palms but members of a primitive family of plants called cycads.

SYMPTOMS   *Leaflets turn yellow or brown* — Overwatering. *Cycas circinalis* should be allowed to dry between waterings. *C. revoluta*'s soil should be kept barely moist. Both plants prefer a slight dormancy when not actively growing: let the soil dry somewhat; when new shoots appear, resume full watering.

INSECT PESTS   Mealybugs, spider mites, scale.

GROWING TIPS   These plants depend on sparkling-clean leaves for their beauty. Wash regularly with soap and water. Feed with high-nitrogen-content fertilizer.

Cyclamen persicum (Cyclamen)

SYMPTOMS   *Leaves develop gray mold and brownish spots* — Botrytis. Keep the leaves dry and the air circulating well.

INSECT PESTS   Did you guess it? Cyclamen mites aren't called that for nothing. Because this is a difficult plant to keep anyway without a greenhouse, you might as well flinch when you see the webs and general unhealthiness caused by the mites and just throw the plant away. Use your energy to keep other plants pest-free. Cyclamen is also prone to aphids and thrips.

GROWING TIPS   This is basically a flowering gift plant. To keep it going as long as possible: Place the plant in bright but not direct sun. It must have very cool temperatures (at least down to 50° F. at night) and the soil must always be kept moist: death comes with dryness. Consider taking the plant to a cool garage at night and enjoying it only during the day.

Some people can keep a plant over for another season of bloom by storing it in a quite cold place until it can be put outdoors. Let it spend the summer outside in a shady spot, being watered daily. Move it back indoors when buds begin to show in early fall. Then give it north light in a cool, almost cold, room. Unfortunately, outdoor plants are prone to rot.

If you don't have an outdoor spot available, let the leaves die back after blooming is finished. Store the pot on its side during summer and keep it cool and dry. About early September you should see new leaves begin to sprout. Repot the tuber, keep the plant cool, and hope a lot.

Cyperus alternifolius (Umbrella plant, umbrella palm)

SYMPTOMS   *Whole stem turns brown* — That happens regularly; just cut it off and it will replace itself.

Stems go limp — Too little light. *Cyperus* likes direct light, except for midday sun in summer.

Brown tips form on umbrella-spine leaflets — Humidity too low, or too little fresh water. Even if this plant is growing in water (where it lives quite happily), it can react to the lack of oxygen in old water by turning tips brown. Change the water frequently to replenish the oxygen supply.

Foliage develops a chewed appearance — Do you have cats? They love this plant, apparently for its resemblance to real grass.

INSECT PESTS   Spider mites, mealybugs, scale, thrips, whitefly.

GROWING TIPS   Keep *Cyperus* out of hot drafts from blowers or radiators; the heat blasts can cause the whole plant to fail.

Cypripedium (Lady's slipper, cypripedium)

SEE   orchids (general)

Cyrtomium falcatum (Holly fern)

SYMPTOMS   *Leaf tips turn brown* — Humidity too low. Increase air moisture as much as possible. Remember: keeping humidity high is easier to do if the air temperature verges on coolness instead of being hot.

New fronds die back — Underwatering. Keep the soil moist at all times.

GROWING TIPS   This plant with leathery leaves and tan, hairy stems is one of the easiest ferns to grow indoors (especially if you obtain the hybrid called Rochefordianum). The

hard leaf-covering protects the fern in the dryness of
house air.

SEE ALSO   ferns (general)

Davallia (Rabbit's-foot fern, deer's-foot fern, ball fern)

SYMPTOMS   *Fronds turn brown gradually and drop off* — That's
natural: the plant occasionally pretends it's a deciduous
tree and sheds its leaflets. Also, fronds last only about
a year under the best of conditions (they are, however,
quickly replaced by new ones growing from different
parts of the rhizomes). If many older fronds turn
brown at the same time, the plant has probably had too
much sun with consequent drying of the soil.

Plant fails completely — Look at the rhizomes; they
are probably rotted. They should never be buried completely. Just lay them on the soil and tamp them in just
slightly to hold them in place. Let the soil dry a bit
between waterings.

Older fronds develop brown leaflets; new fronds wither
— Soil was allowed to dry, or too much sun. This fern
likes no more than an hour or so of direct sun each day,
and it doesn't really need that.

Rhizome doesn't root — Probably needs higher humidity. Cover the pot with a plastic bag and make sure
it receives no direct sun. If the inside of the bag steams
up completely, open it slightly so some moisture can
escape, preventing fungus problems.

Furry rhizomes change color — They probably got
wet. Water with care (which is easier than it might be
with other ferns because the soil can be allowed to dry
slightly between waterings), and if you move the plant
outdoors in summer, give it an umbrella to prevent
sogging of rhizomes in rainy weather.

GROWING TIPS   Rhizomatous ferns develop very sparse roots, so to
avoid excess moisture around them, pot the plant in a

shallow pot (preferably one of plastic, because the rhizome growth can actually break apart a clay pot).

Instead of repotting a big rabbit's-foot fern, just break off rhizome chunks and pot them for new plants.

SEE ALSO   ferns (general)

Dendrobium   (Dendrobium)

SEE   orchids (general)

desert cacti

SEE   cacti, desert

Dieffenbachia   (Dumb cane, dieffenbachia)

NOTE   The leaves of *Dieffenbachia* will cause a loss of feeling in the mouth and tongue if chewed on. The chemical that causes it (calcium oxalate) can be neutralized with vinegar, though it wears off without aftereffects soon anyway. But keep the plant away from children and pets.

SYMPTOMS   *Leaf tips turn brown or leaf edges turn yellow* — Humidity too low. Since these leaves can be spectacular, make sure that humidity is always kept high. Keep the plant on a pebble tray, but don't spray too often because dumb canes are also prone to fungus spots — and big leaves mean big eyesore when they're not healthy.

Older (lower) leaves drop off — Yes, they do. Individual leaves don't last very long (in fact, there is a traditional observation about *Dieffenbachia:* for every leaf you gain, you lose one — but such need not be the case). Changes in environment encourage leaf loss: temperature drop; humidity drop, as when artificial heat is turned on in autumn; soil that's allowed to dry.

Long, bare lower stem develops — The result of too many lower leaves falling. Air-layer the plant top to get

Dieffenbachia *(dumb cane) leaf curled and browned from insufficient humidity or inconsistent watering*

new roots higher up. Keep the cut very near where you want the new base to be, because at least one lower leaf will die during the layering process.

Lower leaves drop off more often than seems reasonable — Probably root rot from overwatering. Check the condition of the roots and let the soil dry. Be sure to water the plant only after the soil has dried.

Thin main stem develops — Probably not enough light, but don't put the plant in constant direct sunlight: the color of the leaves (the only reason to keep this plant) will become dull in overly bright light.

Leaves pucker, curl, ripple, and turn brown — Humidity too low, or underwatering followed by too much water. Be consistent.

Leaves develop spots — Fungal problems from lack of air circulation. Take cuttings of healthy leaves and dust them with fungicide before rooting them for new plants.

INSECT PESTS
Quite vulnerable to spider mites (which may turn leaves yellowish-tan); also gets mealybugs, aphids, and scale. *Do not use* dimethoate (Cygon) or malathion on *Dieffenbachia.*

GROWING TIPS
The hybrid called Rudolph Roehrs grows better than other dieffenbachias in the dryness of our homes. Don't mist its leaves, because it is particularly prone to fungal problems from humidity that's too high; just keep it on a pebble tray.

Dionaea muscipula (Venus flytrap)

SYMPTOMS
Leaf trap turns black and dies — Indigestion: it had a bigger meal than it could cope with. Remove the leaf; a new one will grow to replace it. A trap may also die if you've been teasing it into closing. (A trap dies naturally after several closings.) About indigestion: some authorities say to never feed your plant a fly, much less a meal of hamburger; but most of us can't resist. Never give it more than three meals in any one growing season. And *never, never* use fertilizer on carnivorous plants: their systems aren't equipped to handle it.

If your flytrap does catch an insect (maybe one of the nuisances bothering your other plants), the trap will shut and stay closed for up to two weeks while it digests the meal. Congratulate the plant, but don't rely on it to take care of your insect pests.

Growth stops — The plant is going dormant, which it *must* do every winter; put it in a cool, dim place and keep the moss barely damp until new growth starts.

Dionaea muscipula *(Venus flytrap) with traps blackened and dying from overfeeding*

The plant may also be getting ready to flower (usually in May or June). To get the biggest plant possible, don't let the *Dionaea* flower: pinch off buds as they appear.

General lack of sparkle and health occurs — Probably lack of water. Venus flytrap is a marsh plant and is best grown in a terrarium in *live* sphagnum moss, with all the light it can get. Never use soil (it's too rich in nutrients). Give the plant all the humidity (with circulating air, however) you can garner.

INSECT PESTS Unlikely, but if an attack occurs, do not spray the plant. Dust it lightly with a rotenone or pyrethrum dust, or sink the whole plant in water for several hours to drown the pests.

GROWING TIPS Venus flytrap, as a marsh plant, needs acidic surroundings. Growing it in peat moss, which is slightly acidic, helps, but also add some organic acid source, such as tea, to the water every once in a while.

Dizygotheca (or *Aralia*) *elegantissima* (False aralia, threadleaf)

SYMPTOMS *Lower leaves drop off, leaving stems bare* — This happens easily in reaction to any change in the environment. *Dizygotheca* is generally attractive with bare lower stems, but if you want to have a fuller plant, prune back fairly severely and let the stems begin to grow again (preferably do this in late spring, when you can put the plant outdoors for the summer). You can slow leaf loss by keeping this sensitive plant completely away from drafts, by elevating the humidity as much as possible, and by making sure it has good but not direct light.

Leaves turn yellow and quickly drop off — Not enough water. The soil top should be allowed to dry no more than one day before being rewatered.

Stems develop white specks — Normal to this plant.

Delicate appearance fades as plant broadens and thickens — Normal with maturity. Prune the stems and let the plant regrow for the lacy look.

INSECT PESTS   Aphids, mealybugs, spider mites, scale, thrips.

GROWING TIPS   Don't think you can cure the problem of dropping leaves by moving the plant (unless you discover that it's in an irreparable draft); moving it just makes more leaves fall. If you have to move it, let it live in a plastic bag for some days beforehand. That seems to help it adjust to the shock. Never feed the plant while it's adjusting to environmental change.

Dracaena (general)   (Dragon plant, dragon tree, dracaena)

SYMPTOMS   *Leaf tips turn brown; leaves develop yellow margins* — Humidity too low, a problem to which this family is very vulnerable. Keep plants on pebble trays, spray often, and trim away browned tips.

Older (lower) leaves turn yellow and gradually drop off — Normal slow attrition. If stem becomes bare, cut way down and air-layer the top.

Lots of leaves suddenly turn yellow and drop off — Overwatering; perhaps root rot. Check the roots; let the soil dry or repot the plant. The soil should be kept

Dracaena fragrans
massangeana
*(corn plant) with
brown leaf tips
and edges from
insufficient humidity*

moist but never soggy. Make sure it drains well. These plants are sometimes suggested for growing in poor light. If you keep them in less than bright light, cut way back on watering to avoid root rot. Normally, let the soil get dryish (never totally dry — that makes leaves droop and then fall) every third or fourth watering to let oxygen into the soil.

Leaves develop spots — You probably let the leaves get wet and allowed cold or darkness or too much sun to hit them before they dried. If the spots start near the leaf tips and grow, they are probably fungal. Dust the plant with fungicide and, if possible, remove the spotted leaves. If necessary, cut the stem down and let the plant start over again. Leaf-spot disease can also occur if humidity is too high in poorly circulating air.

Uneven growth occurs — All dracaenas are prone to it. Turn them regularly.

INSECT PESTS	Mainly spider mites and mealybugs; less frequently, scale and thrips.
GROWING TIPS	If you like the height of a tall dracaena but not its bare lower stem, try training a similar-environment plant, such as philodendron, to grow up the stalk.
SEE ALSO	*Cordyline terminalis* (which is closely related), *Dracaena fragrans massangeana*, *Dracaena marginata*, *Pleomele*

Dracaena fragrans massangeana (Corn plant, Massange's dracaena)

SYMPTOMS	*Variegation fades* — Too little light. Gradually move plant to a brighter location.
GROWING TIPS	Never let the soil go dry: roots will die easily and fail to support the large leaves.
SEE ALSO	*Dracaena* (general)

Dracaena marginata (Red-edged or red-margined dracaena)

SYMPTOMS	*Lots of older (lower) leaves drop off suddenly* — Something's wrong: too much or too little water. Don't worry about gradual lower-leaf loss; most *marginatas* are quite attractive with bare stems — they often form unusual shapes — but don't try deliberately to make the bareness happen. Be patient: it'll do it all of its own accord.
SEE ALSO	*Dracaena* (general)

Echeveria (Hen and chickens, echeveria)

SYMPTOMS	*Stem becomes visible* — Normal with these rosette-type succulents after a long period of growth. Cut off the top, leaving a shallow stem to be rooted in sand.

The leafless bottom should develop a new rosette if you don't overwater it.

Leaves develop char marks — Although these plants like lots of sun, they burn in the hot, direct light of south windows in summer. Protect them.

Whole plant goes bad — Maybe crown rot: water was allowed to sit in the heart of the rosette, which then rotted. Cut out bad portion, dust with fungicide, repot, and let plant have a lengthy period without much water so it can take hold again.

Older (lower) leaves drop off — Fairly normal; treat as for exposed stem above. If many leaves fall, check roots for overwatering. These succulents, like others, should be watered only when the leaves start to feel soft.

Dark raised spots form on leaves — Leaf-spot disease. Cut out the spots, dust with fungicide, and improve the air circulation.

Rosette elongates, leaving gaps between leaves instead of a compact crown — Too little light. Gradually move plant to brighter location.

Plant stops growing — Has it bloomed? Echeverias are at the end of their lives if allowed to flower. Blossoms add nothing, so pinch off the buds as they form, especially if you want to develop a large plant.

INSECT PESTS   Mealybugs, scale.

GROWING TIPS   *Echeveria* benefits from having more dryness in winter than it has in summer. In winter, let the soil be dry a day or more before rewatering. Wash the plant occasionally to clean it and to prevent pests.

Epiphyllum (Orchid cactus, tropical cactus, crab cactus, epiphyllum)

SYMPTOMS   *Stems turn yellowish* — Too much light. These plants are not desert cacti and so should never have hot, direct sun.

Stems yellow, develop spots, drop off; all-round bad health occurs — Root rot from overwatering. Let the soil dry completely. Check roots; trim them and repot the plant if necessary. You may want to repot in an orchid mixture or fir bark, which allows air to reach the roots.

Buds drop off — Often happens naturally, leaving only the strongest buds to open. If too many drop, though, check the temperature — coolness is needed — and light, which should be bright, with preferably a little morning or evening sun.

Few flowers form — Plant should be pot-bound, in slightly acidic soil, for best blooming.

INSECT PESTS Not particularly vulnerable, but watch for scale, mealybugs, and aphids. If ants get in the house, they may be drawn to the flower buds.

GROWING TIPS Even though these plants are leafless, don't be fooled into treating them like desert cacti. Their soil needs to be kept moist, except in winter, when it can dry slightly between waterings.

SEE ALSO *Schlumbergera bridgesii* (which is closely related)

Epipremnum aureum (Pothos, devil's ivy)

SEE *Scindapsus aureus*

Episcia (Episcia, flame violet)

SYMPTOMS *Leaves turn black or mushy brown* — Plant got cold; it can't take it below 55° F. and really shouldn't be subjected to temperatures below 60° F.

Leaves turn yellow and drop off — Overwatering; perhaps root rot. Let the soil dry. Check the condition of the roots. If necessary, trim them and repot the plant, using a light, porous soil.

Cuttings rot before they root — The medium is soggy. Try perlite and start again.

No flowers form — Don't worry about it — these plants have gorgeous leaves. But if you really want blossoms, give your plant better light — but protect it from hot, direct sun — and increase the humidity (you might enclose the plant in a plastic bag for several hours a day). Also, remember: if it's busy producing runners (a charming feature of many episcias), it won't produce flowers, too. Pinch back the runners to change the plant's enthusiasm.

Hanging plants develop general shagginess — They're overgrown; prune often to keep them compact and nice-looking. You can cut stems back almost to the soil without hurting the growth.

INSECT PESTS   Aphids.

GROWING TIPS   If you keep stolons and stems pinched back, the growing effort will go into increasing leaf size. It's possible to develop beautiful, plush leaves more than six inches long that way. Under artificial light, *Episcia* leaves take on spectacular color and glow.

SEE ALSO   gesneriads (general)

Euonymus japonicus (Japanese spindle tree, euonymus)

SYMPTOMS   *Plant gets long and spindly* — It tends to; but that's verboten on the spindle tree. Prune back each autumn and repot.

New growth is weak and the plant is lifeless — Temperature too high, especially in winter. If you keep your home above about 72° F., find a cooler home for this plant.

Leaves turn dull-looking — Probably just dirty (they attract dirt easily). Wash them often to keep them shiny.

INSECT PESTS   Spider mites, mealybugs, scale.

GROWING TIPS This plant easily becomes a tree. To keep it small but full, plant pruned stems in the same pot.

Euphorbia pulcherrima (Poinsettia)

NOTE   This is basically a flowering gift plant popular at Christmastime. You can prolong its life with you (some new hybrids last six months or more) by watering when the soil is just dry to the touch (be sure to check it every day — the slightest bit too much dryness can cause leaf loss). Also, give it warmth and some sun, with no drafts; and remove the decorative (but air-stopping) foil from the pot.

SYMPTOMS   *Lower leaves drop off* — Humidity too low; too much water; too warm; too cold (between 65° and 70° F. is just right); not enough light. If leaf loss occurs immediately after receiving the plant, it is probably just adjusting to the move.

Stems turn dark above soil line; leaves turn yellow and drop off — Stem rot from undrained soil. Be sure drainage is sharp and let the soil dry. Check the roots.

Stems develop watery streaks; spots possibly form on the leaves — A bacterial disease called stem canker (usually happens only in greenhouses). Discard suspect plants immediately.

INSECT PESTS   Aphids, mealybugs, spider mites. *Do not use* diazinon or malathion.

GROWING TIPS   Instead of trying to keep the same plant over for another season of color, try this if you have a garden available: Cut the plant way down after it finishes being colorful. Put it outside for the summer, regularly giving it feedings and water, and just letting it grow (though pruning it frequently to keep growth sturdy). About the middle of August, take cuttings of the new, strong growth. Root and pot them separately. After each new cutting has developed six new leaves, put them through a short-day light-and-dark routine: *total* darkness (that means not even a streetlamp outside the window) from dusk to dawn (about 5:00 P.M. to 7:00 A.M.) for the eight weeks during the months of October and November. Give just enough water to prevent leaf loss. Gradually, top leaves will turn color (the red "flowers" are leaves) and buds will set. At the beginning of December, return the plant to normal conditions.

SEE ALSO *Euphorbia splendens*

Euphorbia splendens (or milii) (Crown of thorns, euphorbia)

SYMPTOMS *Leaves turn yellow and drop off* — That's normal for some plants in autumn; the leaves will grow again. If it isn't autumn, you probably didn't water the plant when it wanted and it thought it was autumn. Cut back on water until new growth appears, then resume normal watering: let the soil dry before watering. Leaf drop is almost a way of life for this thorny plant. Overwatering and underwatering both bring it about; so does air that is too dry, although crown of thorns doesn't like a particularly humid atmosphere. You may want to assist the humidity only in winter, when indoor heating makes the air parching. If leaves just turn yellow but don't drop off, you'll have to arm yourself with tweezers to remove them. (See photo, next page.)

No blossoms form — Unless you're content with gnarly spines, you'll want this plant to produce its red or yellow bracts (modified leaves), which are called blossoms. Some people treat crown of thorns like its brother poinsettia, offering special hours of light and dark — but that shouldn't be necessary. Feed with a low-nitrogen fertilizer, keep the soil on the dry side, and preferably let the plant grow pot-bound. Once color shows in the leaves, feed more often than before.

Cuttings fail to root — Let the ends dry for a couple of days before inserting them in rooting medium.

Euphorbia splendens
(crown of thorns)
suffering leaf loss from
inconsistent watering

INSECT PESTS This is a basically pest-free plant, but watch for spider mites, mealybugs, scale, and thrips.

GROWING TIPS When in doubt, treat euphorbias as succulents: they are.

SEE ALSO *Euphorbia pulcherrima*

Exacum affine (Persian violet)

NOTE This plant is usually treated as an annual; discard it when it's past its best. You can extend the blooming period to several months by picking off old blossoms as they fade.

SYMPTOMS   *Leaves turn limp, with brown edges; few or no blossoms form* — Probably drafts are to blame. This violet is incredibly sensitive.

Fatshedera lizei (Tree ivy, climbing aralia)

SYMPTOMS   *Plant won't stand erect* — The *Fatshedera* stem is fairly weak for such a large-leaved plant; put a support in the pot and tie the stem to it loosely.

Plant looks scrawny and weak — That's normal for this plant. Put several in one pot together for a better effect.

Leaves dry out and die — You've probably let the soil dry out. Don't.

INSECT PESTS   Aphids, mealybugs, spider mites, scale.

GROWING TIPS   Tree ivy will gradually die if forced to live in an overheated home in winter. Find a cool location for it — perhaps a hallway.

Fatsia japonica (Japanese aralia)

SYMPTOMS   *Leaves turn yellow, with dry, curling edges* — Temperature probably too high; this plant is much happier when it can live in a cool room, below 70° F. It should never be exposed to hot blasts from a blower, space heater, or radiator.

Leaves turn yellow, often with brown tips, and drop off — Overwatering. The soil should be allowed to dry just slightly between thorough rewaterings.

INSECT PESTS   Very prone to spider mites; also watch for aphids, mealybugs, scale. *Do not use* dimethoate (Cygon).

GROWING TIPS   Keep the leaves glossy and also help prevent spider mite attack with frequent baths.

ferns (general)

SYMPTOMS *Fronds turn brown and die back* — This, the most common problem with ferns indoors, is most likely the result of excessive exposure to dry air. Ferns don't really like our homes, but if you keep them all on pebble trays and spray daily or even more often, plus if you keep them out of direct sun and in coolish temperatures (it's easier to keep humidity high when the temperature is low), they can do well. Ferns also may give up one or more fronds when they are being underwatered; keep their soil moist.

Leaves turn yellow — Too little light or too little moisture or both.

Nephrolepsis exaltata (Boston fern) fronds with lost leaflets from insufficient humidity

Scale insects have apparently lined up on the backs of the fronds — They haven't really, you know. Those little brown or dark lumps in ranks and files are spore cases containing cells used in reproduction. However, if some slip out of the neat lines, they probably *are* scale insects.

INSECT PESTS Fortunately, except for scale, ferns are pretty much pest-free, but keep an eye out for aphids, mealybugs, thrips, and whitefly. Ferns *cannot take malathion or dimethoate (Cygon),* so strive to wash your infested ferns clean with a mild detergent or with alcohol (denatured — not scotch). If a pesticide is required, use nicotine sulfate. And *never* spray an aerosol directly on a delicate fern.

GROWING TIPS If you have difficulty keeping the humidity high enough for most ferns, try *Polypodium;* it requires less moist an atmosphere than the others. Or try only miniature ferns; small spaces stay humid better than big ones do.

Because of the need for moisture in the soil, it's tempting to grow ferns in plastic pots, but don't give in to that temptation (except when growing *Davallia*). Clay pots admit more air to the soil and thus keep the temperature around the plant roots cooler.

Ferns grow best in slightly acidic soil.

Take heart: ferns are generally forgiving (of all but death from total dryness). If things aren't going well, feel free to trim fronds back all the way to the soil and then wait for new ones, perhaps less troublesome, to appear.

SEE ALSO *Adiantum; Asplenium bulbiferum, A. nidus; Cyrtomium falcatum; Davallia; Nephrolepsis exaltata; Pellaea; Platycerium; Polypodium; Pteris*

Ficus (general) (Fig)

SYMPTOMS *Leaves suddenly drop off* — Sudden, drastic change in environment. If you can't make your plant's move gradually, empathize while it repairs itself. New fig

Ficus benjamina
*(weeping fig) with severe
leaf loss, probably from
a sudden change in
environment*

plants that you've just brought home will usually lose leaves in response; a great many newly purchased and expensive plants have been prematurely discarded because of this problem. But if you baby the plant, new leaves will grow and your effort will be rewarded.

Leaves turn yellow, often with brown tips and edges — Sunburn from too much light. Move the plant to a shadier spot and raise the humidity. Remember that an occasional single yellow leaf is probably just natural aging.

Leaves turn dull-looking — Ficus depends on its leaves

for beauty; wash the plant thoroughly and often with soap and water.

Leaves develop spots — Anthracnose and other leaf-spot diseases. Increase the circulation of the air around your plants. Dust with fungicide and cut out damaged spots. Do not mist the plants while you are correcting the situation.

INSECT PESTS   Aphids, mealybugs, spider mites, scale, thrips, white-fly. *Do not use* dimethoate (Cygon) or malathion on your figs.

GROWING TIPS   All fig plants benefit from life in pots that are seemingly too small. Tightness seems to add some protection against leaf loss from sudden environmental change. Almost all problems can be eased if you keep your *Ficus*'s humidity above 30 percent in winter.

SEE ALSO   *Ficus elastica*

Ficus elastica (India rubber plant, rubber plant)

SYMPTOMS   *Leaves turn yellow with brown tips and edges* — Sunburn. Increase the humidity and move the plant to a location with less direct sunlight. You may need to trim off the damaged portions of the leaves.

New leaves have a red covering — That's the nature of the beast. The covering will disappear when the leaf is fully grown and content with its environment.

Lower leaves curl — Probably the soil is not right — either too acid or too alkaline. If you've been using household tapwater for years, the balance has probably leaned toward alkalinity. Use tea or vinegar when watering occasionally to prevent this problem.

Leaves rot, dry up, and drop off — Total decay from overwatering, too much fertilizer-salt buildup in the soil, or both. Safest course is to repot completely if possible (get help if repotting a big plant). Clean the old soil off the root ball before inserting it in fresh soil.

Color in variegated plants disappears — Not enough

light. A variegated India rubber plant needs both more light and more water than the plain green type does.

Leaves develop diseased spots — Anthracnose (see photograph on page 146) and other leaf-spot problems. Remove the damaged leaves. Treat with a fungicide that does not leave any residue: the leaves are too big and impressive to look good with a chemical deposit.

GROWING TIPS   The rubber plant is notorious as a dramatic plant suitable for dark places, but it won't be happy in dim light unless it was originally grown in such light. Check with the greenhouse keeper when you purchase your plant (some plants are deliberately raised as dark-corner plants); otherwise, you and the plant must share a long, painful, leaf-losing period while you both adjust.

SEE ALSO   *Ficus* (general)

Fittonia (Fittonia, mosaic plant, nerve plant)

SYMPTOMS   *Leaves turn brown from tips inward and soon die* — Humidity too low. *Fittonia* has extraordinarily thin leaves that must have continuous moisture around them to retain enough water to carry on life processes. Keep the plant on a pebble tray and spray daily or even more often.

Leaves wilt — *Fittonia* also needs a great deal of water in the soil. But please run a root check before dashing for the watering can — be sure it's not root rot from overwatering that is preventing water use by the plant.

Leaves turn yellow and drop off — Overwatering. Yes, it needs constant moisture, but the drainage must be good, too. Never let water make the soil soggy.

Plant becomes straggly — Fittonias tend to if not kept pinched back for shapeliness. Also, they will grow fuller if you don't let them flower. Pinch off buds when you see them. The flowers add nothing to the plant's charm.

INSECT PESTS   Mealybugs, leaf miners, nematodes, spider mites.

GROWING TIPS   Because of its need for constant moisture, *Fittonia* does very well in a terrarium if you can reach it to pinch it back as it spreads.

Fuchsia (Lady's eardrops)

SYMPTOMS   *Leaves suddenly turn yellow and drop off in autumn* — The plant is probably asking for a rest. Prune back branches and reduce watering to keep the soil just damp; place plant in a cool place. Repot in early spring and return to normal conditions.

Leaves drop off at other times — Air too dry; underwatering.

Buds drop off — Almost inevitable indoors from the combination of air that's too dry and overwatering. Keep the humidity as high as possible (which is difficult with a hanging plant) and keep the soil moist but not soggy.

Flowers drop off — Did you move the plant while it was blooming? Don't. As you might gather from this item and the others above, *Fuchsia* is quite willing to indicate its slightest displeasure by dropping everything.

INSECT PESTS   Whitefly and *Fuchsia* are just about inseparable. It also gets aphids, spider mites, and thrips. With any pest problem, wash the plant under a strong stream of water before spraying under and over the leaves.

GROWING TIPS   If you decide that you really want to bother with this plant indoors, be sure to pinch it back several times for good bloom. Use a high-nitrogen food while it is growing and being pinched; switch to a balanced food when it is time to start concentrating on flowers.

Gardenia jasminoides (Gardenia)

NOTE This is one of those lovely plants that everyone adores the idea of, especially when they see an attractive specimen in a store. But at home almost no one gets a gardenia to bloom successfully indoors.

SYMPTOMS *Top leaves turn yellow* — Chlorosis. If all else is right with the plant, it probably needs iron. Gardenia is an acid-loving plant and it doesn't get its iron when soil turns alkaline. Use acid-type fertilizer or feed with chelated iron. Soil that is allowed to be too wet or too cold can also turn the leaves chlorotic.

Leaves turn brown and drop off — Probably overwatering, combined with not enough light. Repot with a more porous, acidic soil. When new leaves appear give them lots of sun.

Buds drop off — This happens from just about any cause:

· Humidity too low. It must be kept high, especially when the plant is in full sun in winter; plastic bags as temporary greenhouses help.

· Temperatures too high. If necessary to get the temperature down to a cool level at night, move the plant nightly when it is in a budding and flowering stage. It must have a ten-degree-Fahrenheit drop at night — but not to below 60° F. (Unfortunately, such repeated movement can also make buds drop.)

· Drafts — warm ones, cold ones, any in between. Thoroughly analyze the air movement in the location you select for the gardenia.

· Soggy soil from overwatering. Double-check that the soil drains well and that roots are not being damaged. Let the soil dry out thoroughly; then water often in summer. In winter let the soil dry out a bit before rewatering.

INSECT PESTS Just about everything — aphids, mealybugs, spider mites, nematodes, scale. *Do not use* diazinon or nicotine sulfate on gardenias.

GROWING TIPS Feed weekly with an acid-type fertilizer until the plant begins to bud; then use a blossom-boosting food. Do not feed at all when the flowers are open.

Geogenanthus undatus (Seersucker plant)

SYMPTOMS *Leaf tips turn brown; leaves turn yellow and drop off* — Overwatering. The leaves are fairly thick, so this plant can take drying of the surface soil before rewatering. Check the condition of the roots and let the soil dry completely before subjecting the plant to water again. Repot if necessary to repair roots or to change the drainage.

Plant grows stretched out and bushy — Not enough light. Seersucker plant needs some direct light to stay compact, the way it is most attractive.

INSECT PESTS Mealybugs, spider mites.

GROWING TIPS This is a close relative of the wandering Jew (SEE *Tradescantia*). The little side shoots, or suckers, produced by a healthy plant will root easily.

gesneriads (general)

SYMPTOMS *Leaves develop spots* — You probably watered with cold water — it should be at room temperature or slightly warmer. Spots may also be caused by burns from fertilizer drops, or by water drops left on the leaves when the plant was put in bright sun (the drops act as magnifying lenses), or by exposure to cold temperature at night.

Leaves curl — Humidity too low. Gesneriads need a relative humidity of at least 50 percent for best health. Very tight leaf curl may well be caused by accumulation of fertilizer salts in the soil: leach the soil by running water through it for several minutes or repot the plant.

Leaves turn brown and wilt; dark, mushy rot forms in stems and crown — Overwatering, usually after letting the plant be too dry. Cut away all damaged material. You may need to take cuttings of any healthy leaves or stems and start fresh with new plants. Dust them with fungicide before trying to root them.

Plant turns leggy: all stem and little leaf — Not enough light. Gesneriads need east or west light in summer and can take south light in winter. Consider using artificial lights, either full time or to augment the natural light you have available.

New leaves turn pale and break easily; all leaves droop downward around the pot rim — Too much sun. Gesneriads dislike getting more sun than they can cope with and will show their displeasure actively.

Few flowers form — Although gesneriads are among the few plants that like warmth, they sometimes need the shock of a ten-degree-Fahrenheit temperature drop at night to encourage blossoming — but don't let it go below 60° F.

Buds blast (wither); leaf edges turn brown — Usually humidity too low or soil was allowed to dry out or both. Keep all gesneriads on pebble trays and mist them often (but not when they are in direct sun). Be sure, however, that air circulates around them well to prevent fungus growth.

INSECT PESTS The mealybug is most common, but watch for cyclamen mites (a very serious problem), spider mites, leaf miners, nematodes, aphids, and whitefly. Remember that cyclamen mites are not visible, so watch for symptoms (the main one: leaf crown closes in on itself and turns upward). Yes, do wash gesneriads frequently to prevent bugs; just be sure the leaves are dry before nightfall or before returning the plants to direct sunlight.

GROWING TIPS Because all gesneriads easily suffer from overwatering, you might try some built-in protection: plant them in shallow (three-quarter) pots. (Besides, they bloom best when slightly pot-bound.)

SEE ALSO *Achimenes, Aeschynanthus, Chirita sinensis, Colum-nea, Episcia, Nautilocalyx, Nematanthus (Hypocyrta), Saintpaulia ionantha, Sinningia speciosa, Smithiantha, Streptocarpus*

Gibasis geniculata (Tahitian bridal veil)

SEE *Tripogandra multiflora*

Grevillea robusta (Silky oak tree, silk oak)

SYMPTOMS *Leaves turn yellow and drop off* — Overwatering. This can happen fairly easily, because silky oak can't cope with lots of water at one time.

Plant doesn't bloom — It usually won't indoors (it's meant to be a tall outside tree in Australia). You can encourage it by giving it full sun (except at midday in summer) and cool nights; let soil dry a bit between waterings.

Plant grows misshapen — Silky oak often does. Feel free to prune it severely each spring to keep the plant compact and shapely. Use stem cuttings to produce new plants; friends will appreciate receiving them because *Grevillea* isn't one of the readily available house plants.

INSECT PESTS Basically pest-free, but if mites or scale are around they may attack.

GROWING TIPS Do not repot this plant while new growth is appearing: root shock will destroy the fragile new growth.

Guzmania (Guzmania)

SEE bromeliads (general)

Gynura aurantiaca (Velvet plant, purple passion)

SYMPTOMS *Natural purples and greens are not vivid* — Velvet plant needs south light for really good color; keep the soil moist and the humidity high.

Leaves develop spots — Probably from water splashing the leaves. Keep the water in the soil.

Plant grows straggly-looking — This is one of nature's straggly plants. Pinch back often for full growth and big leaves. You may want to start new cuttings each year for nice-looking plants. Also, velvet plant always goes straggly if allowed to produce its strange orange-gold flowers. Pinch out the buds when you see them. (The combination of purple and green and orange-gold is a bit much even for mother nature.)

Leaves fail to reach good size — Probably pot-bound. This is one of the plants that likes room to stretch in its pot. Repot a couple of times each growing season.

INSECT PESTS Aphids and mealybugs are quite passionately drawn to purple passion.

GROWING TIPS If you decide to keep the plant over the winter instead of starting new cuttings, let it have a somewhat dormant period for a couple months: cut back on water until soil is dry; then rewater thoroughly.

Haworthia (Zebra plant, aristocrat plant)

SYMPTOMS *Leaves collapse, with soggy bases and faded color* — Root or stem rot, or both, from too much water. This is a succulent and thus should be watered only when the soil has dried; in winter, when it rests a bit, it can take several days of dryness before being rewatered.

Thick leaves turn yellowish — Almost any cultural problem could be the reason: too much water, too little water, too much heat.

/ THE HEALTHY HOUSE PLANT

INSECT PESTS   Mealybugs, scale.

GROWING TIPS   To help avoid the dangers of overwatering, let this plant get thoroughly pot-bound before repotting it. *Haworthia* is a succulent that will grow in shade as well as in full sun, which is preferred.

Hedera (English ivy)

SYMPTOMS   *Leaf tips turn brown* — Humidity too low. Spray the plant regularly, especially in winter.

Leaves shrivel and dry out — Soil has been allowed to dry too frequently. Don't let the soil ball dry out.

Color differences dim in variegated types — Don't fertilize: food tends to bring out greenness. Once a year should be sufficient for English ivies.

Leaves develop spots rimmed with lighter-color edges — Leaf-spot disease, indicating that something is wrong with the environment. Ivies like coolness (if you can't keep the temperature down, at least spray the plant regularly with cool water), some shade, lots of fresh circulating air, and frequent spraying. The spraying, however, is more to keep the spider mites at bay than to raise the humidity.

Leaves near the soil turn yellow — Overwatering. Be sure the soil drains well and that the plant is watered only after the surface of the soil dries.

Leaves develop dark, dry-centered spots — Anthracnose, a fungus caused by too much moisture in the air or sudden chilling.

INSECT PESTS   Spider mites absolutely adore this plant; they make its leaves turn a sickly gray color. Take the plant to the kitchen sink once a week and wash it thoroughly under a cold-water spray. If you can't do that, at least spray it forcefully with cool water as often as possible. English ivy also attracts scale, mealybugs, aphids, and cyclamen mites. *Do not use* carbaryl (Sevin).

GROWING TIPS — Ivy is quite tolerant of many environments but is happiest in cool temperatures; use English ivy on porches or other areas not used often enough to require continuous central heating.

Helxine soleirolii (Baby's tears, Irish moss)

SYMPTOMS — *Plant dies* — Yes, it does rather tend to do that unless enough water is kept in and around the plant. This is one of the rare house plants that likes to sit in water. If you use a small pot, set the pot in a custard cup or other container full of water so that water can continually seep upward into the soil; a wick-watering pot will help too — but be sure to water from the top occasionally so that there is no chance of the soil drying out. It's probably not really worth mentioning warning symptoms to look for (when this plant dies, it goes quickly), but you might look out for the tiny leaves starting to curl up; they do so in an attempt to retain moisture.

Leaves and stems dry out — Humidity too low.

Foliage drops off — If the leaves themselves dry up and fall, leaving vaguely healthy-looking, wiry stems, the plant is going into dormancy. If you've been keeping the moisture right, hang in there and see if new leaves appear. Cut down a bit on water while you wait.

Stems grow long and erect, looking kind of silly — Not enough light. Baby's tears needs some direct sun or quite bright light in order to stay a thick, compact carpet of ground cover.

INSECT PESTS — Basically pest-less, but may attract spider mites or whitefly.

GROWING TIPS — A healthy baby's tears is a delight as a miniature hanging plant. If the common type is too fragile for you, try the larger-leaved one called English baby's tears.

Hemigraphis colorata (Red ivy, flame ivy)

SYMPTOMS
Leaves drop off — Humidity too low; keep it high in all ways you can.

Plant has no red color — Normal. This plant, victim of misnomering, is actually olive-green with purple veins and leaf backs.

INSECT PESTS
Mealybugs, spider mites.

GROWING TIPS
Flame ivy will grow in north light, but colors are more interesting when it receives some direct sun.

Hibiscus rosa-sinensis (Chinese hibiscus, rose of China)

SYMPTOMS
Buds drop off — Rose of China is sensitive to movement and environment change. Once it has settled in place, don't move it. Also, buds drop (and leaf tips turn brown) in low humidity. Give it all the air-moisturizing help you can. Buds can drop, too, if the temperature is allowed to be too cool; it can't take below about 55° F.

Flowers drop off — Even though a nonblooming hibiscus should be allowed to have its soil dry between waterings, a flowering one must never, never have dry soil.

INSECT PESTS
Aphids, mealybugs, spider mites, scale, whitefly — obviously, this plant is vulnerable. *Do not use* diazinon.

GROWING TIPS
Chinese hibiscus needs a dormant period each winter in order to bloom well in summer and fall. When it stops blooming in the autumn, start cutting back on water and stop feeding completely until later February or March. Then repot and prune the stems severely.

Hippeastrum (Amaryllis)

SYMPTOMS
Leaves grow too much — A good amaryllis ought to send its flower towering far above the leaves. If the

plant is grown in warmth, though, you'll get more leaf than flower. Keep the growing bulb in temperatures below 70° F. until all buds are set.

Plant won't bloom — Sometimes a preplanted amaryllis just won't bloom; perhaps something traumatic happened between planting and the time you got it. Give up and try another bulb later.

Red spots form on leaves and flower stalks — A fungal leaf scorch, called — quite logically — red splotch. Although insect damage may cause red spots, assume, if you can't find insects, that the cause is fungal and spray with a fungicide such as Captan or Zeneb. Be sure not to use the bulb bowl again until it has been sterilized.

INSECT PESTS   Bulb pests, mites, scale, thrips.

GROWING TIPS   You can get a second year of bloom out of an amaryllis bulb: Remove the flower stalk after the blossom dies. Keep the leaves going with sunlight, lots of water, acidic soil, and frequent feeding. Let the leaves get full and large. Then stop all water and food, and place the pot in a warm, dark spot. After the leaves have dried, break them off. Repot the bulb, return it to the dark, and keep the soil damp. When new growth is visible or after about five weeks, return the pot to the sun and resume regular care.

An amaryllis pot must not allow the roots more than two inches of room in any direction. Use a pot so small as to be almost silly-looking: too much room means too much water; too much water means rot.

Howea (Kentia palm, fan palm)

SYMPTOMS   *Leaf tips turn brown* — This may be the reaction to almost anything the plant takes a disliking to: the humidity level, the water supply, the temperature. It wants normal room temperatures that don't get too warm, plus east or west light and extra sand in the soil for good drainage. Kentias can stand coolness better than most palms.

Plant grows too big — Congratulations! You must be doing things right. You can prune the roots to at least one-quarter of the diameter of the soil ball. Repot the plant in a small pot. When it's clear which fronds will die as a result of the pruning, cut them off at the base.

INSECT PESTS Quite prone to scale; remove them from the leaflets at first sight (use a soft brush or your fingernail to free them before they can permanently mark the leaflets with their sucking). Also watch for spider mites and mealybugs. This is one plant that many people put outdoors for the summer; be absolutely certain to wash it thoroughly and spray with malathion before bringing it back indoors in late summer.

SEE ALSO palms (general)

Hoya carnosa (Wax plant, hoya)

SYMPTOMS *New shoots turn yellow and die* — May occur from night cold. Check that the temperature by the window in winter does not go below 50° F.

No blossoms form — A wax plant won't bloom until it is at least three years old. After that it won't bloom until it has been given a winter rest period for several months; water it only enough to keep the fleshy leaves from shriveling. If it still doesn't bloom the following summer, try shocking it: change its light, temperature, or water enough to convince it that it must change its habits. To keep it blooming, never pinch off the dried spur on which previous flowers developed; new blossoms grow from the spurs of old ones. Also, avoid high-nitrogen-content fertilizer at time when the plant should be getting ready to form buds.

Buds drop off — Withhold fertilizer when you first see buds, increase the light, and let the soil dry out on top before rewatering. Do not let the plant get chilled.

INSECT PESTS Basically problem-free, but keep an eye out for aphids, mealybugs, spider mites, and scale.

GROWING TIPS   Instead of letting your *Hoya* hang, train the branches
to grow up a wicker or wire trellis. The plant has to be
straggly to bloom, but the unattractiveness can be
minimized on a trellis (you also lose the temptation to
pinch back straggly stems — a no-no if the plant is to
bloom).

Hoya has a small root system, so keep it in a fairly
small pot with soil that drains very well.

Hyacinthus (Hyacinth)

GROWING TIPS   This plant is usually grown as a forced bulb. To keep
it as long as possible, give it good sunlight in daytime
and cool temperatures at night.

Hydrosme (Voodoo plant, snake palm, devil's tongue)

SYMPTOMS   *Plant smells bad* — You're right: it has an odor sometimes referred to as carrionlike. Not having smelled a
rotting body lately, I can't testify to the accuracy of
that description. However, the smell disappears in a
few days as the spathe (flower-like leaf) ages.

No leaves form before the flower appears — That's normal. The "flower," which is actually the strange spathe
(modified leaf), lasts several weeks. To get the leaf,
transplant into soil, keep moist, and feed often; a spectacularly large leaf that will last for many months will
then appear.

INSECT PESTS   Bulb pests. *Hydrosme* is one of the plants that growers
often advertise heavily; you just might be unlucky and
get an infested tuber. If nothing goes right from the
first, assume it's infested, give up, and throw it away.

GROWING TIPS   This strange plant grows from a tuber. Just put it in
water with the pointed side up. You need a large tuber
to have a large plant.

Hypocyrta (Goldfish plant, candy corn plant)

SEE *Nematanthus*

Hypoestes
sanguinolenta
(or phyllostachya) (Polka-dot plant, freckle face)

SYMPTOMS *Polka dots turn white* — Plant needs better light; give it sun — direct in winter but indirect in summer. The thin leaves can't take the heat of even protected south light in summer.

Stems wither; leaves turn yellow — Old parts do natu-

Hypoestes sanguinolenta
(polka-dot plant) that
has grown top-heavy and
straggly from failure to
pinch back frequently

rally. Just cut back and new growth will quickly appear at the base.

New leaves have no polka dots — Plant needs better light for pink to show.

Plant grows straggly — It certainly does! This is a profuse grower that will be top-heavy (dangerously so) in no time if you don't pinch stems back regularly during the growing season.

Stems won't root — Try rooting cuttings in wet sphagnum moss instead of water. Be sure to keep the humidity high by putting the cuttings inside a partly ventilated plastic bag.

INSECT PESTS Basically pest-free, unless mealybugs or spider mites are around on other plants.

Impatiens (Impatience, patient plant, patient Lucy, busy Lizzie, sultana)

SYMPTOMS *Leaves dry out and drop off* — This can happen from just about anything: humidity that's too low, drafts, soil dryness, insecticides, soil that's too wet, cold air (temperature should not be below 65° F.).

Stems grow limp — Humidity too low.

Clear crystal drops form on leaf edges and stems — That's a normal fluid exuded by the plant, but when the humidity is too low in a room with high temperature more of it becomes visible. Thus, you can use its presence as a clue to what else is troubling the plant.

Plant becomes straggly and overgrown — It's best to take cuttings each year for new plants.

Cuttings rot before they root — Although this plant needs constant moisture, fragile cuttings can't take sogginess. Keep the rooting medium just damp but the humidity high.

INSECT PESTS Spider mites, spider mites, and more spider mites — along with a shot of aphids and whitefly.

GROWING TIPS   If this plant is being healthy and growing normally (which, frankly, it doesn't do very easily in hot, dry houses), it grows abundantly. Feed lightly every week during growing season (which is most of the year) and pinch back frequently except when buds are visible.

Iresine herbstii (Bloodleaf, beefsteak plant, iresine)

SYMPTOMS   *Plant just doesn't grow well* — Bloodleaf must have good light, preferably direct sun, for energy to reach through the red pigmentation to the chlorophyll cells in the leaves.

Leaves dry out and curl — Humidity too low.

Leaves wilt — Too little water. Take care, because eventually the plant won't revive if it is allowed to suffer dryness very often. Because of the need for direct sun, you'll have to check the soil's water supply every day. (Take care, too, not to interpret the normal puckering of the leaf tips as wilting.)

Plant grows straggly — Too much encouragement from food. Feed with a low-nitrogen food and pinch back the stems often. Take cuttings every year for new plants.

Plant sheds leaves — That's normal for old plants, so keep them pinched back for fresh growth.

Stems droop over the pot rim — Old stems often do; pinch them back.

INSECT PESTS   Aphids, mealybugs, spider mites, scale.

GROWING TIPS   Use young plants for upright plants; use older ones in hanging pots. Keep the humidity as high as possible to prevent older stems from shedding their leaves and drooping.

Ixora (Ixora, flame-of-the-woods)

SYMPTOMS   *Leaves turn yellow and mushy* — Overwatering. This plant's soil must drain very well. Check the condition of the roots and repot if necessary.

Leaves turn light yellow with green veins — Chlorosis. *Ixora* needs an acidic soil in order to use iron. Feed with acid-type fertilizer or chelated iron.

New bloom is not abundant — Ixoras need a rest from sun and moisture after blooming in order to do well the next time. Cut back on water for several weeks: water only when leaves are nearly wilting. Then return the plant to normal existence, which includes full sun and high humidity.

INSECT PESTS   Mealybugs, spider mites, scale.

GROWING TIPS   The bigger the pot *Ixora* is in, the bigger the plant you will get — but watch out for the possibility of over-watering in large pots.

Jacaranda acutifolia (Jacaranda)

SYMPTOMS   *Leaves drop off* — That's normal in spring before buds appear.

Plant dies without warning — Temperature too high. Keep jacarandas in a cool location.

INSECT PESTS   Aphids, whitefly.

GROWING TIPS   *Jacaranda* is fairly tall but has a weak stem; stake the plant when it begins to get tall.

Kalanchoe (general) (Panda plant)

SYMPTOMS   *Stems grow elongated and weak, with leaves too small* — Not enough sun.

Succulent leaves turn discolored — Too much sun (although many kalanchoes' leaves turn harmlessly reddish in very bright light).

Cuttings won't root — They won't ever unless they happen to contain a dormant bud. Cut many pieces at once; let them dry a day or longer before inserting them in rooting medium.

Whitish coating forms on leaves — Mildew from humidity that's too high. Wash the plant thoroughly and move it to a drier place with good air circulation.

Dark, usually raised, spots form on leaves — Leaf-spot disease. Also can occur from poor circulation of air that's too humid.

Plant dies unexpectedly — Did you fertilize the plant's dry soil? The roots of kalanchoes can't take such a shock. Never feed unless the soil is damp, and even then use a weak solution.

INSECT PESTS   Mealybugs, ground mealybugs, spider mites, scale. *Do not use* malathion or nicotine sulfate. *Never* spray an aerosol directly at a kalanchoe. With all these Don'ts, it is a very good idea to bathe the plant frequently to help prevent pests.

GROWING TIPS   Use a low-nitrogen-content fertilizer.

SEE ALSO   *Kalanchoe blossfeldiana*

Kalanchoe blossfeldiana (Christmas kalanchoe)

SYMPTOMS   *Leaves turn yellow and squishy* — Overwatering. Kalanchoe needs less water during blossoming than most plants do. Remember, it's a succulent.

GROWING TIPS   This is usually given as a flowering gift plant. To get it to bloom again, cut off faded flowers and prune stems back quite severely. Keep in indirect light and let the soil get fairly dry between waterings. Then, in the fall, you must follow a special day-night schedule: the plant needs about fourteen hours of *total* darkness each night for about eight weeks. Do not feed the plant during this period. About December first resume normal treatment. You should have new flowers for Christmas; however, you don't have to do any of the special stuff except be kind to the plant to get blossoms in early spring (about March) when they normally occur.

SEE ALSO   *Kalanchoe* (general)

Lantana camara   (Lantana)

SYMPTOMS   *Plant grows straggly with no flowers* — Probably over-fertilized. Leach soil by running water through the pot for several minutes. Then feed lightly, perhaps only once a month.

Plant won't bloom — It must have good light. Don't bother with this tricky plant if you can't give it full sun; it is so prone to whitefly and spider mites that it isn't worth bothering with otherwise.

Flowers drop off easily — Don't ever move the plant once buds have set.

INSECT PESTS   Persistent whitefly and spider mites; also mealybugs.

GROWING TIPS   Pinch back after blooming to keep flowers returning later.

Laurus   (Sweet bay, laurel)

SYMPTOMS   *Leaves turn crisp; stems collapse* — Temperature too warm, and underwatering. Keep laurel in cool location (never above 70° F.), with the soil just damp.

Leaves turn yellow — Overwatering. Check the drainage in the pot; do a root check for damage and repot if necessary.

INSECT PESTS   Mealybugs, scale.

GROWING TIPS   Prune back regularly both to control the plant and to have a continuous supply of young leaves for use in cooking.

Lithops (Lithops, living stone, stoneface)

SYMPTOMS *Plant rots and dies, leaving a pile of mush* — This easily happens. These exceedingly unplantlike plants are the epitome of "cactusness." They need water only when they start to shrivel, and then only a tiny bit, not a full drenching of the soil. In summer, when the "rocks" should be getting ready to bloom, you can water a bit more.

Stems grow up off the soil surface and eventually collapse — Not enough light. Living stones like to be parched in bright sun.

GROWING TIPS You must put your finger, or a dipstick, deep into the soil and make sure it is absolutely dry before rewatering. Never fertilize *Lithops*.

SEE ALSO cacti, desert

Mangifera indica (Mango)

NOTE Avoid the sap of this plant if you are allergic to poison ivy — mango is a close relative.

SYMPTOMS *Leaf edges turn dry and brittle* — Too little water.

Leaves develop a grayish, dustlike coating that spreads over their surfaces — A fungus from the soil being kept too wet. Wash fungus off; cut back on watering. Obviously, water balance is important for a mango — keep the soil moist but well draining.

INSECT PESTS Mealybugs, spider mites, scale, thrips.

GROWING TIPS Yes, you can grow this plant with seeds from grocery-store fruit, but don't look for charm or for new fruit . . . just enjoy growing it.

Maranta (Maranta, prayer plant, false arrowroot)

SYMPTOMS *Leaf tips and edges turn brown* — That's almost inevitable in our heated homes with their low humidity.

Maranta *(prayer plant)*
with brown leaf tips
from humidity that's too
low or other extreme
environmental factors

Prayer plants really need humidity levels of about 70 percent or more. Remember, their "praying" leaves fold upward each night to let water that has accumulated on them run down into the roots; so obviously, *Maranta's* natural environment is very humid. Feel free to trim off the damage with clean, sharp scissors, but maintain the pretty oval of the leaves. Actually, any extreme environmental factor will make a prayer plant develop brown tips — too much cold, soil that's too wet, drafts, too much light, whatever.

Leaves develop dark spots that spread from the tips toward the bases — Anthracnose. Humidity is too high; improve the air circulation.

INSECT PESTS   Quite susceptible to spider mite. Wash the entire plant frequently. If necessary, use Kelthane or a similar spray; then keep the humidity high to prevent return of the spider mites. Also, if there are mealybugs loose anywhere in your home, *Maranta* is likely to be attacked. Mealybugs may be difficult to spot because new prayer-plant leaves spend considerable time furled like an umbrella before they open: mealybugs can hide inside the furl, doing unseen damage. *Do not use* dimethoate (Cygon) on prayer plants; it distorts the growth.

Marantas need a winter rest in order to keep glowing the rest of the year. Cut way back on water (which should be given stingily anyway, to prevent brown tips) for several weeks in winter — just keep the plant from wilting.

When removing dead leaves, use scissors, not brute force; stems are quite strong and tugging on them is apt to pull out the roots.

SEE ALSO *Calathea makoyana, Calathea zebrina* (which are closely related)

Marica (Apostle plant, twelve apostles, fan iris)

SEE *Neomarica*

Mimosa pudica (Sensitive plant, humble plant, touch-me-not, mimosa)

SYMPTOMS *Leaves' closing reaction when touched becomes sluggish* — You've probably been teasing the plant or showing off its party trick to friends too often: you've worn the poor thing out. Also, like the best of us (really, like all of us), it slows down as it gets older.

INSECT PESTS Mealybugs, spider mites, whitefly.

GROWING TIPS Sensitive plant doesn't really like being annoyed by its housemates, nor does it particularly like houses — but it is fun. Therefore, take advantage of the ease with which seeds can be sewn and grown. The older ones will probably just give up the ghost for no explained reason, so you might as well be prepared.

Don't overwater. It slows everything down and leads to an earlier demise than usual. Keep the soil moist but draining well.

Monstera
deliciosa
(Philodendron (Split-leaf philodendron, window-leaf
pertusum) philodendron, Swiss-cheese plant,
monstera, Mexican breadfruit, ceriman)

NOTE A potted *Monstera* is unlikely to develop the large
breadfruit for which this plant is grown in Mexico, but
if your plant does grow fruit (it tastes like a combination of banana and pineapple), *do not taste it before it
is fully ripe:* the immature fruit contains a tongue-
paralyzing chemical.

SYMPTOMS *Leaves (this plant's claim to fame) won't grow large and
won't split* — They probably are tolerating existence
in low-level light, where these plants are most often
grown just because they *do* at least tolerate it. Give the
plant some real sunshine (move it gradually) and you'll
be amazed at the growing it does. The leaves are more
likely to split, too, if there is plenty of moisture in the
air. Spray daily. Too low a temperature will also keep
a plant from doing its leaf-splitting thing; *Monstera*
likes warmth.

Leaves turn dry and drop off — If this occurs right
after moving the plant into your home, it means the
plant is having to work too hard at adjusting to the low
humidity. Spray often, and give it an extra-special bath
as frequently as you can (see photograph on page 91,
right). *However, please note:* Ceriman is prone to a
disfiguring fungus if you work too hard at keeping
moisture level up when there is inadequate air circulation. This plant is famed for its ability to reside in dark
corners, but don't make it accept many bad conditions
at once.

Leaf edges turn brown — This is a catastrophe on such
a large-leaved plant; it's probably caused by frequent
overwatering, too much heat, or, less probably, by too
much light. Trim the leaves after solving the problem.

Cuttings won't root — They need heat to help them
root. Place the cutting and its pot containing rooting

mixture high up near a ceiling, where heat accumulates; or on top of a refrigerator or other appliance that gives off some heat. A cutting that includes an aerial root is more likely to root than one without one.

INSECT PESTS   Mealybugs, spider mites, scale.

SEE ALSO   *Philodendron* (general)

Myrtus communis (Myrtle)

SYMPTOMS   *Plant becomes generally unhealthy, perhaps even collapses—* Probably overfed. Myrtle is a very slow grower and so cannot use more than the tiniest bit of fertilizer, perhaps as infrequently as once a year; otherwise, fertilizer accumulates until it poisons the soil. Leach the soil by running water through it for several minutes, or repot.

INSECT PESTS   Scale, thrips.

GROWING TIPS   This boxwood-like shrub will not survive long periods of excessive dry heat. Keep it in a cool place during the winter.

Narcissus (Narcissus)

NOTE   This plant basically offers a short-term bit of color from a forced bulb.

SYMPTOMS   *Buds blast (wither)* — Temperature too high.

More leaf than flower forms — Again, temperature too high. Narcissi will not do well if they are forced to live in rooms with temperature much above 70° F. If necessary, keep your early-spring bulbs on a coolish porch and bring them indoors only when the flowers have safely opened.

INSECT PESTS   Bulb pests such as the maggots of several bulb flies. Discard bulb.

Nautilocalyx (Nautilocalyx)

SYMPTOMS
Stems and leaves turn dry — Normal with aging for this gesneriad. Cut off the dried parts and they will soon be replaced by new, fresh growth.

GROWING TIPS
This gesneriad needs better light than most. It is also taller but has weak stems; stake them when necessary to prevent their collapse.

SEE ALSO
gesneriads (general)

Nematanthus (Hypocyrta) (Goldfish plant, candy corn plant)

SYMPTOMS
Leaves drop off — Dry soil. The soil must be kept damp, and the plant needs high humidity in order to stay healthy.

SEE ALSO
gesneriads (general)

Neomarica (Marica) (Apostle plant, twelve apostles, fan iris)

SYMPTOMS
Fragile flowers last only a day before dying — That's normal for this plant, but more will be along soon.

Plant won't bloom — In order to bloom, *Neomarica* needs to be ridiculously pot-bound and to have spent a period of semidormancy in winter, with cooler temperatures and less water than usual.

Leaf tips turn brown — Humidity too low. Keep the plant on a pebble tray and mist it daily.

INSECT PESTS
Basically pest-free.

GROWING TIPS
The fragile bloom that grows seemingly perched on midleaf is almost ethereal-looking — but it still adds weight to an already long, bending leaf. You may need to prop up the blossoming leaf to keep it in its graceful arch. (However, if you want, let the leaf bend to the soil and pin it down: it will take root and little plantlets will form.)

Neomarica should have cool (about 60° F.) nights in winter.

Neoregelia   (Fingernail plant, painted fingernail)

SYMPTOMS   *Central leaves turn orangish* — Don't panic: it's about to bloom.

Leaf color fades — This bromeliad must have several hours of direct sun each day for it to maintain its vivid color. Since its flower is less significant than that of other bromeliads, work to keep up the leaf color.

SEE ALSO   bromeliads (general)

Nephrolepsis exaltata   (Boston fern, fluffy ruffles, sword fern)

SYMPTOMS   *Leaflets turn yellow* — Bad drainage is probably keeping too much water in the soil. Unpot the plant, check the roots and the drainage, and repot properly.

Leaflets disappear almost overnight, leaving long, wiry stems — Those aren't really stems (and a fallen leaflet will not "disappear" of its own accord, anyway); they are living stolons — specialized reproductive stems that, given a chance, will reach out into other pots and take root. Do not break them off.

Fronds die off more rapidly than seems normal — If you've checked that the water and the drainage are all right, and you aren't keeping the plant too dry, check for drafts. Boston fern does not like air that circulates in gusts.

Whitish mold spreads over the fronds — Botrytis. (Treat as suggested in chapter 7.)

INSECT PESTS   Mealybugs, scale, whitefly.

GROWING TIPS   There's a tendency to place a Boston fern in a central position, where it gets attention but is also exposed to lots of traffic; bruised and broken fronds will not grow again, so be careful. Also, be sure to keep old fronds (as well as broken ones) trimmed off the plant so that the new ones can get as much light as possible.

If your Boston fern likes you and grows well for you, treasure your relationship. Many people seemingly do everything right and still have no success with these particular creatures.

SEE ALSO   ferns (general)

Nerium oleander   (Oleander)

NOTE   All parts of this plant are poisonous when ingested.

SYMPTOMS   *Plant won't bloom* — The plant must be cut back and given a rest after each blooming period in order for it to flower again. Also, buds won't form — or won't open, if they do form — if the soil ball is allowed to dry out.

Leaves develop spots — Oleander is quite prone to various leaf-spot fungi, including anthracnose and others. Keep air circulating well while keeping the humidity level high.

INSECT PESTS   Very vulnerable to scale, but also apt to catch mealybugs and leaf rollers. Be sure to give the plant frequent baths in order to keep pest possibilities to a minimum.

GROWING TIPS   To flower best, oleander needs to be quite tall. It's an ideal plant for a full-sun location such as a porch.

Nidularium   (Nidularium)

SEE   bromeliads (general)

Odontoglossum   (Odontoglossum)

SEE   orchids (general)

orchids (general)

Starting assumption — you are growing as house plants only those orchids that: (1) can stand the warmth of a house, (2) don't need much temperature drop at night, and (3) don't require the humidity of a greenhouse. These include *Cypripedium* with mottled leaves, *Phalaenopsis, Vanda, Cattleya, Odontoglossum,* and some *Dendrobium.*

SYMPTOMS *Young leaves turn yellow* — Too much light or temperature too low.

Leaves turn soft; new ones may be stunted — Not enough light.

Leaves and flowers develop spots — You've allowed the internal temperature of the plant to rise too high; be sure to use a shield on south-facing windows. The leaves should never be allowed to feel warm to the touch. In nature, orchids are quite protected from the sun's blast by trees. Spots may also be botrytis mold; make sure the air circulation around your orchids is good.

Rather large areas of leaves turn brown, then black — Sunburn. If the spots grow, they've been infected by a fungus. Cut out the spots and dust with fungicide. Reduce the environmental humidity.

Flower is misshapen — Too late: the air was too warm and dry when the bud was formed.

Flower dies quickly — Orchid flowers have great lasting power — *unless* the air is polluted or you move the plant enough to change its customary environment. Don't carry around the plant to show off the blossom.

Leaves develop dark green watery spots that turn brown — A bacterial disease called brown spot. Wipe the spots with mercuric-chloride solution (mix 1 part chemical to 1000 parts water).

INSECT PESTS Aphids, spider mites, mealybugs, scale, thrips. *Do not use* malathion or metaldehyde on orchids. Keep leaves and stems wiped with a wet cloth.

GROWING TIPS   The soilless medium in which orchids grow should be fertilized at least every two weeks with a weak food, such as 3-1-1 (plants potted in Osmunda fiber, however, don't need food). Never let the material dry out completely, except for cattleyas, which like an occasional drying period. Because the medium decomposes after a while, be prepared to transplant. You may need to soak the old pot to free roots that have adhered to it.

Orchids bloom best if they spend the summer outdoors, protected from direct sun, perhaps suspended from the branches of a tree. Repot when you bring them indoors, and dip the whole plant and pot in fungicide solution.

Osmanthus (False holly, sweet olive)

SYMPTOMS   *Leaves fall in great numbers* — That's all right if it occurs in late winter (about February or March): it means the plant is going dormant for a few weeks. Cut way back on watering and leaves will soon reappear. The sweet olive is most unlikely to lose its leaves otherwise, because it is generally a trouble-free plant.

GROWING TIPS   Keep the plant pot-bound to encourage its flowers to appear all year.

Oxalis (Wood sorrel, grandmother's shamrock)

SYMPTOMS   *Leaf parts close* — They often do so normally at night. But if they close during the day, the plant is unhappy about something — probably lack of water or low humidity (closing the leaves together conserves the moisture in them).

Plant stops blooming — It needs a rest, after having been faithful most of the year. Repot the plant in fresh soil; cut the stems to about half their normal length. The plant will soon regrow with new vigor.

INSECT PESTS   Very vulnerable to spider mites; also gets mealybugs and aphids. *Oxalis* may seem to die if sprayed with insecticides such as Kelthane, but it will come back with strong new growth if allowed to be cool and dormant for a few weeks.

GROWING TIPS *Oxalis* is a very active plant — lots of flowers, lots of new leaves; groom the plant often to keep it tidy and healthy. Remove all old leaves and blossoms as they stop looking their best.

palms (general)

NOTE In addition to those listed under SEE ALSO, palms include *Chamaerops humilis* and *Chrysalidocarpus lutescens*.

SYMPTOMS *Leaflet tips turn brown* — Humidity too low, along with temperature too high. Palms all depend for their charm on clean-looking, pristine leaflets kept in glowing health. A raggedy palm looks somehow worse than almost any other plant. You may also have let the soil get completely dry — an absolute no-no with palms. Correct the situation and trim off the damaged tips.

Entire older fronds gradually turn yellow, then brown, and die — Too much water. Check that the pot drains well and rewater the plant only enough to keep the soil moist, not soggy. If possible, check the condition of the roots for rot. Fronds can also turn yellow from too little water; soak the whole pot in water for perhaps half an hour to get moisture deep into the heart of the soil ball.

You'll have gathered by now that there is a fine line between the wrong and right amounts of water for an indoor palm. However, the potential damage caused by improper watering can be lessened if you keep the humidity high and the temperature coolish. You might also try keeping the plant in a plastic pot.

Lower fronds die back — There's probably not enough light available for the whole plant to get the sun it needs. Gradually move the plant to a brighter location.

Youngest leaves turn yellow — Probably a lack of iron.

Palms need a slightly acidic soil in order to use the iron in their food. Use an acid-type food every second or third feeding.

Leaves develop spots — Palms are subject to anthracnose and other leaf-spot fungus diseases. Keep the air circulating around them and avoid chilling the plants. Cut out damaged spots and dust plants with fungicide.

INSECT PESTS   Aphids, mealybugs, spider mites, scale, thrips, nematodes. Palms are very vulnerable to red spider mite particularly. Be sure to keep the humidity high to prevent their attack.

GROWING TIPS   Never give palms direct sunlight or let them be in drafts. A well-grown palm will begin to lift from its pot because of new roots, but if all else is healthy, don't move it to a larger pot: that way lies the danger of overwatering.

SEE ALSO   *Caryota mitis, Chamaedorea elegans bella, Howea, Phoenix roebelenii*

Pandanus veitchii (Screw pine, pandanus)

SYMPTOMS   *Aerial-root growth turns the plant unattractive and awkward-looking* — Congratulations, you've managed to grow an old plant. (Most people fail to keep theirs growing long enough to let them get old.) Start anew from cuttings or by separating the mature (six-inch) suckers from the mother plant.

New leaves develop solid green colors (instead of the pretty white stripes for which you bought the plant) — Too little water. The soil should be allowed to dry just a bit between waterings, and when you do rewater, be thorough. Dryness also causes leaf tips to turn an irrevocable brown.

Leaves develop spots — Screw pine is vulnerable to fungal spotting if the humidity is kept too high. Unfortunately, you'll need to cut out the damaged spots and dust the plant with fungicide. Keep air circulating well around the plant.

INSECT PESTS   This is basically a pestless plant, but it might succumb to spider mites if the air is kept too dry.

GROWING TIPS   The development of aerial roots occurs near the base of the plant; given time, these aerial roots can virtually lift the plant out of the soil. Repot when this starts to happen.

Passiflora caerulea   (Passion flower)

SYMPTOMS   *Flowers drop off* — Humidity is not high enough.

No flowers form — Passion flower must have good sun and warmth to bloom.

Leaves develop dark, dry-centered spots — Anthracnose. Keep the air circulating well to prevent fungi from breeding in the high humidity.

INSECT PESTS   Mealybugs, scale.

GROWING TIPS   *Passiflora* passionately wraps its climbing tendrils around anything, including itself. Take care that it doesn't get its clutches on neighboring plants; give it some supports to grab instead.

Pelargonium   (Geranium, pelargonium)

SYMPTOMS   *Leaves turn yellow* — Overwatering. The soil should be allowed to dry some (but *never* let it dry out) before rewatering thoroughly. Too little light can also turn leaves yellow.

Leaves turn crinkled and mottled, with yellow veins — A virus disease. There is no cure. Destroy the affected plants at once.

Leaves develop small watery patches that turn into brown sunken spots — Bacterial leaf-spot disease. Clean the room around your plants thoroughly and keep them spread apart for good air circulation. Discard affected plants and spray others with an antibiotic.

Translucent swellings form on leaves — Edema, probably from too high a humidity level. Don't water or mist *Pelargonium* on sunless days — and never water unless the soil has partially dried.

Plant forms many leaves but no flowers — Too much nitrogen in the soil; use a low-nitrogen fertilizer. Make sure the plant is pot-bound. Give it full sun in the daytime and cool temperature (at least a ten-degree-Fahrenheit drop) at night.

Stems turn black and mushy — Stem rot disease (also called blackleg). You may have gathered by now that geraniums are quite vulnerable to diseases; this one makes the plant not worth trying to save. Take clean cuttings (use absolutely sterile tools or the disease will just spread) and discard the old plant. Promise never to let the new plants sit in soggy soil.

Leaves wilt — First check the roots to be sure they aren't mushy with root rot from being overwatered. If they're firm, the problem may be a temporary afternoon one of too much sun, and the leaves will straighten up in the evening.

Gray, dusty spots coat the leaves — Botrytis mold from too high a humidity level and too little air circulation. Increase air movement, spray with a fungicide such as Benlate, Benomyl, Captan, or Fermate, and always remove old flower stalks as soon as blooming has subsided: they are a breeding ground for mold.

INSECT PESTS   Almost inevitably whitefly, plus mealybugs, aphids, spider mites. *Beware of using* dimethoate (Cygon): your plants may react unfavorably.

GROWING TIPS   Don't mist plants that are budding or flowering — they rot too easily. To keep cuttings from rotting before rooting, use a rooting hormone containing fungicide. In addition, root your cuttings in a solid medium instead of water: they will produce stronger plants.

After all this, why not consider leaving geraniums outdoors — except perhaps for *Pelargonium crispum* (lemon-leaved geranium) and the other geraniums with scented leaves that add a lovely fragrance to your home when you crush them.

Pellaea (Button fern, cliff brake)

SYMPTOMS *Leaflets turn crisp and dry* — The soil has been allowed to dry out.

Leaf fronds turn brown and die — General dryness — and because ferns are generally ornery. Cut the "dead" fronds back to the soil and fresh growth should soon appear.

GROWING TIPS This fern spreads by sending out flat growth along the ground; give it lots of room.

SEE ALSO ferns (general)

Peperomia (Peperomia, pepperface)

NOTE Peperomias are my selection for the hardiest attractive plants you can grow in your home. It is very unusual to have trouble with them. However . . .

SYMPTOMS *Leaves drop off; stem gets squishy near the base* — Overwatering and constant, long-term soil sogginess (it must be constant, because peperomias generally don't react quickly to such mistreatment). Don't even bother to try to save the plant; take cuttings and root them in a rooting medium — or even in the soil where you want them to remain: they take hold very quickly.

Leaves develop spots — Peperomias are subject to the various fungal spots, including anthracnose. Keep the plant out of drafts and keep the air circulating.

If there are definite rings around the spots, or just rings on the leaves, the problem is probably a virus called ring spot. Take clean cuttings for rooting in a sterile medium and discard the remainder of the plant.

INSECT PESTS Basically pest-free, but may get aphids, spider mites, or mealybugs. Rejoice in its essential pestlessness because you must *avoid using* almost all pesticides — especially carbaryl (Sevin), dimethoate, Kelthane, and malathion. They can produce distorted growth.

GROWING TIPS Varieties with light markings on the leaves need more light than the north light that plain green ones can

Peperomia obtusifolia *(peperomia) with leaf spots, probably from too much moisture, both in the soil and in the air*

take. Emerald ripple *(Peperomia caperata)* requires a little more water than the others do.

Persea americana (Avocado, persea)

NOTE Yes, there is indeed a house plant inside the seed of every avocado you buy in the grocery store. But don't feel that you have to grow a plant from every avocado you eat. If you do everything right — or if you're just plain lucky — you may have an avocado plant for fourteen or fifteen years (although it's quite unlikely that it will ever bear fruit while it is growing indoors).

SYMPTOMS *Seed won't root* — Mainly patience is required. I had
one that took four months to produce roots from the
center of the big seed. Be sure that in the waiting time
water is never allowed to drop below the somewhat flat
bottom of the seed. Remember, too, that you needn't
wait for just that specific seed to root unless it has some
particular sentimental value for you: a different one
might root in just a few weeks. Try rooting several
avocados — the effect is much prettier if several plants
are potted together, anyway. As for your other questions:

   · No, it doesn't matter whether you leave the
brown peeling on the seed or gently remove it.

   · Yes, you can start the plant in soil instead of
water; you will, in fact, get a much hardier plant as a
result — especially if its potted in an absurdly large six-
or seven-inch pot. On the other hand, most of the
delight of this plant lies in watching it root — which
rooting in soil prevents. (You pays your money, you
eats your avocado, and you takes your choice.)

   · No, every avocado plant doesn't have to consist of
one out-of-sight stem with a few leaves perched on the
top. After the stem has grown perhaps eight or ten
inches, cut it back ruthlessly to two or three inches in
length. New growth will be lower and fuller. Also, you
can split the stem straight down the middle with a
clean, sharp knife to get the stem to branch.

Leaf edges turn brown — That's almost inevitable
owing to low humidity levels in our houses. Leaf
edges also turn brown from becoming too hot in direct sun, or from not having continuous moisture in
their pot. You'll generally get bleaching of leaves and
grayish scorch marks on leaves that have had too
much sun.

INSECT PESTS Along with its other problems, *Persea* is vulnerable to
aphids, mealybugs, scale, thrips, and whitefly. Why
even bother to try to correct the situation if they get
infested? Just do what you can to protect other plants
nearby and start new avocados from fruit seeds.

Phalaenopsis (Butterfly orchid, moth orchid, phalaenopsis)

SEE orchids (general)

Philodendron (general) (Philodendron)

NOTE This most popular of house plants is generally trouble-free except for the one trouble we inflict on it ourselves.

SYMPTOMS *Leaves turn yellow and drop off* — Overwatering or underwatering. Be sure to let the soil get just slightly dry before rewatering thoroughly. In order to help, too, you can keep philodendrons in smallish pots, although a plant kept too pot-bound for too long can develop brown leaf edges. Keep in mind also that the less light there is, the less water there should be.

New growth is spindly; new leaves are sparse and very small — Not enough light. Gradually move plant to a brighter location; pinch back stems to encourage fuller growth. *Philodendron oxycardium* (sweetheart vine or common philodendron) changes character completely depending on the amount of light it receives.

Leaves curl under; tips may turn brown — Humidity too low. Mist often.

Little brown growths develop along the stem — Those are normal aerial roots. Do not remove them — just keep them damp, and when taking cuttings be sure to include aerial roots for quickest growth.

INSECT PESTS Generally pest-free, but may get mealybugs and spider mites, and perhaps scale. Millipedes or symphylans that sneak into the house may be attracted to philodendrons. In treating for insects, *do not use* dimethoate (Cygon): it can distort new growth.

GROWING TIPS All philodendrons benefit from being misted except *P. selloum,* the tree, or saddle-leaf, philodendron; its leaves disintegrate into mush when subjected to too much water in the soil or the air.

SEE ALSO *Monstera deliciosa (Philodendron pertusum), Scindapsus aureus (Epipremnum aureum)* — which are closely related

Philodendron pertusum

SEE *Monstera deliciosa*

Phoenix roebelenii (Pygmy date palm)

SYMPTOMS
No fruit forms — There won't be any unless you have both male and female plants and they are at least four or five years old.

GROWING TIPS
Grow the plant in a pot that seems too small.

SEE ALSO
palms (general)

Pilea cadierei (Aluminum plant)
P. microphylla (Artillery plant)

SYMPTOMS
Leaves develop brown edges and rusty spots — Too much fertilizer or salt buildup in the pot. Either leach the soil by running water through it for several minutes or repot the plant in fresh soil and a clean pot.

Leaves develop spots — Fungal problems, from keeping the atmosphere too humid with inadequate air circulation or from overwatering. The aluminum plant's soil can take a drying out every four or five waterings.

Plant grows generally shaggy — It's overgrown. Pinch out growing tips of stems frequently to keep growth compact.

INSECT PESTS
Mealybugs, spider mites. *Do not use* carbaryl (Sevin), diazinon, dimethoate (Cygon), or malathion on these plants: they can easily distort new growth.

GROWING TIPS
The artillery plant tends to be dressed in tiny browned leaves if the humidity is too low or the temperature too

high. If the condition gets very bad, prune the branches back and let the plant get a new start.

Pittosporum tobira (Pittosporum, Australian laurel)

SYMPTOMS
Leaves curl under — Probably underwatering, or at least inconsistent watering. The soil should be allowed to just dry between waterings.

Leaves develop spots — Probably a leaf-spot fungus, from keeping humidity too high in noncirculating air. *Pittosporum* does like high humidity — its absence will make leaf tips turn brown, and perhaps the leaf edges will turn lighter in color — but balance is important and good air circulation is vital to the prevention of fungus. Cut out the spots and dust the plant with fungicide.

Plant won't bloom — Probably not enough light. *Pittosporum* is frequently recommended as a good foliage plant for low-level light, but it can't be expected always to form its pretty, white, jasminelike flowers in low light.

INSECT PESTS
Aphids, spider mites, mealybugs, scale. You may first discover pests by noting the presence of lots of sticky, glossy honeydew on the leathery leaves.

GROWING TIPS
In order to keep the humidity high, grow the plant in a cool location and keep it pruned to stay small. *Pittosporum* easily becomes too large — impossible to keep moist. Remember, too, that dry air enhances the chances of attack by red spider mites. The plant benefits from a short resting period in winter, when its soil (which needs to be acidic) should be allowed to dry even more than usual for a few weeks.

Platycerium (Staghorn fern)

SYMPTOMS
The smooth, glossy fronds continually die back — Probably heat, especially drafty heat. This fern doesn't like lots of hot air. Is the plant near a radiator or other

Platycerium
*(staghorn fern) with
dry, browning fronds
from inconsis-
tent watering*

heat source? Dry central heating and the staghorn are not naturally compatible. You have to work at keeping the plant healthy.

Fronds turn brown and dry — Too much sun or inconsistent watering. Staghorn fern has thicker fronds than many ferns, so it doesn't need the constant water supply that others do — but it can't cope with inconsistency in watering. If you have the plant in soil, let it dry between waterings; if you grow it in moss or fiber on a wall bracket, be sure to be faithful about taking it down and remoistening the roots.

GROWING TIPS   When grown in pots, *Platycerium* may need to be watered from the bottom, because a second type of frond — called a shield, or basal, frond — may cover the soil surface. Rather than regularly disturb the shield fronds, fill the pot's saucer with water instead.

SEE ALSO   ferns (general)

Plectranthus (Swedish ivy)

SYMPTOMS   *Growth almost stops after many exuberant months* — That's a quite normal tendency for an older plant. Take cuttings and start new plants; they will root easily and soon have all the exuberance of your old friend.

Leaves turn brown and wither — Underwatering. The soil must be kept moist at all times. Swedish ivy is really quite amiable about its care so long as it has enough water.

New leaves are small and pale — Plant needs more light and food. Swedish ivy's sheer eagerness to grow makes it more greedy than many other plants.

Little translucent blisters form on the leaves — Edema, indicating that the plant's humidity or water supply or both have been kept too abundant in non-circulating air.

Plant won't bloom — Many Swedish ivy plants won't ever bloom, but you might give yours encouragement by feeding with a high-phosphorus-content fertilizer. Keep the plant's soil evenly moist and the humidity high and constant.

INSECT PESTS   Basically a pest-free plant, but keep an eye out for mealybugs.

GROWING TIPS   Swedish ivy, one of the most popular house plants in recent years, is especially useful for growing as a hanging specimen. Keep stems pinched back for full growth.

Pleomele (Song of India)

SYMPTOMS   *Leaf tips turn brown* — Dry air and soil. Spray regularly and keep the soil evenly moist.

INSECT PESTS   A pest-free plant. Enjoy it.

GROWING TIPS   This plant uncannily resembles a dracaena, and some people classify it as such, but it's much easier to care for. If you're not the world's most faithful plant attendant, you might be safer with *Pleomele* than with the plants more commonly called dracaena.

SEE ALSO   *Dracaena* (general)

Podocarpus macrophylla (Southern yew, African pine, podocarp)

SYMPTOMS
Leaf tips turn brown — You've let the soil dry out. Don't.

Newest growth is yellowish — Probably lack of iron. *Podocarpus* is an acid-loving plant and needs to be fed occasionally with an acid-type fertilizer in order for the iron it receives to be used. If feeding with acid-type food doesn't soon correct the situation, give the plant a dose of chelated iron.

Plant looks generally unhappy: it's got spots, curling leaves, and all sorts of other things wrong — It's too warm. This treelike plant prefers its days at less than 70° F., and its nights need a fling with real coolness. At least help it out by turning the thermostat down at night and making sure that hot air from a blower or radiator is not directed at the plant.

INSECT PESTS
Aphids, spider mites, scale, nematodes. *Do not use* dimethoate (Cygon): it can produce distorted leaves.

GROWING TIPS
Podocarpus needs to be pruned regularly to keep it full and attractive. As the tree gets tall, you may need to prop the main stem.

Polypodium (Polypodium)

INSECT PESTS
More vulnerable to scale than most ferns.

GROWING TIPS
This fern is considerably less trouble than most other ferns. Its soil can even be allowed to dry, although if forced to endure extremes of dryness, it won't endure. One problem: because of the denseness with which leaflets grow, air does not circulate well between the growth, making the plant prone to fungus problems. Air the plant as often as possible and don't let humidity get too high if you keep it near other ferns that demand more moisture.

SEE ALSO
ferns (general)

Polyscias balfouriana (Balfour aralia)

SYMPTOMS *Older (lower) leaves drop off in one dramatic swoop —* You've either just brought the plant home or you have moved the plant, even just a bit: it is reacting violently to the change in environment. If you must move your *Polyscias,* give it all the sympathetic help you can. For some days before a move (even just from one room into another) cover the plant with a plastic bag so that it can have high humidity. After the move, leave the bag on for several more days, and then gradually open and remove it, letting the plant adjust to its new surroundings slowly. Never feed the plant until has it completed the adjustment.

INSECT PESTS Spider mites, scale.

GROWING TIPS Anything it dislikes will make this plant shed leaves. Keep its soil moist but draining well, its light bright but not necessarily direct, and its humidity as high as you can without having to devote all day to misting it.

Portulacaria afra (Elephant bush, miniature jade tree)

SYMPTOMS *Leaves shrivel —* Underwatering. The instant you see its leaves start to gather into themselves protectively, water thoroughly. (But don't make a habit of drowning the plant, either.)

Leaves turn yellow and drop off — Probably overwatering. Make sure that the roots aren't rotting; then water only enough to keep the soil moist: perhaps let the top of the soil just begin to dry.

INSECT PESTS This plant is basically pest-free.

GROWING TIPS Have patience when trying to root this slow-growing plant; cuttings may sit for a long time before taking hold. Be sure to use a fungicidal rooting hormone.

Pteris (Table fern, brake fern, ribbon fern)

SYMPTOMS
Leaves turn crisp — You've probably let the soil dry out (see photograph on page 78). You can repair most damage to *Pteris* by cutting back the fronds to the soil level and letting new ones grow.

GROWING TIPS
This is one of the easier ferns to grow indoors because the humidity need not be kept above about 40 percent, a level fairly easy to maintain indoors.

SEE ALSO
ferns (general)

Punica granatum nana (Dwarf pomegranate)

SYMPTOMS
Leaves wilt — You've let the soil dry out. Pomegranate is not a forgiving plant and it may well die as a result of having its soil dry out even once. If you are consistently good to it after letting it dry out, you may get a new set of leaves to develop, but don't count on it.

Plant won't flower — Dwarf pomegranate needs at least four hours a day of direct sun. Keep the plant from getting too hot during the day and let the temperature drop to about 60° F. at night. Obviously, you have to work at getting *Punica* to bloom.

INSECT PESTS
Aphids, mealybugs, spider mites, scale, whitefly.

GROWING TIPS
Don't let a new plant (under four inches) flower: it's too weak. Pinch off the flower buds until the plant reaches five or six inches.

Rhododendron Simsii (Azalea)

NOTE
This is basically a flowering gift plant. To keep it as long as possible indoors, remove the gift-wrap foil. Give the plant bright light, preferably with some direct sun (but not at noon, when the temperature rises).

Water daily and mist with water every time you look at it. At night place the azalea in a location where the temperature drops at least fifteen degrees Fahrenheit (a must for maintaining bloom), and feed with an acid-type fertilizer about every two weeks.

SYMPTOMS *Leaves yellow and drop off* — Plant needs more water.

Leaves yellow and cling to stems — Plant needs iron: feed with an acid-type fertilizer so it can use the iron in its food.

INSECT PESTS Spider mites, scale, thrips, whitefly. *Do not use* dimethoate (Cygon).

GROWING TIPS If you repot a gift azalea, you'll finally get an opportunity to use the short plant container called an azalea pot. However, the rigid requirements (such as several weeks at cold temperatures) for getting the plant to bloom a second year are such that you might as well discard it.

Rhoeo spathacea (or discolor) (Moses-in-the-cradle, boat lily, Moses-in-a-boat)

SYMPTOMS *Flowers last only a day* — That's normal (and the blossoms aren't all that interesting while they are there). The problem in getting the right light balance for *Rhoeo* is that sun can easily char the plant, but it nevertheless needs as much light as possible in order to bloom. It stays interesting and pretty, though, in less than full sun.

Leaf tips turn brown — Humidity too low. It's difficult to keep up the air moisture in the full sun required for blooming.

INSECT PESTS Basically pest-free, but beware if mealybugs are around.

GROWING TIPS *Rhoeo* needs to be kept in moist soil, and it will happily reside in a larger pot than seems necessary.

Rosa chinensis minima (Miniature rose)

NOTE Roses blooming furiously indoors are a glorious sight to behold, but unfortunately roses indoors are prone to just about all the ills that outdoor roses are heir to, as well as an additional one: suffering from humidity that's too low.

SYMPTOMS *Leaves drop off* — They certainly do, for just about everything, but primarily owing to dryness and shock. If you need to transplant the rose, plan to let it live in a plastic bag for several days before and after. As a matter of fact, whenever conditions of sun, constant soil moisture, and high humidity are threatened in some fashion, pull out the plastic bags and drape them protectively over your miniature roses.

Leaves turn yellow and drop off — Probably spider mite, an annoyingly frequent visitor to indoor roses. Look closely for their webs. To keep your other plants safe, you probably should isolate infested roses. Change the miticide you use often, because spider mites easily build up resistance to any insecticide used repeatedly.

Leaves turn yellow and drop off in autumn — Probably normal leaf drop. Keep the plants in a cool place and the soil almost painfully dry until new growth starts. Be sure you prune back severely after the last summer blossoms have faded.

Leaves develop blackspot — Like their outdoor relatives, indoor roses are apt to develop fungus-caused blackspot whenever they've been wet and not allowed to dry properly. Don't water your plants unless they have at least six hours to dry off before nightfall. Don't mist the plants directly: the moisture is too easily trapped and turned into a fungus. Dust regularly with Benomyl or another fungicide suitable for indoor use.

Leaves curl and develop a grainy white coating — Powdery mildew. Treat with Karathane, Benlate, or Benomyl, and keep the air circulating around the plants.

Spider mites, spider mites, and their friends, the spider mites (see photograph on page 139). Also, leaf rollers and thrips, if they happen to be around.

GROWING TIPS Rose roots need air but must never be allowed to dry out. When you get your roses (probably from a mail-order firm), soak the roots in water for at least twenty-four hours before planting them so that the roots are already actively working when put in soil. Don't use plastic pots for roses: they prevent air from reaching the plant roots.

Because roses so readily pick up any fungus that's around, keep your plants sparkling clean. Remove all dead leaves the instant you see them; clip off old blossoms; keep the pebble tray sterile.

Saintpaulia ionantha (African violet)

NOTE Don't panic and give up on African violets when you see the rather long list of possible problems that follows: its length just means that many people have closely observed these pretty plants. African violets (see photographs on page 167) can't get away with anything unusual without being analyzed and diagnosed. If you don't have problems, read through the list and rejoice that you don't have to use it; if you do, be happy to know that you're not alone.

SYMPTOMS *You do everything seemingly right and still your African violets aren't happy — Che sera sera.* I'm firmly convinced that African violets just take to some people and not to others. Don't take it personally if you're one of the "others." Try growing some other gesneriads; many are just as attractive without being so picky.

Ringlike spots, usually yellow, form on leaves — You've watered with cold water. Long thought to be caused by getting water on the leaves, these rings once caused many growers to insist on watering from below.

But it turned out to be the water/air temperature differential that was critical: the water must be at room temperature or slightly warmer.

Leaves are dirty but someone told you washing causes ring spots — See the preceding entry and feel free to wash your plant's leaves, but with room-temperature water and great gentleness: violet leaves are very brittle. Be sure they dry (but not in direct sun) before nightfall.

Leaves in the center of the crown bunch together tightly — If accompanied by yellowing leaves, too much light. If leaves don't yellow, probably too much fertilizer; wash out the soil by running water through it for several minutes, then temper your generosity.

Leaves curl and droop limply over the pot rim — Root rot from letting the soil dry and then vigorously overwatering, probably several times. Remove the plant from pot and soil. Inspect it thoroughly to see if there is a good center section to the leaf crown along with undamaged roots. If there is, cut off all the squishy part, dust with fungicide, and repot the good portion; if there isn't, find one or two unharmed leaves you can root and discard the rest.

Leaf stems turn brown and mushy — This happens from stems rubbing on the unglazed pot rim. These sensitive plants need to be protected. Rub the rim with candle wax or paraffin or cover it with soft tape or plastic.

Leaves turn dry, crinkled, and mottled with two tones of green — A virus. Discard the affected plants.

New leaves are small and don't get larger; older leaves turn downward and are bleached out, especially at the edges — Too much light.

Leaves stand up instead of lying flat — Not enough light, or conditions that are too crowded. African violets need room around them, both for vanity's sake and health.

Leaves curl and lose their color — Probably too cool.

African violets (like other gesneriads) are among the few plants that don't like a nighttime drop in temperature. They can't survive many nights below 65° F. (Also, check closely for the possibility of spider mite when leaves curl.)

Leaves curl under and turn woody; leaf edges may turn brown — Accumulation of fertilizer salts in the pot. Leach by running water through the pot for several minutes, or repot in fresh soil and a clean pot. Remember, African violets do best in plastic pots, which don't show encrusted salts as clay pots do. Try changing the fertilizer occasionally, too. Leaves also turn hard when a plant with dry roots is fertilized. Feed only when the soil is already damp.

Leaves lose their crispness — Too much water. Start checking for root and crown rot.

Variegated leaf colors become blurry — Probably too warm. Keep variegated plants on the cool side (perhaps around 65° F.) for best color and use a low-nitrogen fertilizer.

Large old leaves turn yellow — Normal aging; just pinch them off at the soil level.

Many leaves turn yellow, some wither; flower buds dry up — Too little humidity. Keep air moisture level as high as possible, but don't mist plants with cold water.

Leaves develop a whitish or gray velvety coating — Powdery mildew caused by high humidity in noncirculating air. Wash the leaves; remove any that are damaged; dust with fungicide. Check all other nearby plants.

Stems turn dark with stem rot and flowers don't last — Probably botrytis mold. See chapter 7.

Plant stands up from the soil on a thickened stem — A thick stem called the neck develops naturally on an old plant. Repot the plant, dropping it lower in the soil (unlike most other plants, *Saintpaulia* doesn't mind having its soil level changed); or cut off the crown and

Saintpaulia ionantha *(African violet) with no flowers but lots of leaves. It probably needs more light and a little less water.*

root it anew in fresh soil (hold the plant in place with paper clips).

No flowers form — First check that you're not doing anything grossly wrong, then consult a neighbor who has had success with his or her African violets. Ask the following questions:

· Has the plant put all its effort into leaves and become too large? Remove it from the pot, cut apart separate leaf crowns, and repot them separately.

· Is the plant hungry? Feed with African violet fertilizer that encourages blossoming.

· Is humidity too low? Increase the humidity level to at least 50 percent. Keep a glass of water among your plants; mist often; use a pebble tray — but make sure that air circulates well. Do not keep a lot of African-violet plants close together: that encourages fungus.

· Does the plant get enough sun? *Saintpaulia* usually doesn't need lots — but it does prefer some direct, or at least very bright, light.

· Are the leaves dirty? A layer of dust can quite effectively prevent the leaves from using the sun that does hit them.

· How long have you had the plant? New ones need a period to adjust to the environment you provide. (And don't keep moving your plants around.)

- Are the roots snug? African violets prefer to be slightly pot-bound before blooming.
- Is temperature consistently too high? African violets do like warmth — but day after day of 80° F. or above is unhealthy.

Flowers of different colors form on the same plant — The new hybrids may not be stable; usually only those hybrids that are stable remain on the market for any length of time. Select old favorites.

INSECT PESTS Cyclamen mites (which cause dwarfed, distorted leaves), mealybugs, spider mites (which cause curling leaves), thrips, ground mealybugs, nematodes. Some people recommend a monthly spraying with Kelthane. *Do not use* malathion (Cythion), diazinon, or dimethoate (Cygon); they can distort your plants.

SEE ALSO gesneriads (general)

Sansevieria (Snake plant, mother-in-law's tongue)

NOTE Despite the items below, a generally trouble-free plant.

SYMPTOMS *Leaves are scarce and too long —* When you want a fuller plant, give more sun and fertilize frequently to encourage the growth of new shoots. This is a plant that tolerates dark corners very well, but it really needs some bright light for growth.

Leaves collapse at the base — Crown rot, probably from overwatering. This condition is rare, but it is lethal if it occurs. Retrieve the undamaged leaves and clean away all damaged roots. Repot in well-draining soil and a tight-fitting pot and promise never to overwater again; snake plant needs only enough water to prevent the thick leaves from shriveling.

Round, possibly yellow-rimmed, spots appear on the leaves — Leaf-spot disease, caused by fungus growing where water has accumulated on the leaves or when there is chilling or other environmental shock. Cut out the spots, dust with fungicide and keep your snake plant out of the way when you are misting other plants.

New plants grown from leaf sections lack the yellow stripes of the mama plant — For some reason *Sansevieria* does that. To retain the stripes of *S. trifasciata*, propagate only by dividing the roots.

No blossoms form — Snake plant doesn't bloom very reliably, but letting it get pot-bound might encourage it to put out its fragrant off-white flowers.

INSECT PESTS Basically pest-free, but keep an eye out for scale.

GROWING TIPS Neglect this plant: it and you will be happier as a consequence.

Saxifraga stolonifera (or sarmentosa) (Strawberry begonia, strawberry geranium, mother of thousands)

SYMPTOMS *Plant looks truly less than happy and everything seems to be going wrong* — The plant is probably too warm and is not getting enough air moisture. This little charmer needs lots of fresh air in cool but not blastingly drafty cold temperatures. It's easier at low temperatures, too, to keep the humidity level high — which *Saxifraga* needs for health.

INSECT PESTS Mealybugs, aphids, spider mites.

GROWING TIPS *Saxifraga* does best in a shallow (three-quarter) pot that protects it from being overwatered.

Schefflera (or Brassaia) actinophylla (Australian umbrella tree, umbrella tree, schefflera)

SYMPTOMS *Leaves suddenly drop off* — Probably overwatering after letting the soil get too dry; or perhaps it got too cold when you weren't looking. Scheffleras will also lose leaves when new to a home because of their earlier life in the warm South — they must adjust.

Young leaf tips turn dark — Soil that's consistently too wet. (See photograph on next page.)

Older (lower) leaves gradually drop off — Probably

Schefflera actinophylla *(umbrella tree) with dark tips on young leaves, from soil that's too wet*

normal aging, especially if the plant is kept in less than bright light.

Plant grows too big — Yes, a healthy one does tend to grow. Cut back the stems to the joints. Don't panic when the wounds ooze fluid.

Leaves develop small, blisterlike swellings — Edema from noncirculating air that's too humid. Scheffleras must have lots of fresh air.

INSECT PESTS Very susceptible to spider mites; also attracts aphids, mealybugs, and scale. *Do not use* carbaryl (Sevin), dimethoate (Cygon), Kelthane, or malathion; growth will be distorted if you do.

GROWING TIPS Feed *Schefflera* with a low-nitrogen-content fertilizer to avoid overenthusiastic, spindly growth. This is a very popular plant among people willing to invest big money in dramatic, large trees, but almost inevitably they lose them if the humidity is not kept at a high level.

Schlumbergera bridgesii (Christmas cactus)

SYMPTOMS *Plant won't bloom* — Christmas cactus and its other holiday relatives (*Zygocactus truncatus,* for example) are photoperiodic plants: they require specific hours of light and dark in order for buds to set. Starting about September first, it must have six or eight weeks of nights consisting of at least twelve hours of *total* darkness. That means that *no light* — not even a night-light or reflections from a streetlamp — must be allowed in the room. Consider taping the light switch closed so it can't be flicked on. Water the plant only two or three times during the special long-night period, just barely enough to keep the succulent stems from shriveling. Christmas cactus won't bloom if it gets too much water. Then, after the special days, move the plant to a bright window, begin to water and feed again. Remember, though, that a plant probably won't bloom until it is seven or eight years old. Once it starts blooming, however, don't repot as long as it is doing well each year.

Buds drop off — You've moved the plant, probably to show it off to someone, as you are justified in doing if you got it to bloom — but don't. Even the slightest change in environment will cause buds to drop off.

INSECT PESTS Basically pest-free, but keep an eye open for mealybugs, aphids, and scale.

GROWING TIPS If you conquer the light-dark schedules, rejoice in your accomplishment and keep perhaps twelve plants. Work things right and you can have one in bloom each month of the year.

SEE ALSO *Epiphyllum* (which is closely related)

Scindapsus aureus (Epipremnum aureum) (Pothos, devil's ivy, marble queen, variegated philodendron)

SYMPTOMS *Lower leaves drop off* — This happens easily from overwatering, even if slight. Pinch back the stem ends and new leaves will grow along the sides, keeping the plant full. Overwatering can also make the leaves lose their color patterns.

Leaf tips turn brown — Too little humidity.

Lower leaves turn yellow — Underwatering. Don't let the soil remain dry more than a day or so between waterings.

New growth is solid green and small, usually with leaves a long distance apart — Not enough light. Because of the gold variegations, pothos needs more light than the philodendrons that resemble it.

Leaves develop dead, dry, brown, or yellow spots — Anthracnose or other leaf-spot fungus. Never let the plant get chilled when you've watered or sprayed. Keep the air circulating around the plant. Dust the leaves with fungicide.

INSECT PESTS   Spider mites, mealybugs. *Avoid using* malathion or Kelthane in warm weather: they may distort the growth.

GROWING TIPS   Pothos tends to grow long and straggly, so keep it full and attractive by pinning the vine down at empty places in the pot; each node will take root.

SEE ALSO   *Philodendron* (general)

Sedum morganianum (Burro's tail, sedum)

SYMPTOMS   *Whole sections break off* — They will do so easily, especially if you are careless around the long, fragile stems. However, each broken piece will root. Put it in the pot to fill in a hole.

Fat little leaves break off the stem, leaving a bare patch — They do that for no reason at all — or at least no reason that's apparent. Just break off the stem above the bare patch and let it regrow. Some nice horticulturists have developed a variety called *Sedum* x *orpetii;* its leaves are fatter and not so tightly packed together as the old form, but they cling to the stem more tenaciously.

Leaves develop a bluish, dustlike coating — That's normal for this and some other sedums. It gives them their attractive blue-green color.

Stems turn mushy at base; leaves turn discolored and drop off — Overwatering. This is, of course, a succulent, and it should be watered only when the soil has dried out completely.

INSECT PESTS Aphids, mealybugs, scale, but essentially a trouble-free plant.

GROWING TIPS In winter, let the plant rest in a cool location. Give it water only when the fat leaves are about to shrivel (that might take many weeks; don't forget about your plant).

Selaginella (Irish moss)

NOTE These mosses are primitive plants like ferns and so will never produce flowers.

SYMPTOMS *Leaf tips turn brown* — Humidity too low, or reaction to inconsistent watering. This plant must never have its roots dried out.

INSECT PESTS Basically pest-free, but take care if mealybugs are lurking in the vicinity.

GROWING TIPS Except for *S. lepidophylla* (resurrection plant), these mosses die if humidity is not kept at an adequately high level. They grow best in a terrarium.

Senecio cruentus (Cineraria)

NOTE This is primarily a gift plant, so your main concern involves keeping it going as long as possible. Cineraria does not like temperatures much above 50° F., and not many of us are willing to live in that shivery temperature range. So just enjoy your plant as long as possible, and prolong its life by keeping it on a cool porch when not showing it off as a centerpiece.

Setcreasea purpurea (Purple heart)

SEE *Tradescantia* (which is closely related)

Sinningia speciosa (Gloxinia)

SYMPTOMS

New leaves are small, with dull colors; some old leaves turn yellow — Not enough sun. Gloxinia likes an east or west window so it gets some direct sun each day.

Leaves curl — Probably a reaction to too much fertilizer salt in the soil. Wash the excess out by running water through the pot several times. However, take a close look first, because cyclamen mites can also cause curled-up leaves.

Leaves develop white-ringed spots — You've watered with water colder than the air temperature. Always use tepid water.

Plant growth is lopsided — Gloxinias easily respond to sun; turn the plant every day (except after buds have formed).

Leaves droop down around the pot rim — Too much light (and consequently, probably too much heat). Shield the plant from direct south sun in summer.

Buds blast (wither) — Humidity too low (it should be kept above 50 percent); too much or too little water; shock from quick temperature change. Evaluate what

Sinningia speciosa (gloxinia) with leaves curled, probably from the buildup of fertilizer salts

you've been doing. Do not mist the plant directly after buds start to open.

Flowers open but don't last — That's often the nature of the beast, but check your watering habits; only the very top of the soil surface should be allowed to dry between your thorough waterings (except in autumn, when the tubers go dormant and don't require water).

Plant won't bloom — It needs continuous high humidity and prefers long days. You may want to augment the natural day-length with artificial light.

Stems turn squishy at base and leaves collapse — Crown rot. Take clean cuttings; root them in a warm place and start again, keeping water out of the crown.

INSECT PESTS Cyclamen mites, aphids, thrips.

GROWING TIPS If you're not ready to let the tuber go dormant, you can usually get a repeated blooming by cutting back the stems above the first pair of leaves. However, gloxinias must be allowed a resting period at least after every second blossoming.

SEE ALSO gesneriads (general)

Smithiantha (Temple bells)

SYMPTOMS *Leaves die back and plant begins to go dormant* — You've forgotten to water. This gesneriad regards dryness as an immediate signal to take a nap.

Buds blast (wither) — Humidity too low; try to keep it above 60 percent (that's not easy). Be certain, however, that the humid air circulates well.

Plant won't bloom again — Cut back on water until the leaves die back. Place the plant in a cool, dark place for several months, watering slightly just once a week (enough to prevent the roots shriveling). When new growth appears, gradually return the plant to bright but not direct light and start feeding it again. If nothing happens, check the rhizome: you may have overwatered and allowed it to rot.

The pot size will control the ultimate size of the plant (although you can't get a small variety to turn into a big one). You can acquire more plants by merely breaking the rhizome into sections.

Plants that just aren't doing well may benefit from a rest: cut down on their water and keep them for a few weeks in a place where they receive perhaps half the light usually needed.

SEE ALSO gesneriads (general)

Solanum pseudo-capsicum (Christmas cherry, Jerusalem cherry, solanum)

NOTE The fruit of this plant is poisonous, so don't grow it if you have everything-goes-right-into-the-mouth-aged children.

SYMPTOMS *Leaves turn yellow; leaves and berries drop off* — The cause is probably a blast of hot air from a heater or radiator; Jerusalem cherry can't take being seared.

No fruit forms — The soil must be kept continuously moist to allow the numerous flowers to set. You can help by gently spreading the pollen from flower to flower with a soft paintbrush.

INSECT PESTS Aphids, spider mites, scale, thrips, whitefly.

GROWING TIPS Often a gift plant that flowers, fruits, and fades, you can regain *Solanum*'s beauty for a second year by cutting the plant way back in spring after all fruit has withered. Repot in fresh soil and let it begin growing again.

Never allow Jerusalem cherry to wilt (that means keeping the humidity high and zealously protecting the plant from drafts); any wilting will cause flowers and fruit to drop off.

Spathiphyllum	(Spathiphyllum, peace lily, spathe flower, white anthurium)
SYMPTOMS	*Whole plant collapses around the pot rim and appears dead* — Underwatering. Water at once; the plant will revive, though it may lose a leaf or two. The shock may even prompt it to bloom if it has been reluctant to do so (but I don't recommend that you let it dry out deliberately).
	Leaves develop brown spots — Too much direct sun. Peace lily likes east or west light.
	Plant just isn't doing well — Repot in fresh soil as a pick-me-up. This should be done at least once a year anyway.
	Leaf tips turn brown — Humidity too low. Correct the situation (spray with water often, et cetera) and trim the leaves with sharp scissors, maintaining their pretty pointed shape.
INSECT PESTS	Basically a pest-free plant, but could attract mealybugs, spider mites, or scale.
GROWING TIPS	This plant throws out new leaves all year long. Feed it frequently with a mild solution. Wash the plant often to keep older leaves glossy like the new ones.

Stapelia gigantea	(Aztec lily, carrion flower, stapelia)
SYMPTOMS	*Blossoms smell bad* — Yup, that's the origin of the "carrion" name, but the odor really isn't all that dreadful and it doesn't last long.
	Stems go limp — Underwatering. The soil should be allowed to only partially dry between waterings.
	Plant dies suddenly — Probably caused by rot from a sudden drop in temperature when the soil was wet.
	Plant grows long and distorted, usually with miscolored stems — Too little light; temperature too high.
	Damp spots, dark or yellowish, form on stems — Leaf-

spot disease from a fungus caused by high humidity, lack of air circulation, or chilling.

No leaves form — Normal: this plant is all stem and flower.

INSECT PESTS Well nigh pestless; even insects drawn to real carrion don't frequent this plant.

GROWING TIPS Stop watering, except for a tiny bit, as soon as the flower bud appears (you can't miss it — it's much bigger than the green part of the plant).

Stephanotis floribunda (Madagascar jasmine, wedding flower, stephanotis)

SYMPTOMS *Buds blast (wither)* — Probably underwatering or too little humidity.

Flowers are misshapen and are covered with purplish spots — Botrytis mold.

Plant growth and flowering are poor — Too little light, environmental conditions are not constant, or you forgot to let the plant spend a dormant period during the winter.

INSECT PESTS Highly subject to mealybugs and scale; wash the plant regularly to prevent their attack. Also attracts spider mites. *Do not use* diazinon: it will distort growth.

GROWING TIPS This vine does not need repotting very often, so feel free to train it around windows, especially those where temperatures drop to cool but not cold at night. It should be staked up to give flowers the freedom to open.

Strelitzia reginae (Bird-of-paradise flower)

SYMPTOMS *Leaves curl and split* — Hot, dry air. *Strelitzia* needs all the moisture it can get.

Leaves turn yellow, then dark brown — Hot, dry air (although an occasional single leaf may die this way from normal aging). Cut damaged leaves off at the base and adjust growing conditions if necessary.

Plant won't bloom — It can be very difficult to get bird-of-paradise to flower without the warmth and high humidity of a greenhouse . . . and it won't bloom anyway until it's at least six or seven years old (tradition says: until it has seven leaves), although some new hybrids may bloom after three or four years.

Find a warm (at least 80° F. in the daytime), south-facing location where you can work on keeping the humidity as high as possible without peeling the wallpaper. Keep the plant thoroughly pot-bound in heavy soil that drains perfectly. Water often enough to keep the soil moist but not soggy in summer, a little bit drier (and the temperature lower) in winter. Feed about four times, in summer only, with a low-nitrogen-content food. Then hope.

If you have a garden, remember that your plant is more likely to bloom after a summer spent outside in a protected spot.

Plant stops blooming (I hope you appreciate my assumption that you got it to bloom in the first place.) — Repot in fresh soil and a pot one size larger.

INSECT PESTS | Generally pest-free, but keep an eye out for mealybugs and scale.

GROWING TIPS | Repotting may discourage blooming, so leave the plant in its familiar home for several years at a time once it has grown into a ten-inch pot.

Streptocarpus (Cape primrose, streptocarpus)

NOTE | The flower grows from the midrib of the leaf rather than on a stem of its own.

SYMPTOMS | *Plant just doesn't do well* — This gesneriad prefers it cooler than most others. It especially needs a temperature drop at night.

GROWING TIPS | After blooming is finished, cut back the stems, repot, and let the plant try for new flowers. After that, let it go dormant when it indicates it is ready for a rest by stopping growth.

SEE ALSO gesneriads (general)

Syngonium (Nephthytis, arrowhead, African evergreen)

SYMPTOMS *Color distinctions in leaves begin to fade* — If you are growing the plant in water, it probably needs a break for a while: pot it in soil for a vacation.

Dark, reddish brown, dry-centered spots appear on leaves — Leaf-spot fungus. Take clean cuttings and root them. If you must save the plant, spray with fungicide.

INSECT PESTS Spider mites, mealybugs, scale, thrips — but pretty much pest resistant. *Do not use* carbaryl (Sevin) or malathion.

GROWING TIPS Don't panic if your *Syngonium*'s leaves lose their distinct arrow shape; mature plants tend to broaden out. Older plants also prefer to have something to climb on rather than being left to hang.

Tillandsia (Tillandsia)

SEE bromeliads (general)

Tolmiea menziesii (Piggyback plant, pickaback plant, mother of thousands)

SYMPTOMS *Plant won't grow piggybacks (just plain leaves)* — *Tolmiea* must have cool, even cold, nights, with damp (never soggy) soil to develop the piggyback leaves. The piggybacks are special in that they will propagate, while the plain ones growing from soil level won't.

Old leaves die when the piggybacks appear — The plant needs higher-nutrient-content soil and higher humidity to maintain both kinds of leaves.

Tolmiea menziesii
*(piggyback plant) with
leaf edges turning brown
and crisp from too much
heat and sun*

Leaves turn brown and crisp — Too hot and dry. Cut off the damaged leaves and move the plant to a new location.

Leaves wilt — Underwatering. If the soil dries out too often, some day the plant won't revive.

Leaves develop brown spots — Too much sun when moisture is on the leaves; also humidity that's too low or too much heat.

INSECT PESTS Quite prone to spider mites; also gets aphids, mealybugs, whitefly.

GROWING TIPS Start new plants from piggyback cuttings about every eight or ten months. This isn't a long-lived plant and you'll want a continuous supply because people always ask for them.

Tradescantia (Wandering Jew, inch plant, tradescantia)

SYMPTOMS *Leaves develop too little color —* Not enough light (which also causes long stem growth between leaves). Despite the leaf color, the plant may be healthy: wandering Jews grow well in fairly low-level light.

Leaves closest to the soil die, drop off — Too much or too little water; too much wear and tear from rubbing

Zebrina pendula *(wandering Jew) in generally bad condition. It should be replaced at least once a year by rooting cuttings.*

against the pot rim. Such leaf loss is pretty much inevitable. Just take cuttings and start fresh plants; the problems aren't worth fighting, since these plants root with incredible ease.

Leaves develop spots — Leaf-spot disease from humidity that's too high and noncirculating air.

Brown edges and rusty spots form on leaves (especially on the green-and-white plant varieties) — Probably too much fertilizer buildup in the pot. Leach the soil by running water through it for several minutes or repot in fresh pot and new soil.

INSECT PESTS   Basically trouble-free, but watch for mealybugs and scale.

GROWING TIPS   Whatever goes wrong, don't bother trying to fix it — just take clean cuttings and start over.

When in doubt, pinch back the plants.

SEE ALSO   *Cyanotis somaliensis, Geogenanthus undatus, Tripogandra multiflora* (which are closely related)

Tripogandra multiflora (Gibasis geniculata) (Tahitian bridal veil)

SYMPTOMS   *Leaves nearest the soil turn dry and die* — You've let the soil get dry. This delicate-looking though hardy (all *Tradescantia* relatives are hardy) plant needs its soil kept damp; allow it to dry out briefly only occasionally. Leaves can also die from normal aging and wear and tear from life around a pot rim. Take lots of cuttings and start fresh plants. To develop a full plant, be sure to pinch back *Tripogandra* often as it grows.

INSECT PESTS   Quite attractive to spider mites.

SEE ALSO   *Tradescantia* (which is closely related)

Vanda   (Vanda orchid)

SEE   orchids (general)

Vriesa   (Vriesa, sword plant)

SEE   bromeliads (general)

Zamia   (Zamia)

SEE   *Cycas circinalis, C. revoluta* (which are closely related)

Zebrina pendula   (Zebrina, wandering Jew)

SEE   *Tradescantia* (which is closely related)

Zygocactus truncatus   (Thanksgiving cactus)

SEE   *Schlumbergera bridgesii* (which is closely related)

❧ INDEX AND HOUSE-PLANT COMMON-NAME GUIDE

House-plant common names are cross-referred here to their botanical names. (All page references are listed at the botanical name, even though the common name may be used in the text.) Page numbers in *italic* type indicate illustrations.

fan palm. See *Howea*
Fatshedera lizei, 247
Fatsia japonica, 247
Ferbam, 160, 214
Fermate, 284
fern palm. See *Cycas circinalis*
ferns, 9, 64, 68, 111, 112, 123, 132, 135,
    162, 248–249
fertilizer, 90, 92, 96–108
    acidic, 111, 205, 206, 211, 213, 254,
        281–282, 293, 296
    and flower power, 172–173
    formulas, 99
    organic/inorganic, 104
    salt buildup, 85, 105, 106–108, 155, 300
    time-release, 105–106, 112
Ficus, 112, 180, 249–251
    F. benjamina, 250
    F. elastica, 55, *146,* 181, 251–252
fig. See *Ficus*
fingernail plant. See *Neoregelia*
firecracker flower. See *Crossandra*
    infundibuliformis
fish, insecticides toxic to, 159, 160, 163
fish emulsion, 104, 211
fishtail palm. See *Caryota mitis*
Fittonia, 92, 252–253
flame ivy. See *Hemigraphis colorata*
flame nettle. See *Coleus blumei*
flame-of-the-woods. See *Ixora*
flame violet. See *Episcia*
flamingo flower. See *Anthurium*
flower problems, 42–46 (table), 92, 166–174,
    180, 263
flowering maple. See *Abutilon*
fluffy ruffles. See *Nephrolepsis exaltata*
fluorescent lights, 61
fluorides, 80
freckle face. See *Hypoestes sanguinolenta*
    (or *phyllostachya*)
fronds, 9, 291
Fuchsia, 64, 143, 253
fungal diseases, 144–145, 171, 180–181
fungicides, 13, 146, 147, 150, 152, 160,
    284, 297
fungus gnats, 128, 163

garden centipedes, *129,* 163, 288
Gardenia jasminoides, 110, 111, 169,
    254–255

garlic (as organic pesticide), 163–164
gas leaks, 188
Geogenanthus undatus, 255
geranium. See *Pelargonium*
gesneriads, 93, 130, 173, 255–257
Gibasis geniculata. See *Tripogandra*
    multiflora
gibberellic acid, 115
glory bower. See *Clerodendrum thomsoniae*
gloxinia. See *Sinningia speciosa*
glucose, 11
gold-dust plant. See *Aucuba japonica*
goldfish plant. See *Columnea; Nematanthus*
grandmother's shamrock. See *Oxalis*
grape ivy. See *Cissus rhombifolia*
Grevillea robusta, 64, 257
ground mealybugs, 132. See ALSO mealybugs
growing tip, 9
growth hormones, 115. See ALSO rooting
    hormone
growth problems, 47–50 (table)
    from insecticides, 285, 289, 293, 302,
        304, 306, 312
growth retardants, 115–116
guard cells (of leaf), *10*
Guzmania. See bromeliads
Gynura aurantiaca, 258

hanging-basket plants, 106, 220
Hawaiian ti plant. See *Cordyline terminalis*
Haworthia, 258–259
heartleaf. See *Philodendron oxycardium*
hearts entangled. See *Ceropegia woodii*
heat buildup, 57, 168
heathers, 64
Hedera, 110, 259–260
Helxine soleirolii, 80, 92, 112, 260
Hemigraphis colorata, 261
hemispherical scale, 135
hen and chickens. See *Echeveria*
hen-and-chickens fern. See *Asplenium*
    bulbiferum
Hibiscus, 169
    H. rosa-sinensis, 261
Hippeastrum, 261–262
holly fern. See *Cyrtomium falcatum*
honeydew (insect residue), 120, 122, 131,
    134, 142, 157
Hormodin, 115
hormones, growth, 115, 179

"horticultural therapy," 5
Howea, 262–263
  H. forsteriana, 8
Hoya, 173
  H. carnosa, 263–264
humble plant. SEE *Mimosa pudica*
humidifiers, 84, 140
humidifying trays, 83
Humidiplant, 84
humidity, 62, 64, 80–84, 140, 170–171
hyacinth. SEE *Hyacinthus*
Hyacinthus, 264
Hydrosme, 264
hygrometer, 13, 84
Hypocyrta. SEE *Nematanthus*
Hypoestes sanguinolenta (or *phyllostachya*),
  87, 265–266

impatience. SEE *Impatiens*
Impatiens, 111, 179–180, 266–267
inch plant. SEE *Tradescantia*
India rubber plant. SEE *Ficus elastica*
insecticides, 13, 120, 178, 211
  immunity to, 140
  and plant growth, 285, 289, 293, 302,
    304, 306, 312
  safety precautions when using, 158–165
  SEE ALSO miticides; systemic pesticides
insects, 117–143, 164–165
  predators of, 164
  SEE ALSO INDIVIDUAL ENTRIES
internode, 9
Iresine, 180
  I. herbstii, 267
Irish moss. SEE *Helxine soleirolii;*
  Selaginella
iron, 102, 254, 293
ivies, 92
Ixora, 267–268

Jacaranda acutifolia, 268
Jacob's coat. SEE *Coleus blumei*
jade plant. SEE *Crassula argentea*
Japanese aralia. SEE *Fatsia japonica*
Japanese spindle tree. SEE *Euonymus*
  japonicus
Jerusalem cherry. SEE *Solanum pseudo-*
  capsicum
Jiffy Mix, 113

Kaffir lily. SEE *Clivia miniata*
Kalanchoe, 112, 169, 173, 268–269
  K. blossfeldiana, 56, 269–270
kangaroo vine. SEE *Cissus antarctica*
Karathane, 152, 160, 204, 297
Kelthane, 127, 139, 160, 162, 163, 193,
    197, 220, 222, 224, 227, 272, 281, 285,
    302, 304, 306
Kentia palm. SEE *Howea*
knife (as tool), 13, 90

ladybugs, 164
lady's eardrops. SEE *Fuchsia*
lady's slipper. SEE orchids
Lantana camara, 143, 270
laurel. SEE *Laurus*
Laurus, 270
LD_{50} ratings, 159–160
leaching, 107
leaf axil, 118, 184
leaf blade, 9
leaf midrib, 9
leaf miners, *130*
leaf pores. SEE stomata
leaf problems, 20–38 (table), 80, 98, *179,*
  225
leaf rollers, 130–131
leaf spots, 80, 148–150, *149,* 209, *210,* 283,
  286, 314
leaf stem, 9
leaf structure and function, *9–10*
lemon-leaved geranium. SEE *Pelargonium*
  crispum
light problems, 54–62, *60,* 79, 90, 168–169,
  218, 256. SEE ALSO photoperiodism
lime (soil nutrient), 111, 112
lindane, 159
lipstick plant (or vine). SEE *Aeschynanthus*
Lithops, 271
living stone. SEE *Lithops*
living-vase plant. SEE *Aechmea;*
  Billbergia
Loehr, Franklin, 183
Lucerne angel-wing begonia. SEE *Begonia*
  corallina

Madagascar jasmine. SEE *Stephanotis*
  floribunda
maggots, 128

magnesium, 99, 100–101
magnifying glass, 12
maidenhair fern. SEE Adiantum
malathion, 120
Maneb, 146
manganese, 102
Mangifera indica, 271
mango. SEE Mangifera indica
Maranta, 91, 271–273, 272
marble queen. SEE Scindapsus aureus
  (Epipremnum aureum)
Marica. SEE Neomarica
Massange's dracaena. SEE Dracaena fragrans
  massangeana
mealybugs, 120, 131–132, 157, 163,
  228–229, 272, 284
medicine plant. SEE Aloe vera
mercuric-chloride solution, 279
metaldehyde, 136, 279
Metro Mix, 113
Mexican breadfruit. SEE Monstera deliciosa
midrib (of leaf), 9
mildew, 145
Mildex, 152
millipedes, 288. SEE ALSO garden centipedes
Mimosa pudica, 273
miniature jade tree. SEE Portulacaria afra
miniature rose. SEE Rosa chinensis minima
Mir-Acid, 111
misting, 13, 83, 91, 170
mites, 164. SEE ALSO cyclamen mites; spider
  mites
miticides, 139, 163
mold, 144–145
moldy soil, 150
molybdenum, 102
Monstera deliciosa, 8, 91, 274–275
mosaic plant. SEE Fittonia
Moses-in-a-boat / Moses-in-the-cradle. SEE
  Rhoeo spathacea (or discolor)
mother fern. SEE Asplenium bulbiferum
mother-in-law's tongue. SEE Sansevieria
  trifasciata
mother of thousands. SEE Saxifraga
  stolonifera (or sarmentosa); Tolmiea
  menziesii
moth orchid (Phalaenopsis). SEE orchids
mushroom flies. SEE fungus gnats
music (effect on plants), 183–184
myrtle. SEE Myrtus communis
Myrtus communis, 275

Narcissus, 275
Nautilocalyx, 276
Neanthe bella. SEE Chamaedorea elegans
  bella
Nematanthus (Hypocyrta), 276
nematocides, 151–152
nematodes, 151–152
Neomarica, 276–277
Neoregelia, 277
Nephrolepsis exaltata, 110, 248, 277–278
nephthytis. SEE Syngonium
Nerium oleander, 56, 70, 173–174, 278
nerve plant. SEE Fittonia
nicotine sulfate, 123, 128, 132, 135, 160,
  163, 193, 197, 211, 229, 249, 254, 269
Nidularium. SEE bromeliads
nitrogen, 97–98, 104, 173, 211, 253, 284
Nodampoff, 148
node, 9
Norfolk Island pine. SEE Araucaria excelsa

oblique-banded roller, 130–131
Odontoglossum. SEE orchids
odor (carrionlike), 264, 311
old-man cactus. SEE Cephalocereus senilis
oleander. SEE Nerium oleander
Omite, 139
omnivorous roller, 131
oral contraceptives (effect on plants),
  114–115
orchid cactus. SEE Epiphyllum
orchids, 64, 68, 99, 169, 279–280
Osmanthus, 280
Osmocote, 106
Osmunda fiber, 208, 279
overfeeding, 106–108, 237
Oxalis, 280–281
oxygen supply, 232
oxyquinoline benzoate, 148

painted fingernail. SEE Neoregelia
painted-leaf begonia. SEE Begonia rex
painted nettle. SEE Coleus blumei
palms, 281–282
Pandanus veitchii, 282–283
panda plant. SEE Kalanchoe
paper flower. SEE Bougainvillea
parlor palm. SEE Chamaedorea elegans bella
parrot leaf. SEE Alternanthera amoena
partridge breast. SEE Aloe variegata